CRACKING KEY CONCEPTS *in* SECONDARY SCIENCE

CRACKING KEY CONCEPTS in SECONDARY SCIENCE

ADAM BOXER
HEENA DAVE
GETHYN JONES

CORWIN

SAGE Publications Ltd
1 Oliver's Yard
55 City Road
London EC1Y 1SP

CORWIN
A SAGE company
2455 Teller Road
Thousand Oaks, California 91320
(0800)233-9936
www.corwin.com

SAGE Publications India Pvt Ltd
B 1/I 1 Mohan Cooperative Industrial Area
Mathura Road
New Delhi 110 044

SAGE Publications Asia-Pacific Pte Ltd
3 Church Street
#10-04 Samsung Hub
Singapore 049483

Editor: James Clark
Senior assistant editor: Diana Alves
Production editor: Katherine Haw
Copyeditor: Tom Bedford
Proofreader: Jane Fricker
Indexer: Adam Pozner
Marketing manager: Dilhara Attygalle
Cover design: Wendy Scott
Typeset by: C&M Digitals (P) Ltd, Chennai, India
Printed in the UK

Library of Congress Control Number: 2020951959

British Library Cataloguing in Publication data

A catalogue record for this book is available from the British Library

ISBN 978-1-5297-1645-0
ISBN 978-1-5297-1644-3 (pbk)

At SAGE we take sustainability seriously. Most of our products are printed in the UK using responsibly sourced papers and boards. When we print overseas we ensure sustainable papers are used as measured by the PREPS grading system. We undertake an annual audit to monitor our sustainability.

CONTENTS

PART 3: PHYSICS

203

ABOUT THE AUTHORS

Adam Boxer is the Head of Science at a secondary comprehensive in North London. Somewhat obsessed with educational research, he has lectured and delivered CPD nationally and internationally on evidence-based practice. Adam co-founded CogSciSci – the world's largest grassroots collective of science teachers interested in evidence-based practice, and was its first Managing Editor. Adam blogs at achemicalorthodoxy.wordpress.com and tweets at @adamboxer1.

Heena Dave began her teaching career in 2011 as a teaching assistant and became Head of Science at Bedford Free School in 2015. She is passionate about putting evidence into action and built a department that put powerful science explanations at the centre of its teaching. Prior to 2011, she drove forward an agenda of evidence-informed environmental decision making as a Research Manager for the Environment Agency. She is currently Head of Programmes and Partnerships at the charity Learning through Landscapes, where she is utilising her expertise of learning to influence the future of environmental education and outdoor learning. Heena blogs at https://onesummitmanypaths.wordpress.com/ and tweets at @HeenaDave12.

Gethyn Jones has been a physics teacher and Head of Physics at a number of comprehensive schools and academies in Wales and England over the course of the last 29 years. He is a member of the Chartered College of Teaching and served on the College's council from 2018 to 2020. Gethyn blogs and tweets as @emc2andthat and lives and teaches in London.

ACKNOWLEDGEMENTS

We are all indebted to those who have pioneered and championed the use of evidence-based practice, most notably the leadership and members of researchED and CogSciSci, without whom it's unlikely this book would have ever existed.

Adam would like to thank Shifra, for everything.

Heena would like to thank Graeme Jamieson and Chanda Dave for their unwavering support.

Gethyn would like to say a heartfelt thank you to his beloved *cariad* Laurie for believing in him – always.

INTRODUCTION

'If you can't explain it simply you don't understand it well enough'.

Whether or not Albert Einstein ever said the above has not stopped it becoming a well-loved internet meme, and there are probably few science departments in the country without a glossy poster featuring it imposed on a suitably science-y background. For us, the interesting thing is not whether Einstein ever said it, but whether it is true.

We are most certainly believers in the importance of subject knowledge in crafting powerful science explanations, and it's almost trivially correct that if you don't understand something you can't explain it to another. Understanding is most definitely a *necessary* condition for explaining. But is it a *sufficient* condition? If a person understands something fully, does that mean they possess all they need in order to explain it simply? We think the quote infers this, and we strongly reject it as a proposition. Subject knowledge gets you part of the way, but there is a distinct set of skills and knowledge required before a challenging topic can be explained.

For many years, it seems that teacher explanation has been taken for granted. In a nation-wide focus on pedagogy, activity, student-led learning and social constructivism, the role of the teacher in taking challenging material and explaining it has been de-emphasised, with discovery, enquiry, peer-to-peer tuition and 'figuring things out for yourself' becoming ascendant. Not only that, but a significant number of influential organisations and individuals championed the cause of 'talk-less teaching' where the teacher was relegated to a near-voiceless 'guide on the side', sometimes enforced by observers with a stopwatch and an inflexible 'teacher talk' time limit.

We earnestly hope that such egregious excesses are now a thing of the past; but we must admit that all too often, the mistakes engendered by well-meaning edu-initiatives live on, while whatever good they achieved lies composting with the CPD packs from ancient training days. Even if they are a thing of the past, there has been a collective deskilling when it comes to the crafting of a science explanation – there is little institutional wisdom and few, if any, resources for teachers to use as a reference.

It is in light of the above that this book has been written. We strongly believe that the central part of any science lesson or learning sequence is a well-crafted and executed explanation. But we are also aware that many – if not most – teachers have had very little training in how to actually go about crafting or executing their explanations. As advocates of evidence-informed teaching, we hope to bring a new perspective and set of skills to your teaching and empower you to take your place in the classroom as the imparter of knowledge.

We do, however, wish to put paid to the suspicion that we advocate science lessons to be *all* chalk and talk: we strongly urge that teachers should use targeted and interactive questioning, model answers, practical work, guided practice and supported individual student practice in tandem with 'teacher talk'. There is a time when the teacher should be a 'guide on the side' but the main focus of this book is to enable you to shine when you are called to be a science 'sage on the stage'.

This book will begin with an opening chapter dealing with the nuts and bolts of high-quality science explanations. The rest of the book takes key topics from 11–16 science and shows you how to explain them. The explanations will explicitly draw on techniques which are advocated in the opening chapter, and will essentially serve as worked examples of the skills we are hoping to impart.

We do make claims to being evidence-informed, but we will not be providing a citation for every statement made. Our practice is informed by evidence, but also mediated and filtered by experience in the classroom. There are no randomised controlled trials for how best to explain rates of reaction or the lock and key model. We commit to making clear how the research has informed our practices, but also make no pretence as to being definitive. Rather than being the last word, we hope that this book is the first word in helping you to tailor, adapt and craft your own explanations. In a similar vein, this is not a comprehensive book covering the entire gamut of science education. Expert science instruction relies on many factors that lie beyond our scope, which only focuses on one narrow aspect of a greater whole.

We hope that you find this book enjoyable, thought-provoking and helpful but most importantly we hope that you find it to be empowering.

Adam, Heena and Gethyn

1

CRACKING THE CONCEPTS

THE COMPONENTS OF AN EFFECTIVE EXPLANATION

The DNA of a Powerful Science Explanation

Science teachers are engaged in a truly heroic task: taking some of humanity's greatest and most challenging intellectual treasures and passing them on to the next generation of students. Such acquisition will not come easily to students who will have to overcome the concepts' inherent difficulty and abstractness, as well as how they often conflict with our native understandings of the world around us. Science teachers must master many skills before their students can chart the turbulent waters of school science knowledge, and perhaps none more important than the effective explanation.

How does a science teacher go about crafting an effective explanation? This chapter will explore the key challenges science teachers face when attempting to motivate pupils to understand, value, memorise and apply their nascent learning, and it will outline how you can quickly and easily implement effective instructional strategies in your classroom. All good explanations have model examples, and the later chapters in this book will exemplify all of the theories and techniques mentioned here. Our aim is to summarise and translate research and classroom experience, and there is a further reading section at the end of this chapter.

Throughout the chapter, we have added 'callouts' to model our thinking. There will be times where we have made certain writing and explanatory decisions that won't be obvious to you. We have added these 'callouts' in order to show our thinking explicitly. On your first read through however, please don't look at them. It will become clear in time why you shouldn't, but we recommend you read the chapter once, then go back and read it again with the callouts. You'll just have to trust us for the minute.

1. Know Your Material

As discussed in our introduction to this book, your subject knowledge is a necessary but not sufficient condition for crafting an explanation. In the literature, this type of knowledge is often referred to as *content knowledge* (CK), and it represents the extent to which you know the material that you wish your students to know. However, there is a layer of knowledge that sits on top of your CK, which relates to the way that the CK is taught. For example, knowledge of covalent and ionic substances is part of CK, but the fact that students often struggle to distinguish between them is not.

> **Callout**
>
> We've picked a really straightforward example here: as is discussed below, whenever you use an example to illustrate a new idea, you should pick one that your students are very familiar with so as not to crowd their thoughts too much.

It's vitally important for teachers to be aware of common misconceptions, errors and conceptual difficulties, but you will not find them in the exam specifications or textbooks. Researchers term this knowledge as *pedagogical content knowledge* (PCK), the knowledge not just of the subject but of its pedagogy: the various trials, travails, obstacles and thresholds involved in teaching it.

Increasing your CK is relatively easy: go find a good textbook or online learning platform. Increasing your PCK is significantly harder and, historically, has relied principally on the steady build up of classroom experience. This book attempts to accelerate that process and help you grow your PCK much more quickly than if you were relying solely on time in the classroom.

2. Cognitive Load Theory (CLT)

CLT is the central axis around which a good explanation rotates. It starts by arguing that in order to learn something, information must be passed from your surroundings to your long-term memory (LTM). If the information does not become embedded in your LTM, you can't be said to really have learnt anything. The problem is that in order for the information to move to your LTM, it first needs to pass through your working memory (WM). Your WM is where you think about and process the information from your environment by combining it with things you already have in your LTM. For example, in your LTM you have vast banks of knowledge surrounding general language: letters, words and meanings which are summoned into your WM to be combined with the words you are reading right now.

Callout

In reality, we should have written 'phonemes, graphemes, syntax, semantics and the like' in order to be a bit more true to correct terminology in the science of language. We deliberately didn't use them as it would have resulted in you having to think hard about potentially unfamiliar terms. Choose familiar terms and ideas whenever you are explaining something: it's not about showing off how much you know.

Therefore, as you read this page, information from the text in front of you is being combined with your general language knowledge in order for you to understand what you are reading and for it to be embedded into your LTM.

New information presented to you → moves into WM → old information from LTM moved into WM → WM processes new information → new information moves to LTM.

Callout

Whenever describing a process, use narrative and schematic summary in tandem. A typically good route is to verbally describe what you are talking about as you visually construct a schematic representation in writing. Then, go to a more detailed text and read through as a class, taking opportunities to pause students and check for understanding.

This whole process relies on your WM, which unfortunately is the weak link in the chain. The WM is incredibly constricted, and can only process a few items at any one point. Giving too much information results in cognitive overload: there is too much for your WM to process. And if your WM doesn't process it, it doesn't get learned. This, in a nutshell, is cognitive load theory.

Callout

Throughout this chapter we have used abreviations (most recently WM for 'working memory') but we haven't abbreviated 'cognitive load theory' here to CLT. That's because we introduced the potentially unfamiliar phrase earlier in the chapter, then had a long break from it before returning to it later. If we wrote 'CLT' here, the reader would potentially then have to think 'oh what's that, I'll have to look back to find it' resulting in undesirable processing.

Almost all of the instructional techniques below are effective because of how they respond to CLT. They will help minimise how much new information goes into your students' WM as well as look at some ways to make the processing of that new information more efficient.

3. Prior Knowledge

We said above that new information is combined with old information in your LTM. So when you are reading this page, the new information is being combined with everything you already know about language and reading, but also with everything you already know about learning and the science of learning. New information is combined with relevant old information. There is now a vast academic literature showing that the more relevant old information you have, the easier it is to process the new information. Perhaps counter-intuitively, this means that whilst increasing new information *worsens* processing, increasing old information *betters* processing. The more relevant old information you have, the better your thinking and learning (Table 1.1).

Table 1.1 The effect of prior knowledge on acquiring new knowledge

	New information	Old information
Lots	Cognitive overload: no learning takes place	No cognitive overload: learning takes place
Little	No cognitive overload: learning takes place	Cognitive overload: no learning takes place

What this means is that when you are teaching your students new information, you aren't just teaching it to them because it is important in its own right, but also because it will help them in the future. It's a reinforcing where more knowledge now leads to even more knowledge later.

Callout

We could have done some kind of graphic cycle here showing how knowledge leads to more knowledge, but it probably wouldn't help you understand what we have written. Adding it would then just have been aesthetic, and would result in additional undesirable load.

4. Segmenting

In order to prevent the WM from filling up with too much new information, expert explainers take the content they are due to be teaching and break it up into small parts. They then teach one of the small parts and allow students to practise it before moving on to the next part. We can call this 'segmenting'. For example, it's probably a bad idea to introduce the nuclear model of the atom, subatomic particles, relative masses and relative charges all at the same time. There's just too much new information for anyone to take in at once.

5. Sequencing

Callout

Later in this chapter we revisit sequencing and split it into micro and macro sequencing. This is because when teaching the new term we try to keep it as simple as possible, and add complexity later. In the classroom, this might be something to think about when teaching things like complete/incomplete combustion, contact/non-contact forces and aerobic/anaerobic respiration.

So if you were to be teaching the nuclear model of the atom, how would you order all the different pieces of information you are due to be teaching? Would you show students the nuclear model first and then look at subatomic particles or would you do it the other way around? When would you talk about charges? Normally, that would come after, but is there virtue in doing that earlier so that students can understand why electrons orbit the nucleus? This is where we combine chunking and prior knowledge, where we said that knowing lots of relevant information helps you process new information. You need to think really carefully about how you are going to sequence your explanations so as to build knowledge in a logical way that enables the steady accumulation of concepts without overloading your students.

Callout

It is worth noting that there is no one way to perfectly sequence. You may come up with different routes to the ones your colleagues or we do. There are potentially many valid routes, provided you are balancing the load appropriately.

6. Explicit Instruction

A very common feature of school-based science education is the use of inquiry or discovery approaches to learning. By this point you should be unsurprised to hear that in lab-based studies discovery and inquiry approaches are inferior to ones where the teacher fully guides the class. This finding is replicated in observational analyses of expert teachers as well as in large scale studies like Project Follow Through, PISA 2015 and process-product research.

Callout

This is the first time we have directly mentioned any research literature. Ordinarily we think that such in-text discussion is just distracting when learning new material and can be saved for the further reading. In this case we wanted to put it in because to many it will appear a contentious claim. Note that the next paragraph revisits the claim for the benefit of any reader who decided to break off at this point for further thought/exploration.

That discovery learning is worse than explicit, teacher-led teaching is easily explained by reference to Table 1.1.

By definition, when students are carrying out their own inquiries, discoveries or investigations, they are working with lots of new information and very little old information. There is no outcome in such a scenario that results in learning. This is why the research overwhelmingly supports the craft of teacher-led learning, with an expert and knowledgeable practitioner breaking down the content,

Cracking the Concepts

sequencing it appropriately, feeding it explicitly to students in small chunks and directing students to extensive practice before moving on to the next chunk.

7. Examples and Non-examples

This explanatory principle comes from the analytical philosophy literature Engelmann's Direct Instruction – a work that has been hugely influential on us as authors. In short, it argues that in order for students to fully appreciate a concept, they need to know both what it is, but also what it is not. For example, when teaching particle diagrams it is worth using many incorrect diagrams (non-examples) as well as just using the correct ones.

8. Concrete-Abstract-Concrete Process

Many concepts in science deal with abstract principles and concrete illustrations of those principles. When teaching these, start with a concrete example, then move to the general principle, and then move back down to another concrete example, which can often be used as a check for understanding. You must be explicit with students about what you are doing and the difference between a general principle and its illustration. The more concrete examples you use the better, and you should use a broad range. Ideally, you want to build up towards ones which are maximally different. For example, that polar bears have large feet and that cactuses have small spiky leaves are both concrete examples of the principle of adaptation, but they *look* and *feel* so different that your students may not be able to appreciate that, and using more similar examples (like polar bear then Arctic fox) may be the right place to start.

9. The Multimedia Effect and Dual Coding

Unsurprisingly, empirical lab-based studies show that using pictures and words when explaining concepts aids understanding and long-term memory. This is referred to as the *multimedia effect*. Cognitive scientists believe that the working memory has two separate channels within it which they call the phonological loop and the visuospatial sketchpad. The phonological loop deals with anything to do with language, whether it is reading or hearing. The visuospatial sketchpad deals with things you can see that aren't language, so pictures, movies, animations, etc. Even though the working memory is constricted, these two channels can be used concurrently, effectively increasing how much information can be processed.

So if you use a visual image and you describe it verbally, you are allowing information to be published in both channels, and improving your students' ability to focus (see Figure 1.1). The cognitive process of utilising both channels is called *dual coding*.

This doesn't just work with diagrams, but can be extended to any visual way of presenting information and showing its structure. You can use tables, decision trees, flow diagrams or exploded layering (see Figure 1.2) to show how information is structured. All of these techniques help your students to process new information.

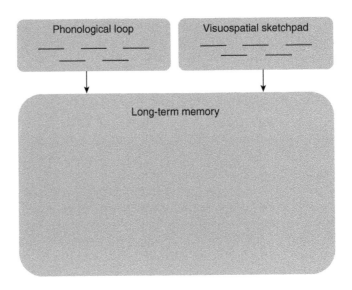

Figure 1.1   A simplified dual-channel model of working memory

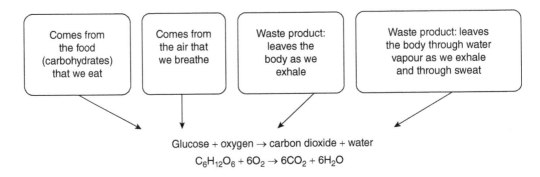

Glucose + oxygen → carbon dioxide + water

$$C_6H_{12}O_6 + 6O_2 \rightarrow 6CO_2 + 6H_2O$$

Figure 1.2   A way of adding levels of detail to a simple equation

10. Redundancy

However, things aren't quite as simple as 'words + pictures = good'. Let's say you put some text on the board and read it out. Your students start to read the text and listen to you. This does not take advantage of dual coding because even though they are listening and seeing, the new information is entirely phonological (language-based). This means that actually you are giving them more than they need: the written words add nothing to what you are saying and vice versa. Having redundant information forces us to devote precious cognitive resources to filtering out information that we don't need and results in weaker understanding and less learning. Therefore, if you are going to have notes on the board or a PowerPoint, resist the temptation to read them out. Allow your students time to read them quietly, then you can go over them again verbally. But if you try to do both at the same time learning will be compromised.

11. Split Attention

When you are using visuals like a diagram, you need to avoid splitting your students' attention. As we have said, working memory is a fragile thing, and if students fail to *attend* to the explanation they will not understand it. Of course, this can be caused by external factors like poor behaviour or a wasp entering the classroom. But it can also come from the best of intentions. For example, if students are presented with a diagram that has a key they learn less than by looking at a diagram where the labels are directly superimposed on the diagram itself.

12. Drawing Attention

In fact, this extends beyond just the use of diagrams and keys. Students will only understand your perfectly sequenced explanation if they *attend* to it perfectly. As a teacher, you must use every in-class tool at your disposal to ensure that students are attending to your explanation. First, ensure that there is no redundant information. Next, make sure your materials themselves do not cause attention splitting. Then, use a gesture to ensure that students are looking exactly where you want them to look. Physically point where you want them to look and say 'this is what I would like you to look at'. It might seem authoritarian, but fundamentally you are the expert in the room, and you must be exacting and particular in what you want your students to be thinking about – without you there is no way your students will know which piece of information is relevant at which point; how could they? Another example of this is students taking notes from the board or your verbal explanation: don't allow them to take notes until you are finished, otherwise their attention will be split between listening to you and writing their notes. Have them drop their pens and listen to you. Then, when you are finished, invite them to pick up their pens and quietly take notes or make summaries.

Callout

Many of the earlier callouts focus on the theme of attention and undesirable processing. This is often called 'extraneous load' and is any processing that your students have to do that isn't related to the material. Any distraction or splitting in attention away from your main narrative thread is going to be detrimental to student learning.

13. Live Drawing

A really simple technique that takes all this into account is called *live drawing*. Instead of projecting a fully drawn diagram onto the board, live drawing involves the teacher starting with a blank canvas and slowly creating a diagram. As the teacher works at the diagram, they are talking aloud about the different parts, and annotating with notes after verbally describing each part. The teacher points to specific areas, drawing student attention to the next step in the sequence. With the students listening in silence, the teacher gradually builds up a complex picture, but one that all students can understand.

Callout

This can also be done using a PowerPoint and ensuring that the animations appear at very controlled times. Make sure that you aren't talking over your notes on the slides and you give students time to look at and digest the material properly.

This is a simple technique to describe, but it is difficult to master. It requires fore-thought and practice. Most of the explanations later in this book will be based around a live drawing approach to instruction.

14. Narrative Structure

Much of the above hints at an overarching principle of narrative structure. Broadly, your explanations should be a bit like a story, in that they start simple and build complexity. Your students must be carried along with your story, this isn't a 'pick your ending' adventure novel. You have a clear destination in mind, but it is for you to carefully weave together the threads that will eventually comprise an entire tapestry.

15. Thinking Aloud

Part of your narrative involves you thinking aloud, and making every step completely explicit. Let's say you are working through a problem like the one below:

> A car has a mass of 50 kg and is moving forward with an acceleration of 4 m/s^2. It experiences a frictional resistance of 120 N. What is the total force from the car's engine?

> Your step 1 has to be to write out $F = ma$. But don't just write it, explain why you have selected that formula.

> Then, substitute your values, being explicit each time 'the mass is given to me in the question here [point to it] as 50 kg...'

Figure 1.3 shows the steps that you might take in order to evaluate the resultant force as 200 N. At this point, you could just write: resultant force = forward force – backwards force, rearrange to forward force = 200 + 120 = 320, but that would confuse some students as they wouldn't know exactly why you were using that equation and where the numbers come from. Far better to live draw a diagram like the one below, explaining at each point:

1. Why you are modelling the car as a square.
2. Why you have drawn the force arrows 320 N and 120 N arrows the way you have done.
3. How we can work out the result of these two forces acting on the object.

Always make what is implicit and obvious to you completely explicit to them. However trivial it may seem, be it rounding a number, substituting a value or writing 'greater' instead of just 'great' when comparing two entities, you must make it explicit. Not only is it important for them to know, but it prevents them thinking 'oh hang on where has that come from?' and losing the thread of your narrative as they desperately search for the answer.

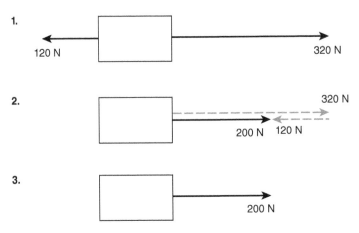

Figure 1.3   Building up a series of diagrams to illustrate calculation of resultant forces

16. Core and Hinterland

It is important to consider both the crucial information that you need your students to learn as well as the stories and contexts that make it come alive. Curriculum theorists call this 'core' and 'hinterland'. For example, when teaching about extraction of metals, you might describe a family holiday to Cornwall where you went down a tin mine and learnt about child miners (hinterland) before discussing the chemical process of using carbon to extract tin from tin oxide (core). The hinterland a science teacher might use is often idiosyncratic – it would be weird for another science teacher to talk about your family holiday – and is therefore beyond the scope of this book and will rarely be used in our explanations here.

17. Misconceptions

Students do not come into our lessons as 'blank slates': they have previously encountered, developed or absorbed many ideas about the universe. In some cases, these conceptions are compatible with the scientific knowledge we wish to teach; for example, the naive idea of electricity as a 'flow' of 'something' is congruent with teaching that electrical current is a flow of charge.

In other cases, these pre-existing ideas are incompatible or even actively hostile with regard to the scientific concepts we wish to communicate; for example, the naive idea that 'no unbalanced force = no movement' makes a complete scientific understanding of the physics of a skydiver falling at terminal velocity next to impossible.

Some misconceptions can be as hard to shift as Japanese knotweed while others seemingly evaporate of their own accord like the morning dew. Predicting with certainty what will happen is therefore often a forlorn hope and may not be a good use of your time. What you cannot afford to do, however, is ignore them completely. The most effective teaching strategy will depend on the nature of the misconception and a number of these strategies will be outlined in this book. Broadly speaking, they will generally involve one or a combination of the following:

- A clear laying out of the positive case for the correct scientific concept using a number of carefully selected and sequenced examples.

- The use of a bridging analogy that acts as a 'stepping stone' between the pre-existing idea and a more complete and correct understanding.

- The deliberate use of words, phrases or examples that 'cue' or encourage the thinking process we are seeking to communicate.

- An exploration of the consequences of what would be the case if the misconception were true, i.e. an attempt to falsify it by a form of *reductio ad absurdum*.

The last strategy should be used with care, as the very act of explaining what the misconception is can strengthen it in the minds of our students.

18. Analogy

An analogy is a comparison between one thing and another, typically for the purpose of explanation or clarification. Analogies are useful in science because they enable us to explain unfamiliar concepts that cannot easily be conceptualised by comparing them to more familiar concepts that share common characteristics. For example in biology, water flowing through a pipe is often used as an analogy for blood flowing in a blood vessel.

Science teachers also make extensive use of models. Models are simplified or idealised representations of the systems found in the physical world and are essential tools not only of the scientific description of the world 'out there', but in supporting students to develop mental models, especially things not directly accessible to the senses, for example the lock and key model in describing the site specificity of enzymes.

Models and analogies can be extremely effective in helping pupils learn about new scientific concepts because they tie a pupil's existing knowledge to new knowledge or to a new concept, helping them to develop new, more concrete or deeper mental models. They can also create attention and enable pupils to value what they are learning through the comparison between new and prior knowledge.

Whilst models and analogies are important within a subject where concepts are not easily visible they should be planned carefully and used with care. It is important that pupils understand when they are participating in analogous thinking, what models and analogies are and how they can be used to develop their understanding. This metacognitive foregrounding prior to utilising models and analogies bridges a pupil's learning between what they don't quite understand and what they do. Given this, it is important that pupils have a contextual awareness of the object you are using as a model or analogy. For example, we often say that 'DNA is the blueprint of life because it contains the instructions needed for an organism to grow, develop, survive and reproduce'. This analogy is rendered ineffective if pupils are unaware of the term 'blueprint'. Finally, it is also important to ensure that pupils are attending to the new content you are teaching them. For example, when using live modelling of the rope model to teach electric current, you need to ensure that pupils are attending to the new knowledge (electricity) and not the surface distractions. In this scenario pupils could be more excited to be up and out of their chairs to play with a rope instead of consolidating their understanding of electric current. With this in mind, throughout this book we will clearly signpost examples of effective models and analogies and how they can be used to create value and attention within the classroom.

19. Checking for Understanding

There is no point moving ahead in an explanation if your students do not understand it, making checking for student understanding through precise and targeted questioning a crucial component of a successful explanation.

In *Teach like a champion 2.0*, teacher educator Doug Lemov explains in detail how teachers must 'reject self-report' when checking understanding (see further reading section). Asking students if they understand or asking if any of them have questions will almost always give you bad data about student understanding. You must carefully prepare your questions in advance, ensuring that they actually test understanding of the specific content you are introducing.

However, too much checking for understanding, or badly timed checking for understanding, can work as a hindrance to your explanation. Any time you ask a question you are breaking up the narrative structure of your explanation. When exactly you choose to break to check is therefore a judgement call that depends on your students and the content. Break too early and you interrupt your flow, break too late and you increase the risk that students will fail to understand the explanation.

Whilst a full discussion of what effective checking for understanding in science looks like is beyond the scope of this book, in each chapter we have included a few questions to help guide your planning.

Further Reading

Cognitive science generally

Willingham, D. T. (2010) *Why don't students like school? A cognitive scientist answers questions about how the mind works and what it means for the classroom.* San Francisco, CA: Jossey-Bass.

Willingham's book has become canonical among the evidence-based community: covering foundational principles of cognitive science simply and with clarity, it is indispensable.

Mccrea, P. (2018) *Memorable teaching: Leveraging memory to build deep and durable learning in the classroom.* Peps Mccrea.

Mccrea's concise and powerful book collates the best available evidence on memory and learning and proposes a set of actionable principles to help pupils build deep, powerful and lasting understanding.

Explicit instruction

Boxer, A. and Bennett, T. (2019) *ResearchED guide to explicit and direct instruction: Working out what works.* Woodbridge: John Catt Educational Ltd.

This primer deals with recent changes in education which bring the teacher back to leading the classroom through the method of explicit instruction.

Clark, R., Kirschner, P. and Sweller, J. (2012) Putting students on the path to learning: The case for fully guided instruction. *American Educator*, 36: 6–11.

Leading authorities in cognitive science, Clark, Kirschner and Sweller here outline the characteristics of fully guided or explicit instruction and why it is the best evidenced approach to teaching.

Lemov, D. (2015) *Teach like a champion 2.0: 62 techniques that put students on the path to college.* San Francisco, CA: Jossey-Bass.

Lemov's *Teach like a champion* is a global bestseller and offers teachers concrete and step-by-step instructions on how to implement effective teaching techniques that keep pupils engaged, focused, and learning.

Multimedia effect

Clark, R. C. and Mayer, R. E. (2011) Applying the multimedia principle: Use words and graphics rather than words alone. In Clark, R. C. and Mayer, R. E., *E-learning and the science of instruction: Proven guidelines for consumers and designers of multimedia learning* (3rd edn). San Francisco, CA: Pfeiffer, Chapter 4.

Chapter 4 provides updated evidence on the multimedia principle. Based on cognitive theory and research evidence, Clark and Mayer argue that people learn better from words and pictures rather than words alone. When presented together the learner is encouraged to build connections and engage in generative processing.

Mayer, R. E. (2019) How multimedia can improve learning and instruction. In Dunlosky, J. and Rawson, K. (Eds.) *The Cambridge handbook of cognition and education* (Cambridge Handbooks in Psychology). Cambridge: Cambridge University Press, Chapter 16.

Mayer has been working on the multimedia effect for decades and has been researching the best conditions for teachers to use visual images as well as verbal exposition. This optimisation is of course especially important for science teachers who already extensively use graphics and diagrams.

ResearchED (2020) *researchEDHome 2020 Adam Boxer: Dual coding for teachers who can't draw: Teacher's explanations*. YouTube. Available at: www.youtube.com/watch?v=16SBht2iF_k [Accessed 21 November 2020].

In this video Adam outlines 'live drawing' and how you can use the multimedia effect to squeeze the most out of your explanations.

Science specific reading

Re, G. D. (2000) Models and analogies in science. *HYLE*, 5 (1): 5–15.

In this paper Re explains the value of physical models in explaining scientific concepts using the example of the spring and ball model in chemistry.

Driver, R., Squires, A., Rushworth, P. and Wood-Robinson, V. (2014) *Making sense of secondary science: Research into children's ideas* (2nd edn). London, New York: Routledge.

In *Making sense of secondary science: Research into children's ideas*, the authors highlight that when children begin secondary school, they already have some scientific knowledge. This book is designed to give guidance both on the ideas which children are likely to bring with them and on using these ideas to help pupils to make sense of their experiences in science lessons. The book is structured into three sections – life and living processes, materials and their properties and physical processes.

PART 1:
BIOLOGY

2

UNDERSTANDING CELLULAR STRUCTURE AND FUNCTION

Relevant ages

11–14

What students should know already

- In biology, an organism is any living being.
- All organisms perform similar roles such as reproduction, growth and development.

(Continued)

- Some examples of organisms are animals, plants, fungi and even microorganisms like bacteria and viruses (these are so small that we can only see them with a special piece of equipment called a microscope).
- To be able to perform their roles organisms rely on a structure called the cell.
- Cells are found inside organisms, they're small and can only be viewed by a microscope.
- Cells do important jobs inside complex organisms, like help to digest food and fight diseases.

What students should know by the end

- Cells are complex structures. They carry out many functions which are needed to sustain the organism throughout its life cycle.
- Cells provide structure and organisation to complex organisms. They contain genetic material to make proteins, provide the energy the organism needs and carry out specialised functions.
- Cells are the basic units of life. Specialised groups of cells work together to form tissue and two or more tissues operating together form an organ.
- Cells are smaller in comparison to tissue and organs.
- Plant cells and animal cells have different structures to carry out specialised functions.

Tips and tricks

The language used to introduce this topic aims to build a concrete and shared understanding of the words 'structure' and 'function' within a biological context. This key terminology should be taught before introducing pupils to plant and animal cells. Structure can be described as the way in which the parts inside a cell are arranged and organised so that it can work. Function can be described as how the parts inside a cell work together to do a specific job.

Explanation

This sequence of learning aims to explicitly distinguish between the structure and function of plant and animal cells. It will also build on a pupil's learning by demonstrating how cellular structure and function are interrelated and integral to enabling life processes within an organism.

Step 1: The Purpose of Cells within an Organism

In biology, an organism is an individual life form; it is a self-sustaining unit of life. Organisms include plants, animals, fungi, protists and prokaryotes. Cells are the smallest unit within a complex organism and are needed to help the organism perform important functions like growth, reproduction and making energy. Complex organisms like plants and animals have different types of cells, with different structures that are specialised to do different jobs like fight disease or enable processes such as digestion or photosynthesis.

Step 2: Organisation and Relative Scale

It is important for pupils to understand that different types of cells need to be well organised in complex organisms to carry out its many different functions. There are five levels of organisation within an organism, each one builds upon the other and in order of size (smallest first) these are: cells, tissues, organs, organ systems and the organism.

At this stage pupils should recognise that cells are so small they cannot be seen by the naked eye. A special piece of equipment called a microscope is needed to provide the magnification for cells to be seen.

Providing two concrete examples, as provided in Tables 2.1 and 2.2 from the plant and animal kingdoms, provides an opportunity for pupils to consolidate their understanding of the terms structure and function and enables pupils to explore how organisms are organised to carry out specialised roles within both plants and animals.

Table 2.1   Exploring the heart within a human

Structure of the heart	Function of the heart
The heart is made up of four chambers consisting of two atria and two ventricles.	An organ that pumps blood throughout the body via the circulatory system, supplying oxygen and nutrients to the tissues and removing carbon dioxide.

Smallest				Largest
Cell	Tissue	Organ	Organ system	Organism
Cardiac muscle cells	Cardiac muscle tissue	Heart	Circulatory system	Human

Table 2.2 Exploring the roots within a rose plant

Structure of the root	Function of the root
The root is made of an outer layer of cells called the epidermis, which surrounds ground tissue and vascular tissue. Root hairs are extensions of root epidermal cells inside the root.	The root has three major functions: anchoring the plant to the soil, transporting water and minerals to other parts of the plant and storing the products of photosynthesis.

Smallest				Largest
Cell	Tissue	Organ	Organ system	Organism
Xylem cells	Vascular tissue	Root	Root system	Rose plant

Step 3: The Structure and Function of Plant Cells

Plant cells have been intentionally introduced first, for two main reasons. Firstly, it is important that pupils view plants as living organisms that share common cellular structures with animal cells. Secondly, teaching cells in this order challenges pupils to learn the cellular structures first and then more independently identify which structures animal cells don't have and why.

To explore the structure and function of a plant cell, create a live diagram that builds in detail (see Tables 2.3–10. At each stage ask pupils what is new about this diagram and take time to explore the key misconceptions that pupils may hold.

Table 2.3 Cell wall

Structure	Function	Misconception
	Provides structure, support, and protection for the cell.	*Misconception: a cell wall is impenetrable.* Reality: there are many small holes in the cell wall. Further detail: the holes are called plasmodesmata. Check for understanding: If I took a plant cell and put it in some water, what would happen?

Table 2.4 Cell membrane

Structure	Function	Misconception
 Cell wall Cell membrane	Protects the cell from its surroundings. The cell membrane is also semi-permeable, this means certain molecules that the cell needs like water, oxygen and carbon dioxide can pass into and out of the cell. The cell membrane therefore regulates the movement of substances into and out of cells.	*Misconception: The cell membrane is a solid structure.* Reality: It is made of millions of smaller molecules that create a flexible and porous membrane. Further detail: Proteins and phospholipids make up most of the membrane structure. Check for understanding: Why is it important for the cell membrane to be flexible and porous?

Table 2.5 Nucleus

Structure	Function	Misconception
 Cell wall Nucleus Cell membrane	Stores the cell's hereditary material (DNA) and coordinates the cell's activities, such as growth, protein synthesis and reproduction.	*Misconception: The nucleus is the 'brain' of the cell.* Reality: The brain is an organ and is made of tissue and cells. It controls thoughts, memory, speech, movement and the function of organs within an animal. Whereas the nucleus is a highly specialised structure inside a cell which stores DNA and coordinates the cell's activities. Further detail: Only the cells of more complex organisms, known as eukaryotes, have a nucleus. Check for understanding: Explain the function of the nucleus.

Table 2.6 Vacuole

Structure	Function	Misconception
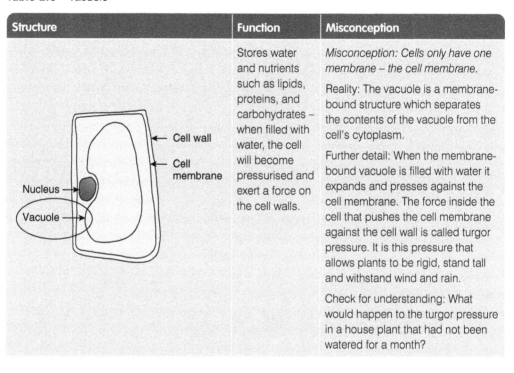	Stores water and nutrients such as lipids, proteins, and carbohydrates – when filled with water, the cell will become pressurised and exert a force on the cell walls.	*Misconception: Cells only have one membrane – the cell membrane.* Reality: The vacuole is a membrane-bound structure which separates the contents of the vacuole from the cell's cytoplasm. Further detail: When the membrane-bound vacuole is filled with water it expands and presses against the cell membrane. The force inside the cell that pushes the cell membrane against the cell wall is called turgor pressure. It is this pressure that allows plants to be rigid, stand tall and withstand wind and rain. Check for understanding: What would happen to the turgor pressure in a house plant that had not been watered for a month?

Table 2.7 Mitochondria

Structure	Function	Misconception
(See diagram with labels: Cell wall, Cell membrane, Nucleus, Vacuole, Mitochondria)	Perform the process of cellular aerobic respiration. This means they take in oxygen and glucose from the cell, break it down, and turn it into chemical energy which is needed by the organism.	*Misconception: Mitochondria burn glucose and oxygen; inaccurately describing the mitochondria as miniature furnaces.* Reality: Mitochondria are involved in a series of complex chemical reactions to create a chemical molecule to provide the organism with energy. Further understanding: The waste products of cellular aerobic respiration are water and carbon dioxide. Check for understanding: What is the name of the process that takes place in the mitochondria to produce the chemical energy needed by the organism?

Table 2.8 Chloroplast

Structure	Function	Misconception
Cell wall Cell membrane Nucleus Vacuole Chloroplasts Mitochondria	Uses light from the sun with carbon dioxide and water to make glucose that can be used by plant cells. This process is called photosynthesis and depends on green chlorophyll molecules inside the chloroplast.	*Misconception: Plants take in all substances they need to grow through their roots.* Reality: Plants take in air (with carbon dioxide in it) through their leaves. Chloroplasts in the leaf and stem absorb the sun's energy for use in photosynthesis. Water and minerals are taken in through the root system. Further understanding: Stomata are tiny openings or pores found in the leaf of the plant that allow air to enter the leaves. Check for understanding: How do plants absorb the sunlight needed for photosynthesis?

Table 2.9 Ribosome

Structure	Function	Misconception
Ribosomes Cell wall Cell membrane Nucleus Chloroplasts Vacuole Mitochondria	Ribosomes make proteins (long chains of amino acids). Proteins are needed for many cellular functions such as to make enzymes to catalyse chemical reactions or in repairing damage to cells.	*Misconception: Amino acids are made by ribosomes.* Reality: Ribosomes make proteins. Proteins are large, complex molecules made from amino acids. Further understanding: Ribosomes direct the steps of protein synthesis by stitching together amino acids to make a protein molecule. Check for understanding: What is the function of a ribosome?

Table 2.10 Cytoplasm

Structure	Function	Misconception
Ribosomes — Cell wall — Cytoplasm — Cell membrane — Chloroplasts — Nucleus — Vacuole — Mitochondria	A gel-like substance where the cell's chemical reactions take place.	*Misconception: Cytoplasm does not have an impact on the cell's structure or shape.* Reality: It provides support to the internal structures of the cell. Further understanding: The cytoplasm is made mostly of water. Water fills the cells around the nucleus and provides structure to the cell. Check for understanding: What are the two main functions of the cytoplasm?

Tips and tricks

Not all this knowledge will be taught in one lesson or over a sequence of corresponding lessons from day one. The aim is to identify the misconceptions pupils hold and to refine your pupils' mental model over time. Cellular structure and function is a foundational topic that should be revisited multiple times and linked to new learning. For example, it would be effective to reactivate prior knowledge about mitochondria when exploring cellular aerobic respiration.

Step 4: The Structure and Function of Animal Cells

Place a diagram of an animal cell alongside the plant cell (Figure 2.1). Ask pupils what they notice about the differences and similarities between the plant and animal cell. It is likely that pupils will focus on surface structures such as that 'the shapes of the cells are different' or that 'the cell wall is missing'. Ask pupils to attend to the specific structures within each cell and ask them to be explicit about whether they are referring to the plant or animal cell and to provide a working hypothesis for the differences or similarities. For example, the chloroplast is missing in the animal cell; this means that animals do not photosynthesise. Or plant and animal cells both have mitochondria; this means respiration takes place in animals and plants.

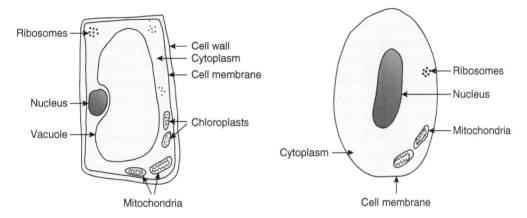

Figure 2.1 Differences and similarities between plant and animal cells

First, highlight that plant and animal cells have structures and functions that are common to both. Ask pupils to identify these structures and explain the cellular functions that are shared by animals and plants. These are:

- Cell membrane.
- Nucleus.
- Mitochondria.
- Ribosomes.
- Cytoplasm.

Then ask pupils what is different. Pupils should respond that animal cells don't have a:

- Cell wall: Explain that this is because animals evolved to develop tissues, organs, and organ systems which needed to be able to connect to each other physically and do not need individual cells to be protected from the outside world.
- Chloroplast: Explain that this is because plants make their own supply of glucose through photosynthesis. Animals, however, get their glucose from the food they eat.

- Vacuole: Explain that this is because one of the key functions of the vacuole is to exert a force on the cell walls, providing structure for the plant. Animal cells do not have this requirement, for example humans have muscles and a skeleton to provide this structure and therefore do not need a large central vacuole.

Check for understanding

The following checks for understanding will help you assess your pupils' knowledge about cellular structure and function:

- Explain the purpose of a cell.
- Describe the differences between cells, tissue and organs providing examples.
- List the structures that plant and animal cells have in common and explain their function.
- Explain the differences between plant and animal cells.

3

BIOLOGICAL ORGANISATION WITHIN COMPLEX MULTICELLULAR ORGANISMS

Relevant ages

11–14

What students should know already

- In biology, an organism is any living being that can function independently.
- All organisms perform similar roles such as reproduction, growth and development.

(Continued)

- Examples of organisms include animals, plants, fungi and microorganisms like bacteria and viruses (these are so small that they can only be seen with a special piece of equipment called a microscope).
- Complex multicellular organisms are made up of many different types of cells which all work together.
- Cells are the basic unit of life; they provide structure and organisation to complex organisms. They contain genetic material to make proteins, provide the energy the organism needs and carry out specialised functions.
- Specialised groups of cells work together to form tissue and two or more tissues operating together form an organ. Organs working together form an organ system and organ systems enable an organism to function.

What students should know by the end

- Complex multicellular organisms need many types of cells to carry out different life processes such as reproduction, digestion or respiration.
- Levels of biological organisation within complex multicellular organisms are arranged from the simplest to most complex. From smallest (simplest) to largest (most complex) these are cells, tissues, organs, organ systems and organism.
- Organisation within complex multicellular organisms occurs through cell differentiation and specialisation. Cell differentiation is the process by which cells specialise, so that they can carry out a specific function within the organism.

Explanation

This sequence of learning focuses on the importance of biological organisation within complex multicellular organisms. Pupils will be supported to understand that biological organisation is hierarchical and highly ordered, so that multiple life processes can be carried out at the same time to sustain the organism. This level of organisation is driven by cell differentiation and cell specialisation.

Step 1: What Do We Mean by Biological Organisation?

Start this sequence of learning by explaining the term biological organisation to pupils and why this is important. Pupils should understand that biological organisation describes the arrangement of cells, tissue, organs and organ systems within complex multicellular organisms that means different life processes such as digestion or respiration can happen both continuously and at the same time. Ask pupils to provide examples of other life processes to highlight that complex organisms carry out many different functions.

Remind pupils that organisms are not randomly organised and are arranged from the smallest, simplest structure to the largest, most complex system. Biological organisation is therefore hierarchical because each level of organisation demonstrates an increase in complexity. This biological hierarchy can be visualised in the form of a table as demonstrated in Table 3.1.

Table 3.1 Biological levels of organisation within complex multicellular organisms

Levels of organisation	Complexity	Size
Cell	Simplest	Smallest
Tissue		
Organ		
Organ system		
Organism	Most complex	Largest

Tips and tricks

Support pupils to engage with the new vocabulary in this sequence of learning. Take time to ensure that they understand the terms hierarchy and hierarchical. A hierarchy is a system in which things are arranged according to their importance. Hierarchical means things are arranged according to the level of importance within a system.

Step 2: How are Complex Multicellular Organisms Organised?

In the next step, help pupils understand how complex multicellular organisms are organised by presenting two examples. Tables 3.2 and 3.3 demonstrate examples of biological organisation from the plant and animal kingdom and aim to provide a concrete context for learning.

Table 3.2 Levels of organisation within the circulatory system of a human

Levels of organisation	Human	Function	Complexity	Size
Cell	Cardiac muscle cells	Specialised to control the pace for pumping blood in the heart.	Simplest	Smallest
Tissue	Cardiac muscle tissue	Allow the heart to pump blood by controlling heart contractions.		
Organ	Heart	Pumps blood through the body.		
Organ system	Circulatory system	Delivers nutrients and oxygen in blood to all cells in the body. It is made up of the heart and blood vessels which run through the entire body.		
Organism	Human	A member of the species *Homo sapiens*.	Most complex	Largest

Table 3.3 Levels of organisation within the root system of a rose plant

Levels of organisation	Rose plant	Function	Complexity	Size
Cell	Xylem cells	Specialised to conduct water and minerals from the root.	Simplest	Smallest
Tissue	Vacular tissue	Transports water from the root.		
Organ	Root	Absorbs and transports water and minerals from the root of the plant to the stem and leaves.		
Organ system	Root system	Absorbs minerals and water, anchors the plant to the ground and acts as storage organ.		
Organism	Rose plant	A rose is a flowering plant. There are hundreds of different species of rose.	Most complex	Largest

Tips and tricks

It is important to provide examples from the plant and animal kingdom so pupils understand that plants are also complex multicellular organisms and carry out life processes such as respiration and reproduction.

Step 3: How are Cells Organised?

In the next steps pupils should explore each level of organisation systematically and understand how each level organises itself. Start by reminding pupils that the first level of organisation within a complex organism is the cell, that cells are made up of smaller structures and each structure has a specific function. Present Figure 3.1 of a plant and animal cell side by side and ask pupils to retrieve knowledge by identifying cellular structures and explaining their function.

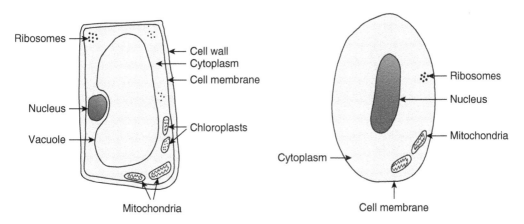

Figure 3.1 Diagram of a plant and animal cell

Step 4: What is Cell Specialisation?

Now that pupils have retrieved their knowledge on cellular structure, it is important to explore cell differentiation and specialisation. Pupils should understand that organisms are made up of many different types of cells. Cells are therefore specialised because they have different shapes and structures which enable them to carry out the different functions and processes within an organism. Pupils should understand that when cells become specialised this is the first step in enabling an organism to organise itself into tissue, organs and organ systems.

Tips and tricks

Emphasise that a specialised cell is a cell that has become differentiated to carry out a specific function within the organism. Differentiation is the process by which a cell becomes more specialised so that it can carry out the job or function it needs to do within an organism.

Table 3.4 provides two examples of specialised cells within a human. Provide context by highlighting that there are over 200 types of specialised cells within the human body and that pupils are only being presented with two examples here.

Table 3.4 Examples of specialised cells within humans

Cell	Structure	Specialisations	Function
Red blood cell	Biconcave shape Does not have a nucleus	Red blood cells do not have a nucleus providing more space for haemoglobin which combines with oxygen.	Red blood cells carry and transport oxygen from the lungs to the rest of the body.
Neurone	Dendrite Cell body Nucleus Myelin sheath Axon Axon terminal	In neurones, dendrites carry impulses to the cell body and down through the axon towards the axon terminal. The myelin sheath electrically insulates the neurone and allows impulses to be transmitted quickly and efficiently.	Neurones are responsible for transmitting electrical impulses to other neurones, muscles or glands to help coordinate and control the functions of the body.

After presenting pupils with these examples, probe understanding by asking what is different about these cells? How does cell structure support function? How would you describe the specialisations of each cell?

Tips and tricks

Providing examples from the plant kingdom will help pupils to understand that differentiation and cell specialisation take place within all complex multicellular organisms, not just animals.

Step 5: What is Tissue?

In this next step make the link between specialised cells and tissue by explaining that tissue is a group of similar cells that are located together and perform a specific function within the organism. Table 3.5 draws out the examples provided in Table 3.4 to scaffold pupils in making the connection between cell specialisation and the formation of tissue.

Table 3.5   Examples of tissue within the human body

Cell	Tissue	Function
Red blood cell	Red blood cells are one type of cell that is found in blood tissue.	Made up of cells that carry and transport oxygen and other substances to cells in the body.
Neurones	Neurones are one type of cell that is found in nervous tissue.	Made up of cells that coordinate and control the functions of the body by sending and receiving impulses.

Step 6: What is an Organ?

Next, support pupils to make the link between tissue and organs by developing the same example. Explain to pupils that an organ is a structure within an organism that can be made up of more than one type of tissue (which in turn is comprised of specialised cells). As a result, organs are more complex than tissue and their role is to carry out specific functions within the body. Take a moment to ask pupils to give examples of organs and to state their function.

Table 3.6 builds on Table 3.5 to provide two examples of organs within the human body and the types of cells and tissue the organs are comprised of. Emphasise that there are 78 organs within the human body all comprised of different types of tissue and specialised cells which enable organs to carry out highly specialised roles.

Table 3.6   Examples of organs within the human body

Example of cells found in organ	Example of tissue found in organ	Organ	Function
Neurones	Nervous tissue	Brain	The brain is an organ made up of nervous tissue and coordinates the functions of the body from building memories to controlling heart rate and regulating breathing.
Cardiac cells	Cardiac muscle	Heart	The heart is an organ made up of cardiac tissue and pumps blood around the body.

Step 7: What is an Organ System?

Next make the connection between organs and organ systems. Ensure that pupils understand that an organ system is a group of organs that work together collectively. By this stage pupils should know that an organ system is more complex than an organ because it involves multiple organs working together. Each organ has its own function, but the organs work together in a system for a collective purpose. Table 3.7 demonstrates how organs work collectively to support the function of the blood circulatory system.

Table 3.7 Exploring the blood circulatory system

Organ	Function	Organ system	Function
Heart	Pumps blood around the body, supplying oxygen and important substances to all cells and removing waste products like carbon dioxide.	Blood circulatory system	Delivers oxygen and other important substances to all cells in the body.
Blood vessels	Arteries are blood vessels that are responsible for carrying oxygen-rich blood away from the heart to the body. Veins are blood vessels that carry oxygen-poor blood from the body back to the heart for reoxygenation in the lungs.		

Remind pupils that there are 11 main organ systems within the human body. For example, the reproductive system is responsible for the production of offspring whilst the digestive system breaks down food so that nutrients and energy can be provided to cells. Each organ system is made up of multiple organs, comprised of specialised tissue and cells, which in turn enable organ systems to complete their function.

Step 8: How Organ Systems Work Together to Support Complex Multicellular Organisms

End this sequence of learning by reminding pupils that an organism is any living being that can function independently. Complex multicellular organisms only function because they are organised by a hierarchy of cells, tissue, organs and organ systems. Each organ system is highly specialised and operates to support essential biological processes within the organism, for example digestion, respiration and reproduction.

Check for understanding

The following checks for understanding will help you assess your pupils' knowledge about biological organisation within complex organisms:

- What is meant by the term biological organisation?
- From smallest to largest what are the levels of organisation within a complex organism?
- Explain how the structures within a cell support a cell's different functions.
- What is meant by cell specialisation?
- What is meant by cell differentiation?
- Explain how a neurone is specialised for its function.
- Explain how a red blood cell is specialised for its function.
- What is tissue?
- Give an example of one type of tissue and how it functions.
- What is an organ?
- Give an example of one organ and how it functions.
- What is an organ system?
- Give an example of one organ system and how it functions.
- Explain why the level of organisation within an organism is hierarchical.

4

MAGNIFICATION

What students should know already

- Cells provide structure and organisation to complex organisms. They contain genetic material to make proteins and provide the energy the organism needs to carry out specialised functions.
- Cells and microorganisms, like bacteria and viruses, are so small that they cannot be seen by the naked eye and can only be viewed once they are magnified by a microscope.

What students should know by the end

- A microscope is a scientific instrument that makes an object appear larger (magnified) and produces an image that is visible to the naked eye.
- The invention and development of the microscope enabled microorganisms and cells to be magnified and observed by the naked eye for the first time.

- Magnification occurs when lenses inside a microscope enlarge an image by a quantifiable amount.
- When using a microscope, the actual size refers to the size of the object before it has been magnified and the image size refers to the size of the object after it has been magnified.
- The image size can be calculated by multiplying the actual size of the object and the magnification.

Explanation

This sequence of learning focuses on the concept of magnification in enabling microorganisms, cells and sub-cellular structures to be observed and studied. It will scaffold pupils to understand the importance of the microscope, as well as what magnification is and how actual size, image size and magnification can be calculated.

Step 1: Introducing Microscopes

Start by introducing pupils to microscopes and explain that a microscope is an instrument that makes an object appear larger (magnified) by producing an image that is visible to the naked eye. Pupils should understand that it is this instrument that enabled scientists to discover and study structures such as cells or mitochondria (within cells) as well as microorganisms such as bacteria and viruses. Pupils should know that there are different types of microscopes and the one that they will become most familiar with is the light microscope. Take time to explain to pupils that in a light microscope, a magnified image is created by light being focused onto an object and through two lenses (the objective and eyepiece lens).

Tips and tricks

A demonstration introducing pupils to the components of a microscope and letting pupils examine specimens through practical work will help them to develop their understanding of how microscopes enable images to be magnified. By the end of the practical, pupils should know how to operate a microscope and magnify images.

Step 2: The Development of the Microscope

When pupils have a clear understanding of what a microscope is and how it works, it is important to explore the hinterland with them and explain that observations of microorganisms and cells only happened after the invention of the microscope. It is important that pupils understand that knowledge of the microscopic biological world developed step-by-step in parallel with advancements made to the microscope.

Tips and tricks

Support pupils to understand that much of what we know about the microscopic biological world has developed over the last four hundred years. One way to exemplify this is by exploring the timeline of the development of the microscope. Key dates to include are:

- 1590: The microscope was invented by Hans and Zacharias Janssen.
- 1665: Using a microscope, the cell was first discovered and named by Robert Hooke.
- 1675: Using a microscope, the first bacteria and protozoa were discovered by Antonie van Leeuwenhoek.
- 1830: Joseph Jackson Lister discovered that using multiple lenses together at various distances improved magnification.
- 1931: The electron microscope was invented by Ernst Ruska and Max Knoll, who discovered that using electrons in microscopy enhanced resolution.

Step 3: What Do We Mean by Magnification?

At this stage it is important to deepen a pupil's understanding of how a microscope works by exploring the concept of magnification in more detail. Remind pupils that magnification occurs when the lenses inside a microscope enlarge an image by a quantifiable amount. Ask pupils to attend to Figure 4.1 and explain that the small squares represent a small object like a cell which cannot be seen by the naked eye.

Figure 4.1 Squares representing a small object like a cell which cannot be seen by the naked eye

Prompt pupils by saying that the image is too small and ask pupils what instrument they would use to help them see an enlarged view of this object, so that they can study it in more detail. Pupils should be able to answer that if they placed the object under a microscope, it would magnify the object and they would be able to view an enlarged image. This process of enlarging an object through a microscope is called magnification.

Tips and tricks

Make sure that pupils understand and are familiar with the words magnify and magnification. The word magnify is a verb and means to make something appear larger than it is. Magnification is a noun and is the process of making something look bigger than it is, for example by using a microscope.

Step 4: Understanding the Process of Magnification

The next step is to ask pupils to think about what the object would look like if it was placed under a microscope and was made two times bigger as demonstrated in Figure 4.2.

Remind pupils that field of view is the area visible through a microscope and is represented by the diameter of the image area.

Take a moment to consolidate learning and remind pupils that the object is not actually two times bigger, it has just been magnified to make the image look like it is two times bigger, so that it can be observed by the naked eye. It is important pupils understand that this process of enlarging an object through a microscope is called magnification.

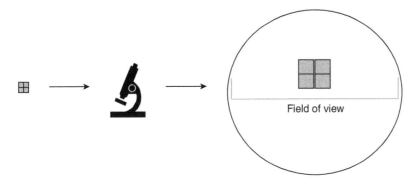

Figure 4.2   The object now magnified by a microscope

Step 5: Understanding Actual Size and Image Size

In the next part of learning, introduce pupils to the terms actual size and image size and how these relate to the process of magnification. Presenting this in a table as demonstrated in Table 4.1 and using the same format of diagram as presented in Figure 4.2 will help pupils to better understand these terms.

Table 4.1   Understanding actual size and image size

Actual size	Image size
⊞	⊞⊞
Explanation: The size of the object before it has been magnified. Remind pupils that the actual size of the object could be so small that it may not be seen by the naked eye and that is why they will need a microscope to magnify the image.	*Explanation:* The size of the object after it has been magnified. Remind pupils that once this image has been magnified it will appear bigger than it is in real life.

Step 6: Calculating Image Size

In the next step explain to pupils that they can calculate the image size if they know the actual size of the object and the magnification provided by the microscope. Support a pupil's understanding of the mathematical relationship between actual size and image size by displaying Figure 4.3, which is presented in the same format and builds on Figure 4.2 and Table 4.1.

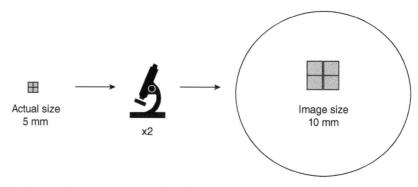

Figure 4.3   Image size once an object has been magnified

In this example, highlight to pupils that the actual size of the image is 5 mm and the magnification from the microscope has made the object appear two times bigger (x2) which means that the image size is now 10 mm. It is important to help pupils understand the mathematical relationship between the actual size, magnification and image size; this can easily be achieved by summarising the information in a table as demonstrated in Table 4.2.

Table 4.2 Calculating image size once an object has been magnified

Actual size	Magnification	Image size
5 mm	x2	10 mm
5	Multiplied by 2	Equals 10

At this stage it is important for pupils to understand that a magnification of x2 means that the image size is two times bigger. Pupils should know that they can easily identify how much an image has been magnified by attending to the number after the x. For example, x50 means that the microscope has magnified the image so that the image size appears 50 times larger than the actual size of the object.

Step 7: Introducing an Equation to Calculate Image Size

In the next sequence of learning, pupils should understand that instead of drawing out their working every time, they can write an **equation**. Explain to pupils that an equation is like a recipe and provides the instructions for how image size can be calculated. Figure 4.4 shows how this is written.

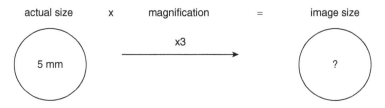

Figure 4.4 Introducing the equation for calculating image size

In this example ask pupils what the image size of the object would be now that it has been magnified x3. Pupils should be able to correctly answer 15 mm.

Tips and tricks

Pupils should consolidate their understanding on how to calculate image size by being presented with additional examples. You can do this by adapting Figure 4.4 and asking pupils to calculate image size with different values for actual size and magnification. Make sure that pupils are supported to explain their thinking process by asking what equation they used, what values they used and how they calculated their final answer.

Step 8: Calculating Actual Size

The next step is to help pupils understand that they can rearrange this equation to calculate the actual size of the object if they know the values for magnification and image size. For example, they may not know the actual size of a plant cell if they are observing it for the first time, but they will be able to measure the image size once magnified and they will know the magnification provided by the microscope. Figure 4.5 shows how this can be calculated by rearranging the equation.

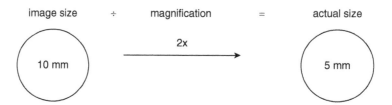

Figure 4.5   Using an equation to calculate actual size

Tips and tricks

Remind pupils that if they are using a microscope, they can work out the total magnification provided by the microscope by multiplying the magnification provided by the eyepiece lens with that of the objective lens.

Step 9: Using an Equation to Calculate Magnification

In the final step, pupils should be supported to learn that they can also rearrange the same equation to calculate the magnification applied by a microscope. This becomes important if they are studying an object and they have the values for image size and actual size but have not been told by how much it has been magnified. Figure 4.6 shows how magnification can be calculated by rearranging the equation.

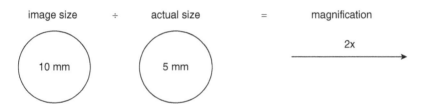

Figure 4.6   Using an equation to calculate magnification

Check for understanding

The following checks for understanding will help you assess your pupils' knowledge about microscopes and magnification:

- Explain why our understanding of cells and microorganisms has developed over many centuries.
- What is the purpose of a microscope?
- How does a light microscope work?
- Explain what happens during the process of magnification?
- What is the field of view?
- What is meant by the actual size of the object?
- What is meant by the image size?
- How do you calculate image size?
- How do you calculate actual size?
- How do you calculate magnification?

(Continued)

- The actual size of an *E. coli* cell is 0.002 mm and it is magnified x500. Calculate the image size.
- The image size of a cell is 3 mm and has been magnified x100. Calculate the actual size.
- The actual size of a pollen grain is 0.2 mm and its image size is 40 mm. Calculate the magnification.

5

ENZYME FUNCTION

What students should know already

- Cells provide structure and organisation to complex organisms. They contain genetic material to make proteins, provide the energy the organism needs and carry out specialised functions.
- Ribosomes make proteins (long chains of amino acids).
- Enzymes are made of proteins. They have a complex 3D shape and have a region called an active site.
- Enzymes are biological catalysts, which means they speed up reactions without being used up. They catalyse reactions which means that something new is made that the organism needs to survive.
- Enzymes are required to catalyse many of the chemical reactions that happen in complex organisms. Examples of chemical reactions include respiration and photosynthesis.

(Continued)

- Some of the reactions catalysed by enzymes may involve the breakdown of chemical molecules whilst others are involved in building chemical molecules, for example:
  - Amylase found in the saliva catalyses the reaction to break down starch into glucose.
  - Catalase found in the liver cells catalyses the reaction to break down harmful hydrogen peroxide into harmless water and oxygen.
  - Starch synthase found in plants catalyses the synthesis (building) of starch from glucose.
  - DNA polymerase found in the nucleus of cells catalyses the synthesis (building) of DNA from its monomers.

What students should know by the end

- Enzymes catalyse new chemical molecules.
- Enzyme molecules work on substrates and the molecules that are made by this reaction are called products.
- For a new chemical molecule to be catalysed the substrate needs to fit into the active site.
- Each enzyme's active site is substrate-specific.
- The lock and key model provides a concrete representation of how enzymes function by comparing the key to a substrate which needs to be matched to a specific lock (the enzyme's active site) before it can work.
- The active site on an enzyme is affected by changes in pH and temperature, this leads to the active site changing shape. If this happens the substrate will no longer fit into the active site and the enzyme is said to be denatured.

Explanation

The most effective way to teach enzyme function is to use a series of well-annotated diagrams, drawn live in lesson. The diagrams used should become sequentially more complex to avoid cognitive overload. Challenge pupils to attend to the new knowledge in each diagram before moving on to the next, more complex diagram. Key questions to ask pupils throughout include: What's new here? What do you think is happening and why? What do you think will happen next?

Pupils should have a concrete understanding of both the structure of an enzyme and the purpose of an enzyme, with some clear examples, before moving on to focus on enzyme function. This will enable you to create depth in your pupils' knowledge by sequencing learning that becomes more complex over time. Ask pupils to retrieve what they already know about enzyme structure, its purpose and some examples before exploring enzyme function.

Step 1: The Active Site

Start by retrieving prior knowledge that enzymes act as biological catalysts, meaning they speed up reactions without being used up. They catalyse reactions to make new molecules, these molecules are needed by an organism to perform life-sustaining biological processes. Highlight that in this sequence of learning, pupils will learn how an enzyme functions.

As demonstrated by Figure 5.1, start by drawing a diagrammatic representation of an enzyme and introducing key vocabulary. Note the simplicity of this figure. At this stage pupils are only focusing in on the enzyme, the active site and the name of the enzyme, amylase.

Pupils must be able to recognise that the active site is the part of an enzyme where substrate molecules bind and where the chemical reaction takes place. Remind pupils that enzyme molecules work on substrates and the molecules that are made by this reaction are called products.

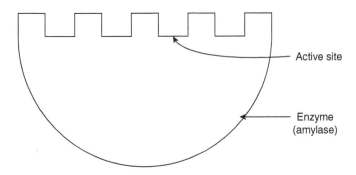

Figure 5.1 Simplistic representation of the enzyme amylase

Step 2: The Substrate Molecule

Introduce Figure 5.2 and ask pupils to explain what is happening here and what is new. The only addition to the figure here is the inclusion of the substrate molecule. Ensure that pupils understand that a substrate molecule is the molecule that the enzyme is acting on. In this example the substrate molecule is starch.

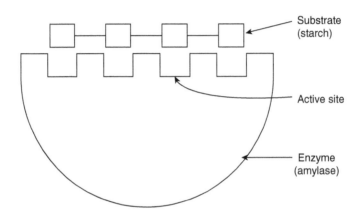

Figure 5.2 Introduction of substrate molecule to explore enzyme function

Then pose a question: What do you think will happen when starch collides with the active site of the enzyme amylase? Some pupils may be able to utilise their prior knowledge and provide a surface response along the lines of 'starch will be broken down into glucose'. Support pupils to develop their understanding further by explaining that when the enzyme's active site and substrate molecules collide, they form an enzyme–substrate complex, meaning that a chemical reaction will take place and something new will be produced, in this case glucose.

Step 3: The Shape of the Active Site

Introduce Figure 5.3 and ask pupils to attend to the shape of the active site and substrate molecule. Pupils should be able to identify that the substrate molecule has a shape that will fit specifically into the active site. Explain to pupils that an enzyme will only work if the substrate molecule has a shape that matches the shape of the active site. Ask pupils to attend to the chemical reaction that will occur because of this collision, and what will happen to the starch.

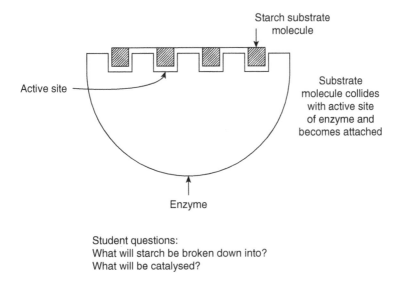

Student questions:
What will starch be broken down into?
What will be catalysed?

Figure 5.3 Substrate molecule (starch) binding to the active site of an enzyme (amylase)

Step 4: Exploring Which Product Has Been Catalysed

Present Figure 5.4 and, before annotating it with text, ask pupils what has happened in this figure? Responses elicited should reflect that something new has been made. Pupils should be able to state that starch has been broken down into glucose. However, it is important to develop a deeper understanding by explaining that the complex starch molecule has been broken down into a simpler molecule, glucose, by the enzyme amylase. For pupils to understand why enzyme function is important in organisms, ask them what biological process glucose is necessary for. Pupils should be able to identify that glucose alongside oxygen is required for cellular aerobic respiration to make chemical energy.

Step 5: Consolidate Learning

Figure 5.5 consolidates learning by displaying Figures 5.2, 5.3 and 5.4 at the same time so that pupils can understand the clear sequence involved in enzyme action. Ask pupils here to recap: What is happening? Why is this important? What has changed by the end of the chemical reaction?

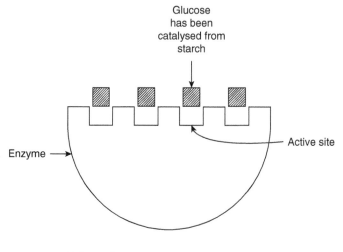

Figure 5.4 Product catalysed by the enzyme

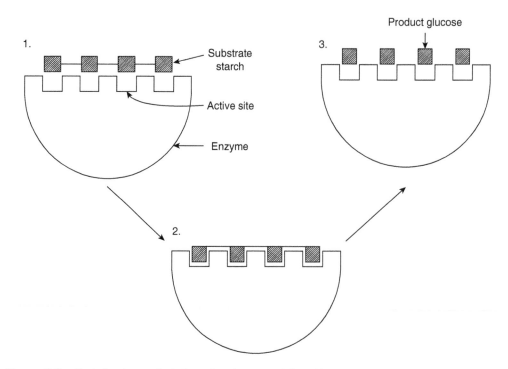

Figure 5.5 Exploring how substrate molecules are catalysed by enzymes

Step 6: Exploring the Site-specific Nature of the Active Site in an Enzyme

Display Figure 5.6 and explain to pupils that the purpose of this figure is to check for understanding. Ask pupils why the protein substrate molecule will not be catalysed by amylase. Pupils should be able to explain that the shape of the protein substrate molecule does not match the shape of the active site and so will not be able to bind with the active site, therefore the substrate molecule cannot be catalysed.

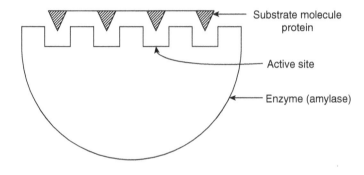

Will amylase be able to break down protein? Explain your answer.

Figure 5.6   Exploring the site specificity of an enzyme

Tips and tricks

Observe how each figure is building in detail from simple to complex. This conscious design decision manages cognitive load, builds a pupil's knowledge, summarises the key scientific words and can also be used to check for understanding.

Step 7: The Lock and Key Model

The purpose of Figure 5.7 is to introduce the concept of the lock and key model. This model aims to support pupils' understanding by comparing a key that only operates on one lock to the idea that a substrate molecule will only bind with an enzyme with an active site that complements the shape of the substrate. The key has a specific shape which will fit the lock in the same way that a substrate molecule has a specific shape which fits into the active site. Figure 5.7 demonstrates the substrate molecule acting as the key which fits into the lock or the active site.

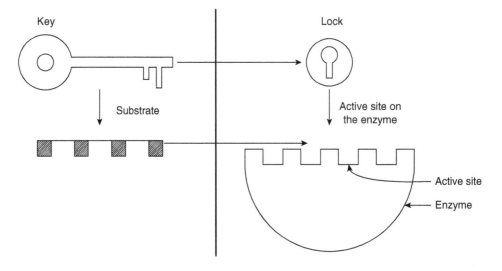

Which is the lock and which is the key?
Explain the lock and key model.

Figure 5.7   Exploring the lock and key model

Before annotating the figure, ask pupils why the substrate fitting into the active site of an enzyme can be compared to a lock and key. Pupils should be able to respond that only the right shaped key (substrate) will fit into the lock (active site of the enzyme) to open the door (or catalyse the substrate).

Tips and tricks

The representation of the substrate molecule and active site is drawn as an exact copy to previous figures to create consistency, consolidate learning and build upon previous knowledge.

Step 8: Denatured Enzymes

To consolidate learning, Figure 5.8 can be drawn fresh, without the aid of Figures 5.1–7. Check for understanding by asking pupils to label key parts of the figure whilst preparing them for the next sequence of learning on the effects of temperature and pH on enzymes.

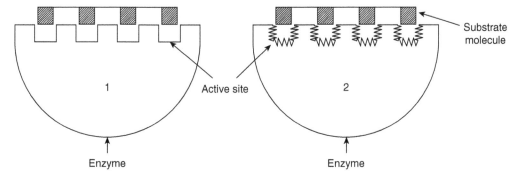

Why would we say that enzyme 2 has become denatured?
What has physically happened to the shape of the active site?

Figure 5.8 Exploring denatured enzymes

Start by introducing pupils to the word denature and explain that this word means to destroy or take away the characteristic properties of a biological structure so that its function is disrupted.

Explain that enzymes can be denatured if they are exposed to extremes of pH or temperatures above the enzyme's optimum temperature. The temperature at which the enzyme's rate of reaction is the highest is referred to as the optimum temperature whilst the pH is a unit of measurement which describes the degree of acidity or alkalinity of a solution.

If the temperature increases above the enzyme's optimum temperature or there are extreme variations in the pH, the shape of the enzyme's active site changes and the substrate molecule can no longer fit into the enzyme's active site. This means the key will no longer be able to fit into the lock. The enzyme is said to be denatured; its function has been disrupted because it can no longer catalyse the biological reaction.

Step 9: Exploring Pupils' Misconceptions

As you progress through this sequence of learning, it is important to identify and correct pupils' misconceptions. When teaching enzymes, misconceptions fall into four main categories:

1. Function: Enzymes have an important job to do because they sustain life by building molecules like DNA or breaking down molecules like starch.

2. Context: Enzymes are found in all organisms because all organisms need to build or break down molecules needed for essential life processes to take place.
3. Scale: Enzymes are made inside cells and are therefore smaller than cells.
4. Location: Enzymes are protein molecules produced by ribosomes that are then stored within the cytoplasm of the cell.

Check for understanding

The following checks for understanding will help you assess your pupils' knowledge about enzyme structure and function:

- What is the purpose of an enzyme?
- What happens at the active site of an enzyme?
- What is the difference between a substrate and a product?
- What does it mean when we say that an enzyme is substrate-specific?
- Explain how the enzyme amylase works.
- Explain why amylase will not break down a protein molecule.
- How can the lock and key model can be used to represent enzyme function?
- What do we mean by the term denatured?
- What two factors will cause an enzyme to denature?
- When we say an enzyme has denatured, what does this mean?

6

CELLULAR RESPIRATION

What students should know already

- Cells provide structure and organisation to complex organisms. They contain genetic material to make proteins, provide the energy the organism needs and carry out specialised functions.
- The four molecules necessary for life are proteins, carbohydrates, lipids and nucleic acids. Without these four molecules, cells and therefore organisms would not be able to function.
- In chemical reactions atoms are rearranged. Reactants are the substances that go into a chemical reaction and products are the substances that are made at the end of a chemical reaction.

(Continued)

- Exothermic reactions are chemical reactions during which some of the energy is also transferred into the thermal energy store of the surroundings, resulting in the temperature of the surroundings increasing.
- In chemistry a word equation models a chemical reaction, using the names of the reactants and products.

What students should know by the end

- Cellular respiration is a fundamental life process.
- The purpose of cellular respiration is that it provides cells the energy they need to function for the organism to carry out essential life processes.
- Cellular respiration is a series of chemical reactions that transfer energy from the chemical energy store of glucose.
- There are two types of cellular respiration: cellular aerobic and anaerobic respiration.
- The main type of cellular respiration is cellular aerobic respiration.
- Cellular aerobic respiration requires oxygen and takes place in an organelle called the mitochondria.
- In the absence of oxygen anaerobic respiration can take place in the cytoplasm but smaller amounts of energy are released in comparison to aerobic respiration.
- There are two types of cellular anaerobic respiration: anaerobic respiration that occurs in the muscles of animals and anaerobic respiration that occurs in plants and microorganisms (also known as fermentation).

Explanation

It is important to reflect on the knowledge pupils require to develop a full understanding of this topic. Often it is taught as an over-simplified and standalone biological topic. However, for pupils to develop a depth of understanding, the links between biology, chemistry and physics should be made by helping pupils to learn that respiration involves a series of chemical reactions and involves energy transfers.

Step 1: What is Cellular Respiration?

Cellular respiration is a series of chemical reactions that transfers energy from the chemical energy store of glucose. This energy is used by the cells of the organism to power all its functions. Some of the energy is also transferred into the thermal energy stores of the cell and its surroundings. Therefore, we can also say that respiration is an exothermic reaction; this is because the chemical energy store of the products is smaller than the store of the reactants.

Step 2: What is the Purpose of Cellular Respiration?

Cellular respiration provides the energy for all cellular processes to take place in complex organisms. Energy is needed by cells in complex organisms for a wide variety of reasons, for example reproduction, growth and digestion. Ask pupils if they can identify any other life processes that require energy – these could include excretion and movement.

Respiration, therefore, is an essential process which powers the work of all complex organisms. Most cells in complex organisms require energy because every cell has a job to do. The purpose of respiration therefore is to provide the energy for cells to complete their function.

Providing concrete examples will help pupils to develop their understanding. Two examples are included:

- Sperm cells: During fertilisation, the sperm requires energy to swim to the egg cell, fuse and form a new diploid organism.

- Thigh muscle cells: Require a constant supply of energy to enable people to walk and run.

Step 3: Understanding Cellular Respiration

Pupils should understand that there are two types of cellular respiration: aerobic and anaerobic. By presenting the two pathways in a flowchart like Figure 6.1, pupils can more easily distinguish between the two processes. Remind pupils that all cellular respiration starts with breaking down glucose to release energy from the chemical energy store, but in complex organisms this breakdown of glucose can happen in two different ways, depending on the energy demands placed on the organism.

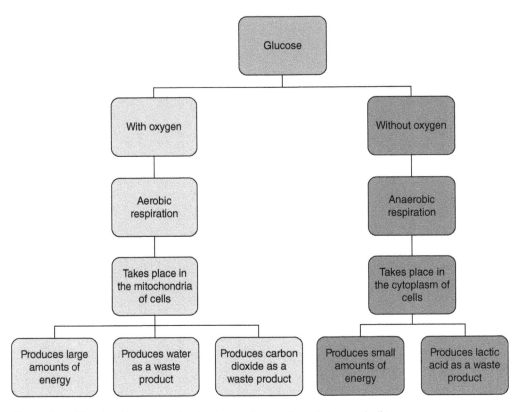

Figure 6.1 Flowchart to summarise the two pathways for cellular respiration

Step 4: How Does Cellular Aerobic Respiration Take Place?

Start by breaking down the left-hand part of the flowchart by explaining cellular aerobic respiration. When there is a plentiful supply of oxygen, most complex organisms favour aerobic respiration because a lot more energy is released.

Check that pupils understand what the word aerobic means. Some may say needs air, but this is an inaccuracy that needs to be corrected. Aerobic means relating to, involving, or requiring oxygen. The word aerobic should immediately indicate to pupils that oxygen (not air) is an essential part of the chemical reaction involved in cellular aerobic respiration.

Scaffold a pupil's learning by encouraging them to apply their new knowledge to the concrete example of aerobic respiration in humans. Start by asking what two substances are required by cells before respiration can take place. Pupils should be able to correctly identify oxygen and glucose. Start by explaining how oxygen is transported to the cells by presenting a simplified diagram of the respiratory system in humans to help pupils visualise how oxygen is transported to individual cells, as demonstrated in Figure 6.2.

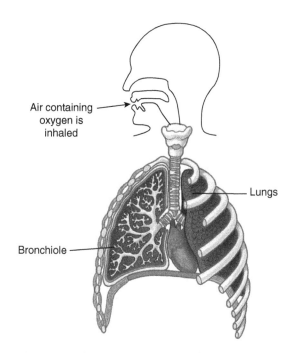

Air containing oxygen is inhaled

Lungs

Bronchiole

The bronchial tubes divide into smaller air passages called bronchi and then into bronchioles.
The bronchioles end in tiny air sacs called alveoli, where oxygen is transferred from the inhaled air to the blood.

Figure 6.2 Simplified diagram of the respiratory system

Then ask pupils to consider where the glucose comes from that is required for aerobic respiration. Explain that we eat food that contains carbohydrates, and the body will break these down into smaller molecules called glucose. This happens during the process of digestion as demonstrated in Figure 6.3. Like oxygen, glucose is absorbed into the blood and transported throughout the body, so that cells can be provided with a continuous supply of glucose and oxygen for cellular aerobic respiration to take place.

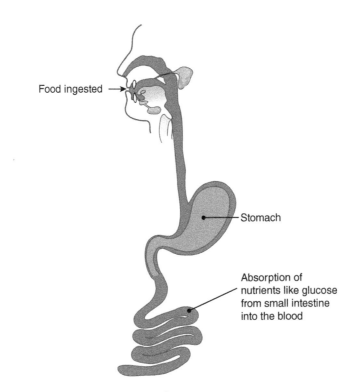

Food ingested →

Stomach

Absorption of nutrients like glucose from small intestine into the blood

Figure 6.3 Simplified diagram of the digestive system

Step 5: Where Does Cellular Aerobic Respiration Take Place?

Retrieve prior knowledge by asking pupils where cellular aerobic respiration takes place. They should remember from their study of plant and animal cells that it takes place in an organelle called the mitochondria. Highlight that this means that both plants and animals must respire, because plants also have mitochondria in their cells and need energy for functions like growth and reproduction.

To help them locate and contextualise their learning, support pupils by presenting them with a diagrammatic representation of a plant and animal cell as in Figure 6.4 and ask them to identify the site of cellular aerobic respiration.

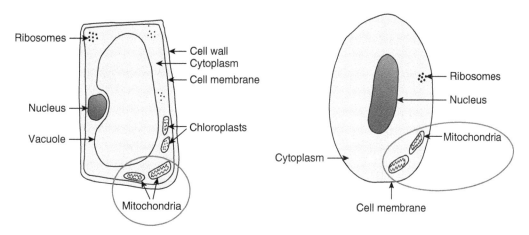

Figure 6.4 Identifying mitochondria in plant cell and animal cells

Step 6: Cellular Aerobic Respiration as a Chemical Reaction

During aerobic respiration, the oxygen combines with glucose inside the mitochondria of the cell to transfer energy from the chemical energy store of glucose. Carbon dioxide and water are waste products and need to be expelled by the cell. This chemical reaction is shown in Figure 6.5.

Reactants		**Products**
glucose + oxygen	$\longrightarrow$	carbon dioxide + water

Figure 6.5 Word equation for cellular aerobic respiration

Remind pupils that aerobic respiration is an exothermic reaction. This is because not all the energy produced by cellular respiration is transferred into the chemical energy stores of the products; some of the energy is also transferred into the thermal energy store of the surroundings, resulting in the temperature of the surroundings increasing.

Step 7: What is Anaerobic Respiration?

To explore the second pathway for cellular respiration, present and break down the right-hand part of the flowchart in Figure 6.1 to outline the key features of anaerobic respiration.

Explain to pupils that there are times when oxygen is in short supply; when this happens complex organisms can switch from aerobic respiration to anaerobic respiration. Ask pupils to attend to what they think the word anaerobic means. Pupils should be able to more easily identify that the word anaerobic indicates that cellular respiration will take place in the absence of oxygen.

At this stage pupils should be introduced to two types of cellular anaerobic respiration – anaerobic respiration that occurs in the muscles of animals and anaerobic respiration that occurs in plants and microorganisms.

Step 8: Anaerobic Respiration that Occurs in the Muscles of Animals

Ask pupils to imagine sprinting 100 metres, they will need to transfer energy from the chemical energy store of the glucose to the cells of their leg muscles very quickly. They will also need a continuous supply of oxygen for the chemical reaction to happen and provide the energy needed for the sprint. During hard exercise like sprinting, weightlifting or cycling uphill, the demand for energy increases and a person cannot supply enough oxygen quickly enough to the muscles that need it for cellular aerobic respiration to occur. To cope with this additional energy requirement on the body, cellular anaerobic respiration happens as well – this means respiration can still take place, but without oxygen.

Using the same process as you did to explain aerobic respiration, explain to pupils that cellular anaerobic respiration does not take place in the mitochondria but in the cytoplasm of the cell; it occurs without oxygen and the waste product is lactic acid.

It is important for pupils to understand that cellular anaerobic respiration in animals releases less energy than aerobic respiration and is therefore less efficient, but is useful if an animal needs a sudden burst of energy, for example if escaping from a predator.

Ask pupils to analyse the word equation in Figure 6.6 and what is different to aerobic respiration here. Pupils should be able to recognise that glucose is broken down without oxygen and lactic acid is the waste product that needs to be removed from muscle cells when strenuous exercise occurs.

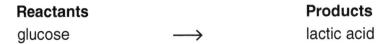

Reactants		**Products**
glucose	$\longrightarrow$	lactic acid

Figure 6.6   Word equation for anaerobic respiration in the muscles of animals

Step 9: Anaerobic Respiration that Occurs in Plants and Microorganisms

Some plants, microorganisms and fungi also respire anaerobically; this reaction can be referred to as fermentation. Fermentation is the process by which plants, microorganisms and fungi produce chemical energy in the absence of oxygen. Present pupils with the word equation for fermentation in Figure 6.7 and ask them what is different when compared to anaerobic respiration in the muscles of animals.

Reactants		**Products**
glucose	$\longrightarrow$	carbon dioxide + ethanol

Figure 6.7   Word equation for anaerobic respiration in plants and microorganisms

Remind pupils that like cellular anaerobic respiration in the muscle cells of animals, smaller amounts of energy are released in comparison to aerobic respiration. However, unlike anaerobic respiration in animals, the waste products of fermentation can be useful to human society. For example, during anaerobic respiration in the fungi yeast, the ethanol produced is used to make alcoholic drinks like beer, whilst in bread the carbon dioxide gas expelled makes it rise.

Check for understanding

The following checks for understanding will help you assess your pupils' knowledge about cellular respiration:

- How are oxygen and glucose transported to cells in humans for aerobic respiration to take place?
- Explain what happens during the process of cellular aerobic respiration.
- Where does aerobic respiration take place?
- What are the reactants and products in cellular aerobic respiration?
- What will the energy released be used for?
- The thigh muscles of professional marathon runners have been found to contain more mitochondria than those of non-professional runners. Explain this finding.
- Under what conditions does anaerobic respiration take place?
- Where does anaerobic respiration in animals take place?

(Continued)

- What are the benefits of anaerobic respiration in animals?
- What are the differences between aerobic and anaerobic respiration in animals?
- What are the differences between anaerobic respiration in the muscle cells of animals when compared to anaerobic respiration in plants, microorganisms and fungi?

7

PHOTOSYNTHESIS

Relevant ages

11–14

What students should know already

- Cells provide structure and organisation to complex organisms. They contain genetic material to make proteins, provide the energy the organism needs and carry out specialised functions.
- The purpose of cellular respiration is that it provides cells the energy they need to function for the organism to carry out essential life processes.
- In chemical reactions atoms are rearranged. The substances that go into a chemical reaction are called reactants and the substances made at the end of a chemical reaction are called products.
- Endothermic reactions are chemical reactions in which more energy is absorbed when the bonds in the reactants are broken than is released when new bonds are formed in the products.
- In chemistry a word equation models a chemical reaction, using the names of the reactants and products.

What students should know by the end

- Photosynthesis is a fundamental life process in plants, which creates biomass and drives energy transfer for almost all life on Earth.
- The purpose of photosynthesis is to provide plant cells with glucose.
- Photosynthesis is a series of chemical reactions that takes place in plants, in which energy is transferred into the chemical energy store of glucose via the light pathway.
- The light required for photosynthesis is absorbed by a pigment called chlorophyll, which is green in colour.
- Chlorophyll is found in the chloroplasts of plant cells in the leaves of a plant.
- The carbon dioxide needed for photosynthesis enters the cell through microscopic pores called stomata in the leaves.
- The water needed for photosynthesis enters through the roots and is transported to the leaves through vessels called xylem.
- Glucose is a sugar molecule and is used by the plant for respiration, to make other vital substances and as a storage material.
- The waste product of photosynthesis is oxygen. The oxygen is used by plant cells for respiration. Any excess oxygen leaves the leaf through microscopic pores in the plant leaf called stomata.

Tips and tricks

Reactivate prior knowledge by asking pupils to retrieve knowledge on chemical reactions, cells and respiration. Some teachers opt to teach photosynthesis within the chemistry curriculum, this provides a good opportunity to consolidate endothermic reactions through exemplification. However, the primary purpose of photosynthesis is as a biological process which creates biomass and drives energy transfer for almost all life on Earth. This biological context should be the focus of a pupil's learning when exploring the process of photosynthesis.

Explanation

This sequence of learning aims to build a pupil's knowledge about the importance of photosynthesis as a biological process in creating biomass and driving energy transfer for almost all life on Earth. It also supports pupils to understand how photosynthesis takes place and how the products are utilised by the plant.

Step 1: What is Photosynthesis?

Photosynthesis is a series of chemical reactions that takes place in plants, in which energy is transferred into the chemical energy store of glucose via the light pathway.

Pupils should be reminded that glucose is a simple sugar and is an important molecule needed to sustain life in all organisms. Glucose and other molecules like starch, a polymer made from glucose, are important to plants and animals in providing the essential energy stores needed for respiration.

Step 2: Why is Photosynthesis One of the Most Important Life Processes?

It is important for pupils to understand that there are many reasons why photosynthesis is an essential process for all life on Earth. These are:

- Plants are the first step in the food chain; they are called producers because they make their own organic nutrients/food in the form of glucose.

- The energy stored in glucose is transferred from plants through the food chain to consumers. Photosynthesis is therefore essential in providing the energy needed by consumers and sustains all life on Earth.

- The oxygen released during photosynthesis is essential because it will be used by animals during respiration.

Step 3: Understanding the Importance of Glucose

Before asking pupils to learn about the process of photosynthesis, it is important to:

- Provide context and unpick why glucose is an important molecule for both plants and animals.

- Explain how plants and animals differ in the way they acquire glucose, so that pupils understand why photosynthesis is so essential. This can easily be presented in a simple table such as in Table 7.1.

Table 7.1   How do animals and plants acquire and use glucose?

	Plants	Animals
Why is glucose needed?	• Respiration. • To make new materials like lipids or proteins. • To convert into a storage molecule in the form of starch.	• Respiration.
How is glucose acquired?	Plants make their own supply of glucose during photosynthesis.	Animals get glucose from the food they eat.
What biological processes are involved?	Photosynthesis is a series of chemical reactions in which plants use carbon dioxide, water and light to make glucose.	In animals, complex carbohydrates are broken down during digestion into the simple sugar molecule glucose.

Step 4: Where Does Photosynthesis Take Place?

Before exploring photosynthesis as a chemical reaction, ask pupils to locate where photosynthesis takes place. Pupils should be able to recall this from previous knowledge on plant cells and correctly identify that photosynthesis takes place in an organelle called the chloroplast. To help pupils contextualise their learning, present them with a diagrammatic representation of a plant cell as in Figure 7.1 and ask them to locate the chloroplast.

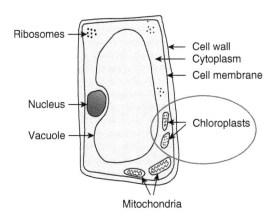

Figure 7.1   Plant cell

Build on pupils' knowledge by explaining that chloroplasts contain a green pigment called chlorophyll. It is in the chlorophyll that energy is absorbed from the light and transferred into the chemical energy of glucose during the process of photosynthesis.

With this information, ask pupils which part of a plant is green and therefore contains chlorophyll. All pupils should be able to recognise that leaves and stems are green in colour and therefore contain the pigment chlorophyll. A follow-up question to this should be, what does this tell you about what is going on in this part of a plant? Pupils should be able to recognise that chlorophyll is green in colour, is found in chloroplasts and indicates that this is the part of the plant where photosynthesis takes place.

Step 5: Photosynthesis as a Chemical Reaction

Develop pupils' knowledge further by explaining that the chlorophyll within chloroplasts absorbs the energy transferred by light and uses this energy to make glucose from carbon dioxide and water. Oxygen is the waste product in this chemical reaction. Remind pupils that because photosynthesis is a series of chemical reactions, we can represent photosynthesis as a word equation as shown in Figure 7.2.

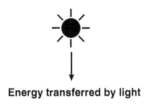

Energy transferred by light

Reactants	Products
carbon dioxide + water $\rightarrow$	glucose + oxygen

Figure 7.2 Word equation for photosynthesis

At this stage in the sequence of learning, highlight that photosynthesis is an example of an endothermic reaction. A reaction is endothermic when more energy is absorbed to break the bonds in the reactants than is released when new bonds are formed in the products. A constant input of energy via the pathway of light is needed to keep this endothermic reaction going. In this case the energy required for photosynthesis comes from light sources such as the sun.

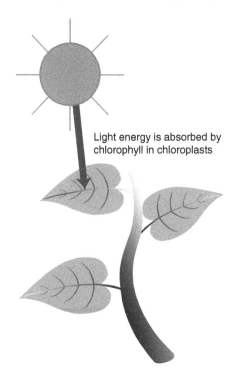

Tips and tricks

Help pupils to distinguish between natural and artificial sources of light. In the natural environment plants will use the sun as a source of light energy. However, plants can also use the energy contained in artificial light sources such as LED lamps for photosynthesis.

Step 6: How Does a Plant Get Carbon Dioxide, Water and Light to Enable Photosynthesis to Take Place?

Once pupils understand the process of photosynthesis and have explored how glucose is made, it is important to explore how a plant gets the reactants it needs and how they are transported to the chloroplast for photosynthesis to take place. This is most effectively done through building up a diagram of how each reactant enters a plant. Start by presenting Figure 7.3 and explaining that energy from light is absorbed by the chlorophyll in the chloroplasts found in the green parts of a plant.

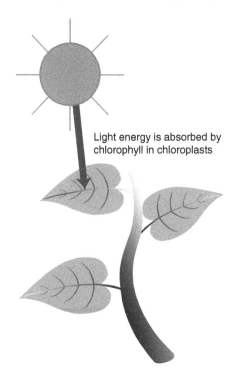

Light energy is absorbed by chlorophyll in chloroplasts

Figure 7.3   How light enters a leaf

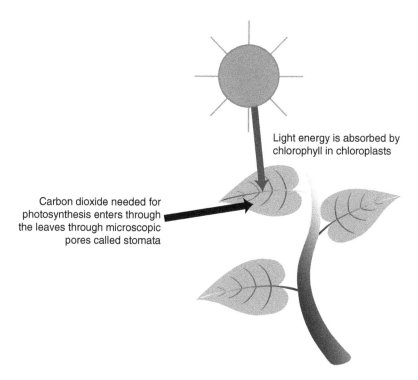

Light energy is absorbed by chlorophyll in chloroplasts

Carbon dioxide needed for photosynthesis enters through the leaves through microscopic pores called stomata

Figure 7.4 How carbon dioxide enters a leaf

Present Figure 7.4 to demonstrate that the carbon dioxide needed for photosynthesis enters through microscopic pores in the leaf called stomata. Remind pupils that microscopic means that the openings or pores called stomata are so small they are only visible with a microscope.

Tips and tricks

At each stage, when building this sequence of diagrams, ask pupils what is new here so that they are being directed to focus on the three requirements of photosynthesis in small steps. Ask pupils to focus on the two new words introduced and provide explanations for each before continuing:

- Stomata are microscopic pores (pores are small openings), found at the surface of leaves and stems. Stomata control the amount of carbon dioxide entering the leaf.
- Xylem vessels transport water and dissolved nutrients from the roots to the stems and leaves of the plant.

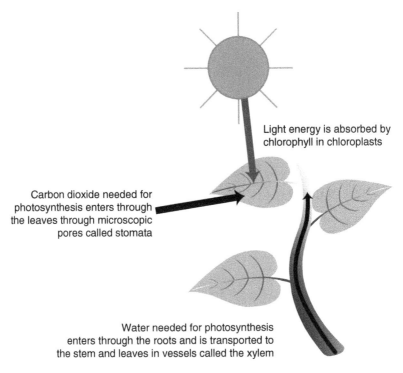

Light energy is absorbed by chlorophyll in chloroplasts

Carbon dioxide needed for photosynthesis enters through the leaves through microscopic pores called stomata

Water needed for photosynthesis enters through the roots and is transported to the stem and leaves in vessels called the xylem

Figure 7.5 How water enters a leaf

Finally, present Figure 7.5 to demonstrate that the water needed for photosynthesis enters through the roots and is transported by vessels called the xylem to the stem and leaves of the plant.

Tips and tricks

Ask pupils to focus on the word phloem and provide a clear explanation before continuing. The phloem is a network of vessels in a plant that transports sucrose from the leaves to the rest of the plant.

Step 7: What Happens to the Glucose Produced During Photosynthesis?

Pupils should understand that the glucose produced during photosynthesis is vital for the structure and function of the plant and is used in several ways. This can be more easily explained in a structured diagram as demonstrated in

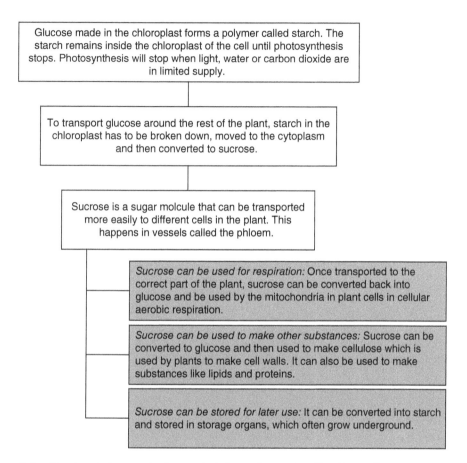

Figure 7.6 Structured diagram to demonstrate how glucose is utilised by a plant

Figure 7.6. Pupils should understand that glucose is needed by all cells in the plant and will therefore have to be transported. This transportation takes place in a network of vessels called the phloem. Before this transportation can happen, glucose produced in leaf cells must be converted to sucrose, another type of sugar molecule.

Step 8: What Happens to the Oxygen?

Ask pupils what the waste product of photosynthesis is. Pupils should be able to identify that oxygen is the waste product. It is important for pupils to understand that one of two things will happen to the oxygen:

- The oxygen will be used by the plant in respiration.
- Any excess oxygen will be removed from the leaf through microscopic pores called stomata. It is this excess oxygen that is used by animals in respiration.

Tips and tricks

Remind pupils that both plants and animals respire. Plants will use the glucose and oxygen produced during photosynthesis as products for cellular aerobic respiration. The energy released from the chemical energy store during respiration is essential for important cellular functions in plants, such as reproduction and growth.

Check for understanding

The following checks for understanding will help you assess your pupils' knowledge about photosynthesis:

- Why is photosynthesis a fundamental life process?
- Where does photosynthesis take place?
- What reactants are needed for photosynthesis?
- How do the reactants of photosynthesis enter a plant?
- What is the useful product of photosynthesis?
- What is the waste product of photosynthesis?
- Why can photosynthesis be described as an endothermic reaction?
- In the natural environment what time of day would you expect photosynthesis to stop? Explain your answer.
- What happens to the glucose made in chloroplasts and how is it transported to other parts of the plant?
- What is the glucose from photosynthesis used for in a plant?
- What roles do stomata and xylem vessels have in photosynthesis?
- Explain why plants need to photosynthesise and respire.

8

IMMUNITY AND THE IMMUNE SYSTEM

Relevant ages

14–16

What students should know already

- Cells provide structure and organisation to complex organisms. They contain genetic material to make proteins, provide the energy the organism needs and carry out specialised functions.
- Enzyme molecules work on substrates and the molecules that are made by this reaction are called products.
- For a new chemical molecule to be catalysed the substrate needs to fit into the active site.
- Each enzyme's active site is substrate-specific.

(Continued)

- Some examples of organisms are animals, plants, fungi and even microorganisms like bacteria and viruses (these are so small that we can only see them with a special piece of equipment called a microscope).
- A non-communicable disease is a disease that is not infectious; it cannot be passed from person to person. They are caused by genetic faults or the lifestyle of the person.
- A communicable disease is an infectious disease (it can be passed from person to person), caused by a pathogen and harms the host.

What students should know by the end

- A pathogen is any microorganism that causes a disease and harms its host. There are five main types of pathogen: viruses, bacteria, fungi, protozoa, and animal parasites.
- The immune system protects complex organisms from pathogens. It is made up of different organs, tissues and cells that are specialised to destroy pathogens.
- An antigen is a protein on the surface of a cell. A foreign antigen found on the surface of a pathogen will produce an immune response by the host and induce white blood cells to produce antibodies to destroy the antigen.
- White blood cells are part of the immune system and are found in blood. Their function is to help the host fight infection from pathogens.
- A lymphocyte is a type of white blood cell that produces antibodies.
- Antibodies are proteins found at the surface of lymphocytes; they attach to antigens from the pathogen to destroy it.
- Memory lymphocytes remain in the blood stream after an infection has been fought and when exposed to the same pathogen again can quickly produce many antibodies to destroy the pathogen, before it has had time to reproduce and cause disease within the host.
- Being immune means that you are protected against that disease. Getting a second infection of the same disease means that you can produce antibodies rapidly because of memory lymphocytes, which destroy the pathogen before a host has symptoms of the disease.

Explanation

This sequence of learning focuses on the immune system's response to an infection caused by a communicable disease. It will deep dive into how the immune system is triggered when foreign antigens on the surface of a pathogen are detected and how antibody production by the host's own lymphocytes requires a series of stages before the pathogen is destroyed. It also explores how a subsequent infection by the same pathogen can be destroyed more rapidly by the function of memory lymphocytes.

Step 1: What are Pathogens?

Start by introducing the importance of the immune system in complex organisms, by explaining that the immune system protects complex organisms from communicable diseases caused by pathogens. Ensure that pupils understand that a communicable disease is an infectious disease (it can be passed from person to person), is caused by a pathogen and harms the host.

Tips and tricks

Help pupils to retrieve prior knowledge by exploring that the immune system is like all biological systems found within complex organisms. It is made of cells, tissue and organs that work together to perform a specific function. The immune system functions to destroy foreign objects like pathogens.

Take a moment to frame learning for pupils by highlighting that the immune system is extremely complex and this sequence of learning specifically deep dives into how white blood cells, called lymphocytes, produce antibodies to destroy pathogens. Pupils will explore why this immune response is important in fighting communicable diseases.

Pupils should understand that a pathogen is any microorganism that causes a disease and therefore harms its host. There are five main types of pathogen: viruses, bacteria, fungi, protozoa, and animal parasites. A disease caused by a pathogen is known as a communicable disease because it is infectious. By infectious, remind pupils that this means it can pass from person to person and cause the same harmful symptoms in all people with that disease. Provide pupils with examples of pathogens so that they have a concrete foundation for their learning. Table 8.1 outlines a series of examples.

Step 2: How is a Pathogen Detected?

All cells and pathogens have antigens. An antigen is a protein on the surface of any cell or pathogen. For example, the surface of red blood cells is coated with antigens. When a pathogen enters our body, its antigens are identified by the body as foreign. Ensure that pupils understand that in terms of biology, being foreign means something that is unfamiliar to the host. It is the presence of a foreign antigen found on the surface of the pathogen that triggers a response in our immune system to fight and destroy the pathogen.

Table 8.1 Types of pathogens, examples of diseases caused by pathogens and their symptoms

Type of pathogen	Example of a disease caused by this type of pathogen in humans	Symptoms of this disease
Virus	Flu	A high fever, aching body, runny nose, sore throat, headache, cough and sneezing.
Fungi	Athlete's foot	Itching, stinging, and burning between toes as well as cracking and peeling skin on your feet.
Protozoa	Malaria	A high fever, chills, headache, nausea, vomiting, muscle pain and fatigue.
Bacteria	E. coli	Abdominal cramping, diarrhoea, loss of appetite or nausea, fatigue and fever.
Animal parasites	Tapeworms	Nausea, diarrhoea, abdominal pain, fatigue and weight loss.

Introduce Figure 8.1 to provide an example of a pathogen and the location of the antigens at the surface of the pathogen. Ask pupils to describe the shape of the antigen and highlight that the shape of the antigens is unique to that pathogen. Each type of pathogen will have differently shaped antigens. Indicate that this detail will become important as they progress through the sequence of learning.

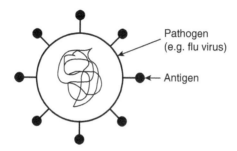

Figure 8.1   The location of antigens on the surface of a pathogen

Step 3: Which Cells are Responsible for Detecting Antigens on the Surface of a Pathogen?

The cells responsible for detecting antigens on the surface of a pathogen are white blood cells. These cells are found in the blood and are part of the immune system. Pupils should understand that it is these cells that help people to fight an infection from a pathogen like the flu virus.

Extend pupil learning by introducing Figure 8.2 to highlight that lymphocytes are a type of white blood cell and are an important part of the immune system. Lymphocytes also have protein molecules on their surface, called antibodies. It is these antibodies that are responsible for destroying a pathogen like a flu virus. At this stage ask pupils to attend to the shape of the antibodies and ask them to make a link between the shape of the antibody and the shape of the antigen on the surface of the pathogen.

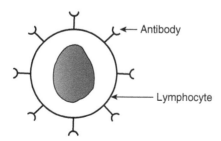

Figure 8.2   Lymphocytes with antibodies at their surface

Step 4: How are Antibodies Activated?

Pupils should understand that an antibody is a protein molecule produced by lymphocytes and responsible for destroying pathogens. However, before antibodies can do this, a lymphocyte with the right antibodies needs to be activated. Figure 8.3 demonstrates that a lymphocyte is activated only when it has antibodies at its surface that match the shape of the antigen on the pathogen. When this happens, the lymphocyte becomes activated and can start to produce lots of antibodies in order to seek out and destroy the pathogen.

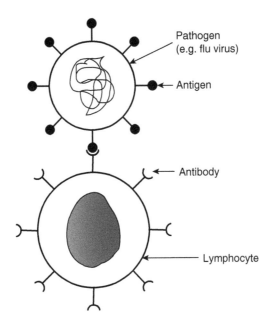

Figure 8.3   Lymphocytes with antibodies at their surface that match the shape of the antigen on the surface of the pathogen

Tips and tricks

Highlight that the body produces lymphocytes with differently shaped antibodies. It is only when the shape of the antibody matches the shape of the antigen on the pathogen that the lymphocyte will be activated and the pathogen can be destroyed. Remind pupils that they have come across this concept of shape specificity when they explored the active site of an enzyme.

It is important to consolidate learning about the importance of shape specificity in relation to lymphocyte activation and antibody production before moving on. Present Figure 8.4 and ask pupils to identify why the lymphocyte cannot be activated by the antigens on the hepatitis B virus. Pupils should recognise that the shape of the antibodies do not match the shape of the antigens on the surface of the pathogen; they are not complementary. Each antigen has a distinct shape and must match the shape of the antibodies on the surface of the lymphocyte.

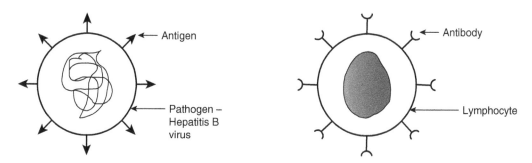

Figure 8.4   A hepatitis B virus with distinct antigens on its surface

Step 6: How do Antibodies Destroy Pathogens?

Once the lymphocyte with the correct antibody has been matched to the antigen on the surface of the pathogen, pupils should understand that three stages must take place before the pathogen is fully destroyed.

Figure 8.5 demonstrates stage 1. During this stage, the activated lymphocyte will divide rapidly to produce more antibodies. The shape of all the antibodies produced will match the shape of the antigen and will therefore be able destroy the pathogens that have entered the body and have since been reproducing.

To explore stage 2, ask pupils to attend to Figure 8.6, which demonstrates how antibodies are released from the lymphocytes, so that they can locate and destroy the pathogen.

In stage 3, ask pupils to attend to Figure 8.7, demonstrating multiple antibodies attaching onto the foreign antigen on the surface of the pathogen. This must happen until all the pathogens are destroyed.

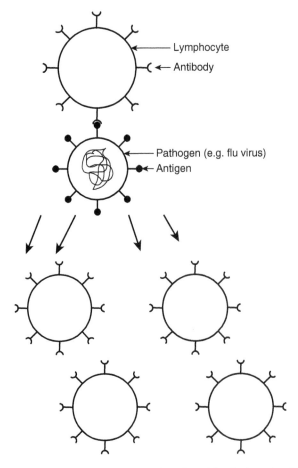

Figure 8.5 Stage 1: lymphocytes divide rapidly to produce identical copies (clones) to make antibodies that match the shape of the antigen on the surface of the pathogen

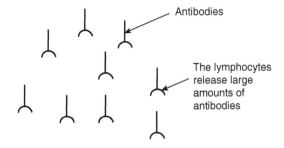

Figure 8.6 Lymphocytes release large amounts of antibodies into the blood stream

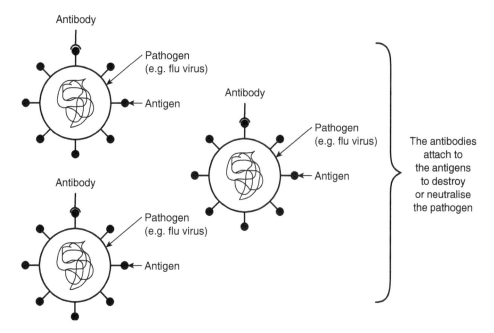

Figure 8.7 Antibodies destroying pathogens

Step 7: What is the Role of a Memory Lymphocyte?

Pupils should understand that while all the pathogens may have been destroyed in stages 1–3, the host is not yet fully protected from another infection of the same pathogen until memory lymphocytes have been produced. Once created, memory lymphocytes remain in the blood stream for some time after the initial infection. They carry the matching antibodies and can quickly respond to a reinfection by the same pathogen and will stop the host from having the symptoms of the disease caused by the pathogen. At this stage, the host is immune which means they are protected against that disease.

Tips and tricks

Pupils should understand that the memory cells will only protect them from that one infectious disease. If they were infected by another type of pathogen then a new lymphocyte

(Continued)

with an antibody that is complementary to the shape of the new pathogen's antigen would have to be activated – would need to undertake rapid cell division to make copies and release antbodies into the blood stream for the pathogen to be destroyed. Finally, memory lymphocytes would need to be released into the blood stream before a body is immune to the new disease.

Check for understanding

The following checks for understanding will help you assess your pupils' knowledge about immunity and the immune system:

- What is a communicable disease?
- What is the role of the immune system?
- What is a pathogen?
- What is an antigen?
- What is a lymphocyte?
- What is an antibody?
- When will the immune system be activated?
- When will a lymphocyte be activated?
- Once a lymphocyte has been activated, what are the three stages involved in destroying a pathogen?
- What is the role of memory lymphocytes?
- What would happen if the body were infected by the same pathogen?
- What would happen if the body were infected by a different pathogen?
- If you are immune to a disease what does this mean?

9

THE HEART

What students should know already

- Cells provide structure and organisation to complex organisms. They contain genetic material to make proteins, provide the energy the organism needs and carry out specialised functions.
- There are five levels of organisation within a complex organism, each one builds upon the other and in order of size (smallest first) these are – cells, tissues, organs, organ systems and the organism. Cells are smaller in comparison to tissue and organs.
- The blood circulatory system delivers nutrients and oxygen to all cells in the body. It is made up of the heart and blood vessels which run through the entire body.
- Molecules transported in the blood like oxygen and glucose are needed for cellular aerobic respiration. Cellular aerobic respiration provides cells with the energy they need to carry out essential life processes.
- Arteries are blood vessels that are responsible for carrying oxygen-rich blood away from the heart to the body. Veins are blood vessels that carry oxygen-poor blood from the body back to the heart for reoxygenation in the lungs.

Explanation

This sequence of learning aims to support pupils in understanding the structure, function and flow of blood into and out of the heart. It will gradually build up a pupil's knowledge on how the heart is organised through a careful sequencing of diagrams that become more complex.

Step 1: What is the Blood Circulatory System?

Start by retrieving knowledge on the blood circulatory system as an important system that delivers oxygen and other substances to all cells in the body. It is made up of the heart and blood vessels (veins and arteries). The arteries carry oxygen-rich blood away from the heart whilst the veins carry oxygen-poor blood back to the heart. Remind pupils the transportation of blood around the body is important for three main reasons:

- Blood transports molecules like oxygen to cells. The oxygen is needed for cellular aerobic respiration.

- Blood transports waste products like carbon dioxide (a waste product of cellular aerobic respiration) back to the lungs, where it is then exhaled.

- Blood provides cells with nutrients like glucose (needed for cellular aerobic respiration) and transports hormones.

Step 2: Exploring Structure, Function, Organisation and Location of the Human Heart

Start by reminding pupils that the heart is one of the main organs in the blood circulatory system. This overview can be achieved by displaying Table 9.1, which provides the key knowledge pupils need to give their learning context.

Table 9.1 Exploring the structure, function, organisation and location of the human heart

Structure of the human heart	Function of the human heart
Divided into four chambers consisting of two atria and two ventricles.	An organ that pumps blood throughout the body via the blood circulatory system, supplying oxygen and nutrients to cells and removing waste products like carbon dioxide.

Location of the human heart
Found in the front and middle of your chest, behind and slightly to the left of your breastbone.

Organisation inside the heart				
Smallest				**Largest**
Cell	Tissue	Organ	Organ system	Organism
Cardiac muscle cells	Cardiac muscle tissue	Heart (roughly the size of a clenched fist)	Blood circulatory system	Human

Step 3: Introducing the Right and Left Side of the Human Heart

To reduce cognitive load, build a diagram of the heart's structure and explain corresponding function in incremental steps; this builds the level of complexity gradually.

Tips and tricks

At the outset explain to pupils that the right and left sides of the heart appear reversed when in diagrammatic form. This is because the right and left side of the heart appear as if pupils are facing a person, from the perspective of observing the heart in another person. Pair pupils up and ask them to explore this reversal with a partner before they are exposed to a diagram of the heart.

Introduce a diagrammatic representation of the human heart as in Figure 9.1 to help pupils understand what a human heart looks like and begin by explaining that the heart has two sides: the left side and the right side. Explain to pupils that the heart is always split into these two sides and each side of the heart has a specific function. The right side of the heart pumps oxygen-poor blood to the lungs to receive oxygen, whilst the left side receives oxygen-rich blood from the lungs and pumps it to the cells in the rest of the body via the aorta.

Right side of the heart pumps oxygen-poor blood to the lungs to become oxygenated

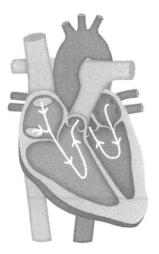

Left side of the heart receives oxygen-rich blood from the lungs and pumps it to the cells in the rest of the body via the aorta

Figure 9.1 Left and right sides of the heart

Step 4: Introducing the Four Chambers of the Human Heart

Next introduce pupils to the four chambers of the human heart. The top two chambers are called the atria (the singular of atria is atrium) and the bottom two chambers are called the ventricles, as demonstrated in Figure 9.2. Each chamber is preceded by the words left or right to indicate which side of the heart the chamber is located.

Then link structure to function by introducing Table 9.2 alongside Figure 9.2. Present each chamber based on the sequence of blood flow through the heart and highlight how each side of the heart has a specific role. This is the sequence pupils must learn to understand the importance of the chambers working together to perform the core function of pumping blood round the body. Utilise and ask pupils to attend to the white line in Figure 9.2 to support pupils' understanding about the flow of blood through the human heart.

Figure 9.2 and Table 9.2   The structure and function of the four chambers of the heart

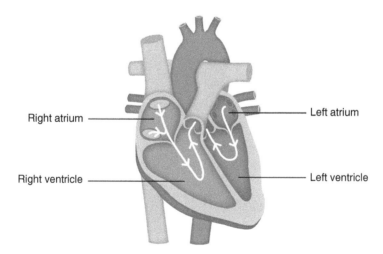

Side of the heart	Chamber	Function
Right	Right atrium	Receives oxygen-poor blood from the veins in the body.
	Right ventricle	Pumps oxygen-poor blood to the lungs to be reoxygenated.
Left	Left atrium	Receives oxygen-rich blood from the lungs and pumps it to the left ventricle.
	Left ventricle	Pumps oxygen-rich blood under high pressure through the aorta to the rest of the body.

Step 5: The Major Vessels of the Heart

To show how blood flows into and out of the heart, introduce pupils to the five major blood vessels connected to the heart as demonstrated in Figure 9.3. Notice the new knowledge (the major vessels of the heart) are in a darker font on the diagram, so pupils can more easily locate what is new.

Link structure to function by introducing Table 9.3 alongside Figure 9.3 to demonstrate how the vessels of the heart work together to maintain the flow of blood through the body. Ask pupils to attend to the order in which the vessels are presented in Table 9.3. Explain to pupils that this order is important because it demonstrates the direction in which the blood flows through the heart.

Figure 9.3 and Table 9.3 The major vessels of the heart

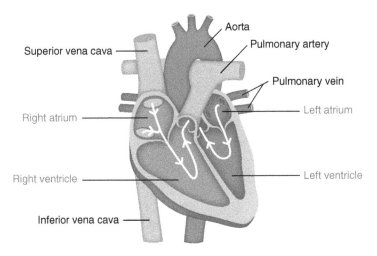

Side of the heart	Vessel	Function
Right	Superior vena cava	Transports oxygen-poor blood from the upper part of the body into the right atrium.
	Inferior vena cava	Transports oxygen-poor blood from the lower part of the body into the right atrium.
	Pulmonary artery	Transports oxygen-poor blood from the right ventricle into the lungs, where oxygen enters the blood stream.
Left	Pulmonary veins	Transports oxygen-rich blood to the left atrium.
	Aorta	Transports oxygen-rich blood to the body from the left ventricle.

Step 6: How is the Heart Specialised for its Function?

Pupils should explore that the heart is also highly specialised organ. Figure 9.4 demonstrates four main specialisations which enable the heart to carry out its function. Notice the new knowledge (the specialisations of the heart) are in a darker font on the diagram, so pupils can more easily locate what is new.

Link structure to function by introducing Table 9.4 alongside Figure 9.4 to demonstrate how the specialisations of the heart maintain the flow of blood through the body.

Figure 9.4 and Table 9.4   Specialisations of the heart and their function

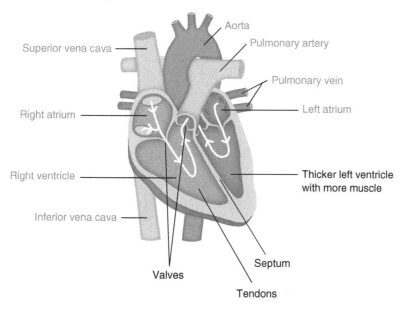

Side of the heart	Structure	Function
Right and left	Valves	Maintain the direction of the flow of blood by stopping blood flowing in the wrong direction.
	Tendons	Stop the valves from turning inside out.
Middle	Septum	Separates the atria and ventricles and forms a barrier between the left and right chambers of the heart. This prevents mixing of oxygen-poor and oxygen-rich blood.
Left	Left ventricle	Is thicker with more muscle, because it must pump blood around the body against higher pressure, compared with the right ventricle.

Step 7: The Flow of Blood in the Heart

By this stage in the sequence of learning it is important for pupils to understand how blood flows into and out of the heart. Figure 9.5 demonstrates how this takes place. Ask pupils to attend to the fact that the top two chambers (the atria) fill up and contract at the same time whilst the bottom two chambers (the ventricles) fill up second and also contract at the same time. The arrows indicate the direction of flow which is maintained because the heart valves only allow blood to flow in one direction.

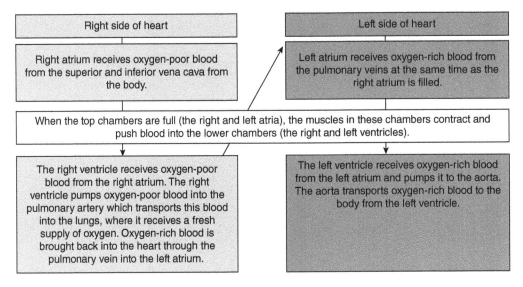

Figure 9.5   How blood flows and is pumped through the heart and around the body

Check for understanding

The following checks for understanding will help you assess your pupils' knowledge about the heart:

- What is the role of the blood circulatory system?
- What is the role of the heart in the blood circulatory system?
- Why are the right atrium and right ventricle always drawn on the left side?
- What is different about the blood on the right side of the heart when compared to the left side of the heart?

- Name the four chambers of the heart and explain their role.
- Name the five major vessels of the heart and explain their role.
- Name four specialisations of the heart and explain their role.
- Explain the structure and function of the heart.
- Starting from the inferior and superior vena cava explain how blood flows through the heart.

10

EVOLUTION BY NATURAL SELECTION

Relevant ages

14–16

What students should know already

- Cells provide structure and organisation to complex organisms. They contain genetic material to make proteins, provide the energy the organism needs and carry out specialised functions.
- A genetic mutation is a change in a gene or chromosome. It is a rare, random change in the genetic material and it can be inherited by offspring.
- Sexual and asexual reproduction is the biological process by which offspring are produced.
- Living organisms are classified or arranged into categories or groups depending on their structure and characteristics.

What students should know by the end

- Evolution is both a complex process and end result; it is driven by three processes: genetic variation, inheritance and natural selection.
- Our current understanding of evolution is built on the research and observations of Charles Darwin.
- Darwin's theory of natural selection was published in 1859 in the book called *On the origin of species by means of natural selection*.
- Genetic variation is the difference in genes between individuals and populations. Genetic mutations occur and DNA sequences change resulting in genetic variation, for example eye colour and blood groups.
- Inheritance is when genes are passed from parent to offspring through the process of reproduction to produce genetically distinct individuals.
- Natural selection is a process during which advantageous genes are inherited and passed on to offspring. As a result, a species changes over time in response to changes in its environment, enabling a species to survive new conditions.

Tips and tricks

A full grasp of this topic relies on a pupil's concrete understanding of a range of new scientific words and terms, for example genetic variation, inheritance and natural selection. Keep revisiting key vocabulary and explore pupils' understanding of this throughout the sequence of lessons to assess that pupils are using complex scientific terms accurately.

Explanation

Evolution is a complex topic because it is both a process during which a species develops gradually in response to a change in the environment and is also the end result in which an organism has developed from an earlier form over time. This sequence of learning aims to build a pupil's knowledge about the genetic basis underpinning this process and how this links to an end result whereby a whole species is able to adapt to the constraints posed by its environment.

Step 1: Introducing Evolution as a Process

Start by ensuring that pupils understand that a biological process is a series of steps that take place to enable a change to happen and that evolution is one such biological process. Provide pupils with concrete examples so that the process of evolution is rooted within a biological context. Some examples are provided in Table 10.1.

Table 10.1 Examples of biological processes

Biological process	Purpose of process	End result
Respiration	A series of chemical reactions that occurs in the mitochondria of cells combining oxygen and glucose.	Energy is transferred from the chemical energy store of glucose.
Photosynthesis	A series of chemical reactions that takes place in the chloroplasts of plant cells in which the energy from light is captured and used to convert water and carbon dioxide into glucose and oxygen.	Energy is transferred into the chemical energy store of glucose.
Sexual reproduction	A process in which the sperm cell combines with the egg cell. This fusion of gametes is called fertilisation.	New offspring is formed.
Evolution	A process by which the heritable characteristics of whole populations of a species over successive generations change in response to a shift in environmental conditions. New genes are passed on from parent to offspring through reproduction.	A new species is formed.

Step 2: Visualising Evolution

Introduce pupils to two concrete examples of evolution first, so that they understand the types of changes that take place over time. Table 10.2 provides two examples, one from the plant kingdom and the other from the animal kingdom.

Table 10.2 Examples of evolution

End result of evolution	What did they evolve from?	When?	How did they evolve?
Land plants	Aquatic algae	Approximately 500 million years ago.	Underground parts developed into root systems; shoots and vascular tissue developed to transport water and the sugar sucrose. Stems and branches were strengthened by lignin and leaves were protected by cuticle.

End result of evolution	What did they evolve from?	When?	How did they evolve?
Humans	Primates	Modern humans, *Homo sapiens*, originated in Africa sometime between 200,000 and 100,000 years ago.	Developmental trends include decreasing arm length, increase in skull volume resulting from increasing brain size, walking upright and the use of tools.

Step 3: Introducing Darwin's Theory of Natural Selection

It is important for pupils to understand that evolution, as exemplified above, does not happen randomly and occurs because of a set of processes that have a genetic basis. This distinct model of evolution is called the theory of natural selection, which was published by Charles Darwin in 1859 in the book *On the origin of species by means of natural selection*.

Step 4: Why Does Evolution Happen?

Evolution occurs because organisms need to adapt to changes within their habitats, such as changes to weather patterns over time, increasing pollution levels or changes in the abundance of food. Ask pupils if they can think of any other environmental changes that may lead to a species evolving – this could include factors such as increased competition for mates, distribution of food sources or increased predation.

Step 5: How Does Evolution Happen?

For evolution by natural selection to happen, three fundamental processes must take place:

1. Genetic variation: These are differences in genes between individuals and populations. Genetic mutations occur and DNA sequences change resulting in genetic variation, for example eye colour and blood groups.
2. Inheritance: The process by which genes are passed on from parent to offspring via sexual or asexual reproduction.

3. Natural selection: The process by which those members of a population with genes that are advantageous and therefore better adapted to their environment tend to survive and produce more offspring. Over time this genetic advantage is passed on and inherited by more and more of the population. This is called survival of the fittest.

Tips and tricks

Exploring the hinterland with pupils around Darwin's life and the period in which his theory was developed will enrich pupils' understanding of the challenges associated with the development of scientific theory during the Victorian era. Key themes around religion, his voyages and the observational methods he utilised will give pupils a richer understanding of how Darwin created new knowledge.

Step 6: Understanding Genetic Variation

To explain each stage of Darwin's theory, use a table that builds in complexity gradually, introducing each of the three processes sequentially. Start with the concept of genetic variation in Figure 10.1.

Genetic variation
What is it? Differences in genes between individuals and populations caused by genetic mutations. This is when DNA sequences change, resulting in genetic variation, for example eye colour and blood groups.
Example: Hares predominantly have white fur colour in Arctic conditions. A few have a mutation for grey fur colour.

Figure 10.1 Introducing genetic variation

Pupils often have a misconception that genetic mutations are always detrimental to life. Some mutations will have no impact whilst others may lead to the adaptations which result in the evolution of a new species and make them better suited to new environmental conditions, in which case mutations may also be beneficial.

Step 7: Understanding Inheritance

Build on this by presenting Figure 10.2 to explore the concept of inheritance and how this relates to genetic variation.

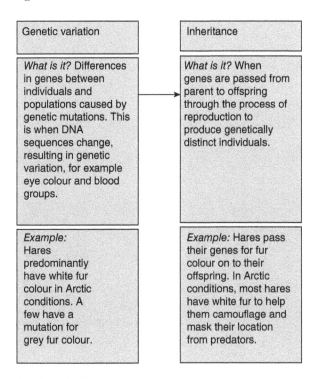

Genetic variation	Inheritance
What is it? Differences in genes between individuals and populations caused by genetic mutations. This is when DNA sequences change, resulting in genetic variation, for example eye colour and blood groups.	*What is it?* When genes are passed from parent to offspring through the process of reproduction to produce genetically distinct individuals.
Example: Hares predominantly have white fur colour in Arctic conditions. A few have a mutation for grey fur colour.	*Example:* Hares pass their genes for fur colour on to their offspring. In Arctic conditions, most hares have white fur to help them camouflage and mask their location from predators.

Figure 10.2   Understanding inheritance

Step 8: Understanding Natural Selection

Present Figure 10.3 to explore the concept of natural selection and how this relates to inheritance.

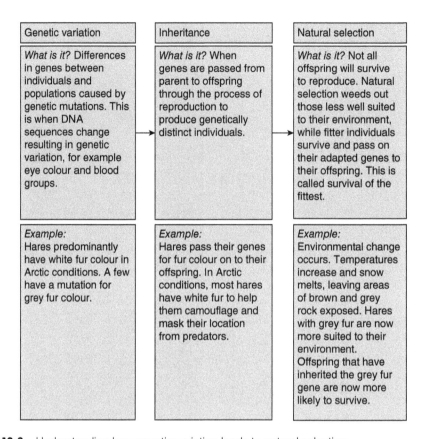

Genetic variation	Inheritance	Natural selection
What is it? Differences in genes between individuals and populations caused by genetic mutations. This is when DNA sequences change resulting in genetic variation, for example eye colour and blood groups.	*What is it?* When genes are passed from parent to offspring through the process of reproduction to produce genetically distinct individuals.	*What is it?* Not all offspring will survive to reproduce. Natural selection weeds out those less well suited to their environment, while fitter individuals survive and pass on their adapted genes to their offspring. This is called survival of the fittest.
Example: Hares predominantly have white fur colour in Arctic conditions. A few have a mutation for grey fur colour.	*Example:* Hares pass their genes for fur colour on to their offspring. In Arctic conditions, most hares have white fur to help them camouflage and mask their location from predators.	*Example:* Environmental change occurs. Temperatures increase and snow melts, leaving areas of brown and grey rock exposed. Hares with grey fur are now more suited to their environment. Offspring that have inherited the grey fur gene are now more likely to survive.

Figure 10.3   Understanding how genetic variation leads to natural selection

Step 9: Natural Selection as a Process and End Result

Finally, consolidate understanding by presenting Figure 10.4 to differentiate between evolution as a process and end result, as well as demonstrating the links between genetic variation, inheritance and natural selection.

Tips and tricks

It is important for pupils to understand that evolution is a continual process and is still happening. The example of antibiotic resistance exemplifies this well and can be presented in the same way to build and consolidate understanding.

Genetic variation	Inheritance	Natural selection	The end result
What is it? Differences in genes between individuals and populations caused by genetic mutations. This is when DNA sequences change resulting in genetic variation, for example eye colour and blood groups.	*What is it?* When genes are passed from parent to offspring through the process of reproduction to produce genetically distinct individuals.	*What is it?* Not all offspring will survive to reproduce. Natural selection weeds out those less well suited to their environment, while fitter individuals survive and pass on their adapted genes to their offspring. This is called survival of the fittest.	*What is it?* Evolution has occurred when natural selection occurs repeatedly over many generations. A new species evolves and most individuals in the population are now better adapted to the new environment.
Example: Hares predominantly have white fur colour in Arctic conditions. A few have a mutation for grey fur colour.	*Example:* Hares pass their genes for fur colour on to their offspring. In Arctic conditions, most hares have white fur to help them camouflage and mask their location from predators.	*Example:* Environmental change occurs. Temperatures increase and snow melts, leaving areas of brown and grey rock exposed. Hares with grey fur are now more suited to their environment. Offspring that have inherited the grey fur gene are now more likely to survive.	*Example:* Hares with the grey fur gene reproduce repeatedly, their survival is now favoured because they are better adapted to their grey, rocky environment.

Figure 10.4 Differentiating between evolution as a process and end result

Check for understanding

The following checks for understanding will help you assess your pupils' knowledge about evolution by natural selection:

- Provide two examples of evolution and explain the changes that took place.
- Using examples, what drives evolution to take place?
- What are the three fundamental processes that are involved in Darwin's theory of natural selection?
- Explain how evolution can be described both as a process and end result.
- Peppered moths are normally white with black speckles across the wings, giving them their name. This patterning makes them well camouflaged against lichen-covered tree trunks. However, in the nineteenth century when industrialisation caused sooty air pollution, lichens were killed off and urban tree trunks and walls were blackened. The black form of the moth became more common in towns and cities. Using what you know about Darwin's theory of natural selection, explain how this change came about.

PART 2: CHEMISTRY

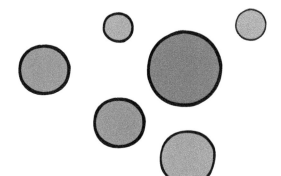

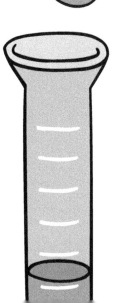

11

BALANCING EQUATIONS

What students should know already

- Familiarity with word equations.
- Familiarity with terms like 'reactants' and 'products'.
- How elements have a symbol.
- Understanding of the principle of conservation of mass.
- That atoms can be joined by chemical bonds.

What students should know by the end

- How to balance equations.
- Why balancing equations is important in terms of conservation of mass.

There are many methods to use for students to learn to balance equations. Most of them tend not to be 'fool-proof' and at a certain point particular questions and errors become common. This is normally because of the number of 'rules' involved in terms of which operations are possible and which ones are not. So one operation might be 'you cannot touch the small numbers' and another might be 'a big number means you increase the number of atoms by the big number multiplied by the small number'. Increasing the number of operations increases the likelihood that students will make an error in failing to apply one or more of them.

As a fairly abstract topic, it is widespread to use physical models to aid in balancing. This is not necessarily a helpful route, as the cognitive jump from physical models → symbolic representation can be another area for error to be introduced.

The method below limits the number of operations and provides a straightforward route to balancing equations. Provided the preparatory work is done adequately, it is a highly effective and efficient method that should reduce student error.

Knowledge of conservation of mass is very helpful in explaining why balancing is necessary. Do not introduce conservation of mass at the same time as teaching balancing equations, as this will lead to students becoming overloaded.

Step 1: Formulae into Drawings

Show students a formula like H_2O. Students should recognise the elements hydrogen and oxygen. Explain what the sub-script 2 means with the help of a diagram (Figure 11.1).

Figure 11.1 A molecule of water, showing two hydrogen atoms and one oxygen atom

The order to draw the atoms in is not important at this point i.e. HHO or HOH. If students worry about it, it causes further undesirable cognitive load. When going over examples be sure to sample a few student answers so they can see that it doesn't matter how it is drawn.

It will be helpful for students to know that it does not matter which order the atoms are in, provided that they are touching each other. Do another couple of worked examples (I), then give students a couple of examples to do on whiteboards or in their books (we); sample a couple of answers and correct if necessary, and when satisfied give students a number of examples to practise independently (you). In the examples, try to include a range of elements and orders: NaCl, $AlCl_3$, AlF_3, NH_3, TiO_2, Na_2SO_4, $KMnO_4$, $NaHCO_3$ are all good options.

Step 2: The Symbol Equation

Write a word equation on the board; the best example to start with would be hydrogen + oxygen → water. Do not do a demonstration of this reaction now, as it is not relevant to understanding the process of balancing equations, and is therefore cognitively distracting. Underneath the word equation, write up the symbol equation:

$$H_2 + O_2 \rightarrow H_2O$$

Students may ask how you know that hydrogen is H_2. Do not go into it now too much, just say that that's its formula and it will be explained at a later date.

Step 3: Drawing it Out

Students should by now have no problem drawing out the pictorial representation, or understanding why you are doing it (Figure 11.2).

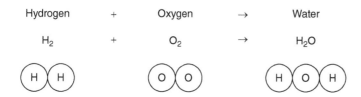

Figure 11.2 Multiple representations of substances in an equation

Step 4: The Problem

Draw a dotted line down the centre, and discuss with students the fact that there are two oxygens on the left and one on the right. Because you have taught conservation of mass already, this should not be difficult for students to understand.

Step 5: The Boxes

This is the step at which this method differs from other methods. Draw a thick box around each molecule, and explain that what is in the box cannot be touched under any circumstances (Figure 11.3).

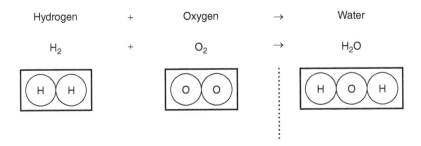

Figure 11.3 The addition of boxes to the molecules shows their boundedness

Step 6: The Operation

There is now only one operation possible: adding a new entire box. There is nothing else students are 'allowed' to do. If there is an atom missing somewhere, they should add a box as necessary. In this case, we need two oxygens on the right side, so we add a new entire box on that side (Figure 11.4).

Step 7: Repeat the Operation

We now have four hydrogens on the right, and two on the left. So we reiterate the operation rule from step 6: all you can do is add another box, which leaves us with Figure 11.5.

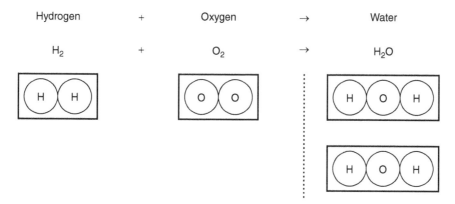

Figure 11.4 Add an extra box to balance the number of oxygen atoms

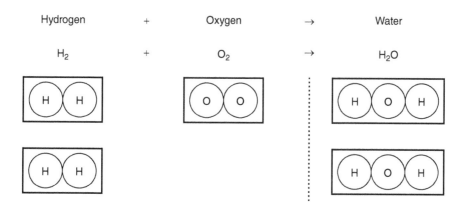

Figure 11.5 A final box is added to balance the hydrogens

Tips and tricks

Despite your emphasis on the operation, students will *still* try and change what is in the boxes (e.g. try to squeeze another oxygen in). Make sure you are attentive to this issue.

Step 8: The Numbers

Count up the number of boxes you have, and put the numbers underneath (Figure 11.6).

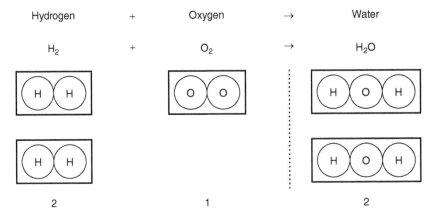

Figure 11.6 Addition of stoichiometric numbers

Step 9: Copy and Paste the Symbol Equation

Rewrite your symbol equation next to the numbers, and your equation is now balanced (Figure 11.7).

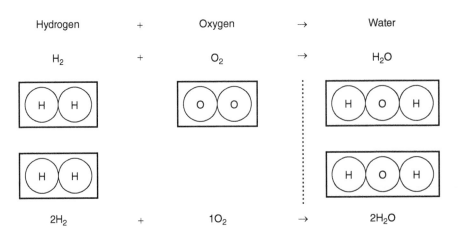

Figure 11.7 The final balanced equation

Of course at this point you will want to do another couple of worked examples and prepare students for plentiful practice. Follow an I/we/you format to guide your students towards being able to practise independently.

12

THE DEVELOPMENT OF THE PERIODIC TABLE

Relevant ages

11–16

What students should know already

- Definition of an element.
- Basic familiarity with element symbols.
- Basic knowledge of chemical properties.

- How the periodic table was arranged before Mendeleev.
- What Mendeleev did:
  - Grouping based on properties.
  - Gaps for undiscovered elements.
  - Position swapping of elements to keep group order.

Explanation

This topic is an interesting case study in science explanations for two intertwined reasons. Firstly, in general, teachers assume that this is one of the 'easy' topics in the course to teach. Secondly, teachers often use a categorisation bridging analogy to help students understand the topic; giving students fruit, or vehicles, or some other objects to categorise, and explaining that this is what Mendeleev did. Sometimes, teachers will use element cards with properties on them to do this as well. The use of such an analogy, however, misses the point in this topic. An analogy is there to help students grasp a complex and abstract concept. The idea of grouping elements together based on their properties is neither complex nor abstract. Indeed, grouping and categorising is such a common activity in human cognition that scientists since the pre-Socratics have been engaged in it. Grouping and categorising is not, therefore, what students find challenging about this topic.

It is more likely that what students find difficult about this topic is how the periodic table developed in a dynamic sense. The periodic table as we look at it is a static object, and saying that 'iodine and tellurium are switched' does not help our students form a mental image of what is taking place; what it looked like before and what it looked like after. Knowing what a gap would look like and why it was innovative necessitates showing students a gap in a way that is readily intelligible to them (i.e. not by showing an artefact image of Mendeleev's actual table) and what it would look like had Mendeleev *not* left a gap.

As such, the explanation below does not use an analogy. Rather it uses a concrete physical model that builds up slowly over time to represent the dynamism of the process of formulating the periodic table.

Tips and tricks

This explanation makes a number of gross simplifications and historical inaccuracies in terms of which elements Mendeleev had access to. This is perfectly acceptable as in this case it's unlikely that students will remember the inaccuracies (for example that Mendeleev had access to the Noble gases). You can make this clear to students with phrases like 'I'm not going to do exactly what he did because the list of elements he had was a bit different, but I'm going to show you the type of thing he did.'

Step 1: Get Your Arts and Crafts Out

For this explanation, you will need small cards with elements looking like Figure 12.1 below. These particular elements have been carefully chosen to make the dynamic process as clear as possible, but do not show students the cards laid out like this. Tell students that they represent all the elements they knew about at that time, with their symbols and their weight (as above, you can simplify this as 'which is about how heavy the atoms are [note also that the correct term here for pre-Mendeleev is atomic weight not atomic mass]). Have one blank card spare.

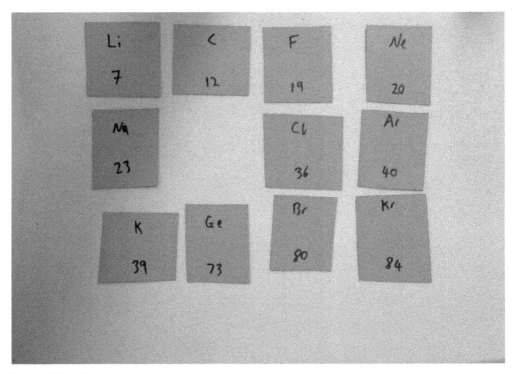

Figure 12.1   The elements we will use

Step 2: What Came Before

Tell students that before Mendeleev, scientists arranged the atoms by their weight, something like Figure 12.2. You can arrange them vertically too if preferred.

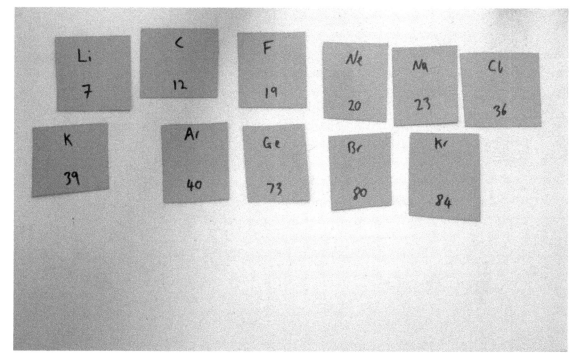

Figure 12.2 Elements ordered by atomic weight

Emphasise that even though the numbers don't go up by regular amounts, they clearly increase progressively.

Step 3: Properties

Discuss how Mendeleev looked at these elements and thought he could arrange them better. First, he took lithium, sodium and potassium and put them in a pile. They are metals that are very reactive, but nothing else there is. So he put them in a family together – a group. Fluorine, chlorine and bromine go together as they are colourful and poisonous. Carbon and germanium go together as they are solid non-metals, and neon, argon and krypton go together as they are colourless gases (see Figure 12.3).

Give each group a little sticker as shown in Figure 12.4. This is a lot easier to recognise than text describing the group, and at this point the specific property which unites them is less relevant than the point that they are united based on their properties.

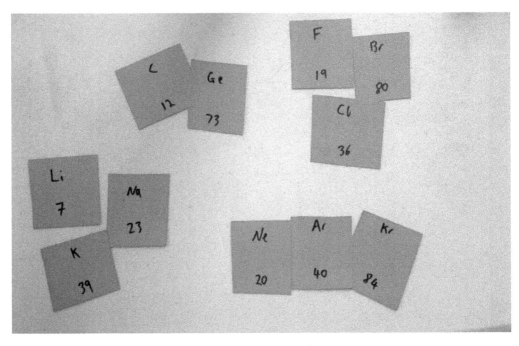

Figure 12.3 Elements grouped together based on properties

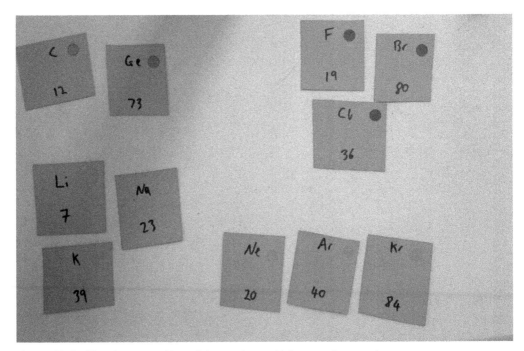

Figure 12.4 The elements with a sticker to show which group they are in

Step 4: Weight and Group

Next, Mendeleev ordered them by their group and their weight, getting something that looked a bit like Figure 12.5.

Obviously, though, something is wrong with Ge and with Ar and K. Start with the latter and show them swapped around as in Figure 12.6.

This is what other scientists would have done, but was not in line with Mendeleev's model. He made sure that K and Ar were in the group based on their properties, even if it meant going out of weight order.

Germanium was a bigger problem, as dropping it down to its weight order left a gap as in Figure 12.7.

Other scientists will have shifted everything back as in Figure 12.8, but as before, that would ruin the property grouping.

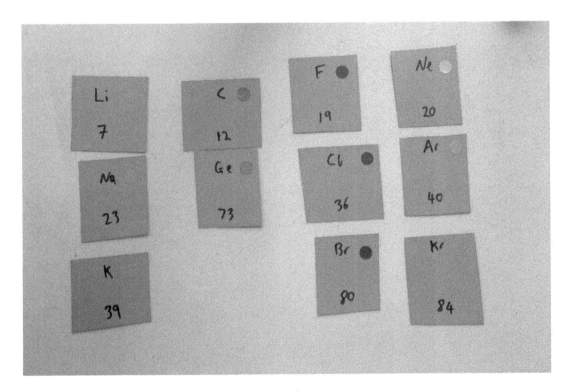

Figure 12.5   Elements ordered by weight and properties

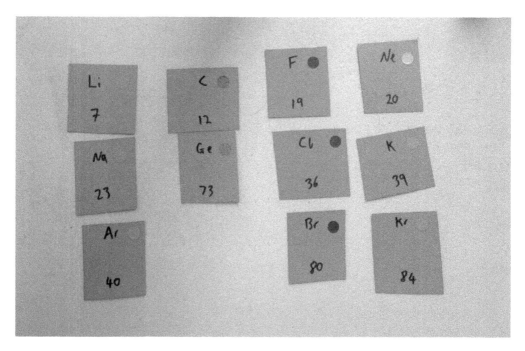

Figure 12.6 Illustrating how other scientists will have had the elements out of their correct groups by following their weights only

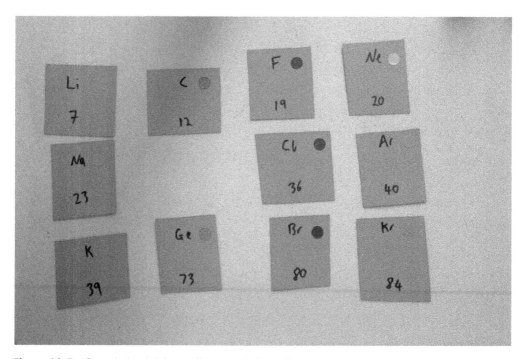

Figure 12.7 Gaps being left for undiscovered elements

Chemistry

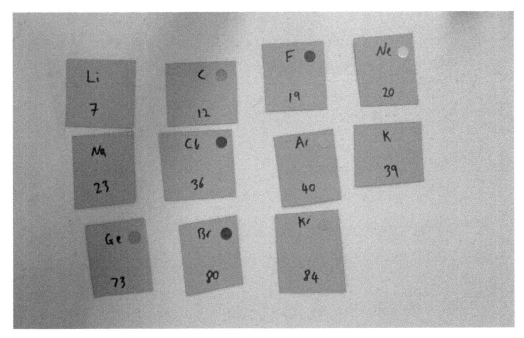

Figure 12.8 Shifting the elements without accounting for undiscovered ones

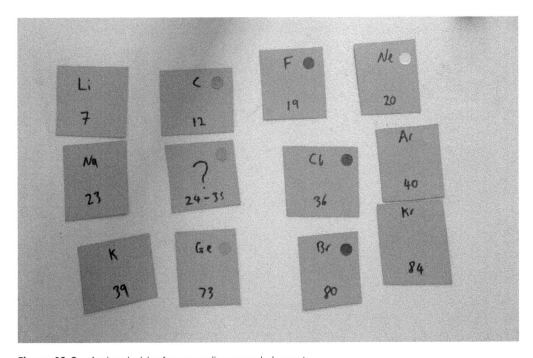

Figure 12.9 A placeholder for an undiscovered element

Instead, Mendeleev returned to Figure 12.7, but left it as a gap. He hypothesised that there was an element that had not yet been discovered that would fit there. Place your blank card in the gap with a question mark on it, and say that you know it would be similar to C and Ge, so would take a blue sticker, and its mass would be between 24 and 35 (Figure 12.9).

Say that in the fullness of time, that element was discovered, and flip the card to reveal the other side, where you have previously written Si, 28 and added a blue sticker. Your periodic table is now complete and has illustrated all of the steps and innovations made by Mendeleev.

Check for understanding

As discussed in the Introduction, the key areas for understanding are not necessarily why he put them in groups, but how that differed from what others did. Good questions to check then would be along the lines of:

- Identify the atomic weights of iodine and tellurium.
- Before Mendeleev, which would have come first?
- Why would Mendeleev have swapped them?

You can test understanding of the gaps with questions like:

- In Mendeleev's time, boron had not been discovered. Between which two elements would there have been a gap?
- What could Mendeleev have predicted about boron?

13

BONDING, STRUCTURE AND PROPERTIES

Relevant ages

11–16

What students should know already

- States of matter.
- Familiarity with ionic, covalent and metallic bonding.

What students should know by the end

- How there are different types of bonds, which leads to different types of structure, which leads to different properties.
- How to identify the difference between a bond, a structure and a property.

Bonding, structure and properties cuts right across the heart of school science, and could be considered its backbone. It is immensely explanatory and contains elements and concepts from a wide range of foundational chemical knowledge. In general, how the bonds and structures are formed is taught well, as are the resulting properties. However, as an overarching framework, the distinctions between the three strands and the relationship between them are not always made explicit. Students calling diamond a 'covalent bond' or saying 'a property of solids is that the particles are touching' shows that there is some knowledge there, but as a whole understanding is lacking. Bonding works in very specific ways, and *leads* to specific kinds of structures which *explain* specific properties. That logical chain from bonding to structure to properties must be unearthed and made explicit.

It is beyond the scope of this chapter to explain in detail how to teach every part of that logical chain. Instead, we will consider its application to five main areas which span secondary school science. As such, this chapter is a *supplement* to your normal teaching of these topics, not a replacement for it.

Area 1: The Simple Particle Diagram

Generally introduced early on in students' scientific careers, the familiar particle diagram seems principally aimed at describing different states of matter. As a simplified model, it is extremely limited and can even potentially cause misconceptions and misunderstandings when students are exposed to more sophisticated structural models.

Bonding

In the simple particle diagrams, the bonding is generally undifferentiated and referred to as 'bonds' between particles. No explanation is given as to what causes the bonds, and no distinction is made between bonds and intermolecular forces. For this reason, schools might use a different term like 'forces of attraction' and tell students that these will become more sophisticated with time. As such, in a solid the forces of attraction are strong, in a liquid they are less strong and in a gas they are weak.

Tips and tricks

It may be clear by now that from a chemistry perspective, the simple particle model is deeply problematic both in terms of how it only actually represents one type of substance (Noble gases) and how the language around it is fraught with difficulty (are liquids' forces described as 'less strong'? Why do solids and gases have absolute descriptions whilst liquids only have relative ones?). It is, however, a valid and useful model in physics. There is therefore a strong curricular argument to completely omit it from early instruction, and instead to use simplified versions of true structures like molecular and giant early on. This is not too demanding for students, and changes of state can be done separately for each, i.e. learning sequences on state changes for giant substances and sequences for state changes in molecular substances. Later on, students can be exposed to the limited particle model and told that 'we are going to simplify what you have learnt already for this particular application'. Discussion of limitations can also then be more fruitful as students have seen other models and can appreciate better the limits of the particle model. In many settings, such a curricular shift will not be possible, and as such this chapter assumes that the simple particle diagram is taught early on, with other models taught later. However, where possible, shifting to a different model is strongly advised.

The key at this point is to emphasise that the forces of attraction are to do with *bonding*. That this results in particles in a solid all touching is taking you into the structure. It may be worth starting by just drawing a couple of particles touching and describing the force between them, then slowly adding more and saying that these forces *result* in a very specific structure forming. Non-examples will also help, if you add three particles close to each other and touching, and then a fourth floating at a distance, students will immediately be able to see not only that this is incorrect, but *why* it is incorrect: if the bonds are strong they hold the particles tight and close to each other.

Tips and tricks

You must anticipate poor use of language. For example, students will commonly refer to 'solid particles', whereas the state of something should really be better construed as a bulk property (i.e. of a whole material) and not a property of individual atoms. If such language is used, it must not only be corrected to 'particles in a solid' but the explanation of the difference be made explicit.

You can now move on to properties. Draw a particle diagram of a solid on the board, and ask students what they think would happen if you pushed it at the top, as in Figure 13.1.

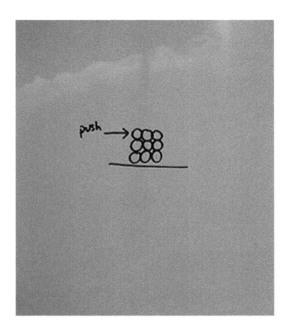

Figure 13.1 What happens when you push a solid?

Students should be able to predict that it will not collapse, but will either slide or be caused to roll (using a physical manipulative may help here). This is because the forces are strong, so the particles won't just break away from each other.

At this point you *must* emphasise that 'solids do not flow' is a *property* and is *explained by* its bonding and structure. A useful sentence frame throughout could look something like this:

In _____, the forces are _____, leading to a _____structure. Therefore it has a property that _____.

Which in this case would fill out to:

In solids, the forces between particles are strong, leading to a fixed structure. Therefore it has a property that it does not flow.

The last part of the sentence does not scan particularly well as far as prose is concerned, but it rams home the causative chain. Using a sentence like this, and then perhaps highlighting the three parts (forces/bonds, structure, property) will help your students develop the conceptual understanding that we seek.

This approach can then be replicated for liquids and gases as well as for other properties like compression, with Table 13.1 showing how it would apply to the 'flow' property (it is probably not best yet to use the word 'fluidity').

Table 13.1 A schematic representation of how you would tackle various properties of solids, liquids and gases

State	Bonding	Structure	Property: Does it flow?
Solid	Strong forces of attraction.	Particles all held together tightly.	No, the particles cannot move away from each other easily.
Liquid	Middle-strength forces of attraction.	Particles are touching, but free to move.	Yes, particles can move around.
Gas	Weak forces of attraction.	Particles do not touch and are free to move.	Yes, particles can move around.

You would then repeat the process for other properties, again starting with bonding, then moving to structure, then moving to the property.

Tips and tricks

It is probably worthwhile to spend an entire lesson on what 'properties' are. Too often students are not provided with a list of items which count as properties as well as non-examples. Among other examples, words like 'hard' and 'strong' are used interchangeably, so a lesson and accompanying reference table could help your students greatly. Assuming that students will either come to the lesson with this knowledge already or they will somehow pick it up tacitly will end up causing or exacerbating already extant gaps in attainment.

Once you have covered the properties you wished to, you can use a series of diagrams like in Figure 13.2 to consolidate and show students the 'big picture'.

Area 2: Ionic Bonding, Structure and Properties

In a sense, the route to be taken here is extremely similar to that in Area 1. First, you will need to look at the formation of ions. The most common route is at this point to describe how atoms transfer electrons one to the other to result in the formation of ions, but it may be better to hold that off till later. The key problem in the understanding of bonding and structure in ionic substances is that the electrostatic force of attraction works in all directions, and it is *that* which leads to the formation of a giant lattice. Students struggle to make the link from one or two ions to an entire structure, so whilst the electron transfer is a part of the process to be sure, it tends to reinforce the conception that we are only dealing with a few ions, thus hindering understanding of how the bonding results in the structure. Because it isn't really prerequisite knowledge (whereas conceptions of what ions are is), it can be pushed off till later.

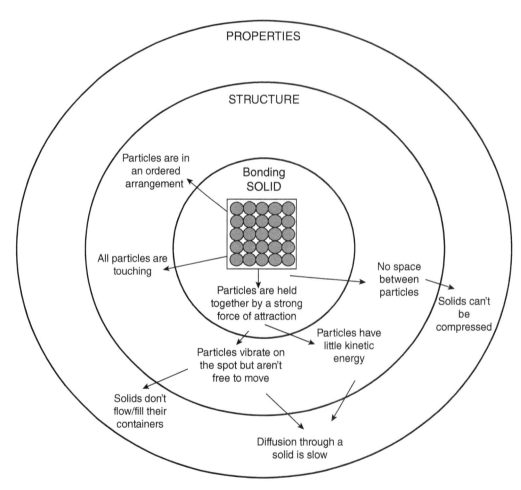

Figure 13.2 A concentric circles diagram showing students how bonding and structure lead to properties

A good understanding of the electrostatic interactions between charges explains properties like brittleness as well. Using the sentence frames similar to the one earlier, we can construct sentences like:

'In ionic substances, the electrostatic forces of attraction are between opposite ions leading to a regular positive-negative structure. If it is hit by a force, the ions are no longer in the positive-negative structure and repel each other, leading to a property of it being brittle.'

As ever, this can be emphasised through diagrams, for example like the one in Figure 13.3. This is a property that actually serves to help students better understand the principle of a giant ionic structure, as it is in itself a non-example.

The electrical conductivity of ionic substances is an interesting case in point in terms of sequencing the teaching properties. Ordinarily, it is taught at this point in terms of the movement of ions in liquid or aqueous forms. Later on, students are exposed to delocalised electrons (either in graphite or metals). These substances conduct electricity due to the similar characteristics of:

1. Having charged particles.
2. Those charged particles being able to move.

In general therefore, the overarching principle of 'Ions free to move' emerges from an exploration of the specific instances in which it applies.

Another route would be to first teach all the different structures, ignoring electrical conductivity, and then teach it in one go and apply it to the various substances that conduct electricity, as well as those which do not. This will allow you to use a range of examples and non-examples to illustrate an overarching principle.

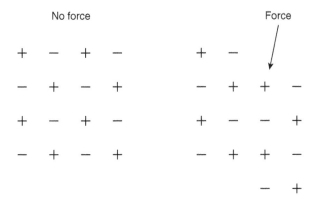

Figure 13.3 A diagram illustrating how applying a force to a giant ionic lattice results in misalignment of ions

Which route is better is hard to decide definitely. The advantage of the first route is that it enables you to drill deeper into the structure of the substance currently under discussion. However, it could be that the hardest thing to teach in this sequence is the overarching principle. If so, then it is best to teach it at the point where students have enough knowledge for you to be able to build a meaningful example and non-example sequence. Constructing a table like Table 13.2 really helps students embed the new understanding through their drawing on an already broad understanding of bonding and structure.

Table 13.2 A table showing electrical conductivity in a range of substances that can be used as a springboard for deeper understanding and student practice

Substance	Charged particles?	Particles free to move?	Does it conduct electricity?
Diamond	No	No	No
Water	No	Yes	No
Solid sodium chloride	Yes (ions)	No	No
Liquid sodium chloride	Yes (ions)	Yes	Yes
Aqueous sodium chloride	Yes (ions)	Yes	Yes
Iron	Yes (delocalised electrons)	Yes	Yes
Graphite	Yes (delocalised electrons)	Yes	Yes

A third approach would then be to take a mixed route, introducing conductivity early on, but going very light on detail and then returning to the topic later on. The advantage of this approach is that you slightly increase your students' knowledge for when you revisit it in more detail, but run the risk of them being confused and not fully understanding the processes involved.

Area 3: Giant Covalent Substances

Traditionally, small molecules (simple molecular) are taught before giant covalent substances; however, it may be best to swap the order as teaching small molecules means adding two new elements – covalent bonding and intermolecular forces – whereas starting with giant covalent substances only introduces one new element – covalent bonding.

When it comes to the teaching of graphite, ensure that students know that it is an exception to the normal rules governing giant covalent substances. If you are following route 2 above, you may want to leave any discussion of its conductivity until later. In fact, a case could be made to leave it out entirely until the end of the unit. Graphite's bonding is covalent, but each carbon atom only forms three bonds. The spare electron then contributes to the *structure* in a similar way to a metal. The first part here (bonding: three bonds per atom) will always be new content, but leaving the teaching of graphite entirely till later on means that this second part (the delocalised electron) is at least not new content.

As above, throughout this area you must ensure that the bonding → structure → properties chain is maintained, with a sample sentence for the property 'hardness' being something like:

'In giant covalent substances, the covalent bonds are very strong leading to a fixed structure. It is therefore very difficult to separate the atoms, leading to the property of being very hard.'

Before moving on to area 4, ensure you have spent a good amount of time on the melting and boiling points of ionic and giant covalent substances. You can even write comparison sample sentences like:

'In giant ionic and giant covalent substances, the bonds are very strong leading to a fixed structure. It therefore requires lots of energy to break those bonds, leading to a high melting and boiling point.'

Tips and tricks

Students tend to learn that certain substances have high or low melting and boiling points, but they tend not to be taught how to tie that to typical substances. It is worth making 'high melting point means it is a solid at room temperature' into a curricular item, along with 'low melting point means it is a liquid or gas at room temperature'. This will allow students to make stronger links between the concepts of states generally, melting/boiling points and typical contextual states.

Area 4: Small Molecules

The key, and classic, error here is failing to understand the difference between the covalent bonds *within* molecules and the intermolecular forces *between* molecules.

Following our *bonding → structure → property* approach, we can apply the framework to preempt this error (to an extent). The covalent bonds within the molecules are part of *bonding*. The forces between the molecules are part of the *structure*. If you have been heavily emphasising the division of these ideas until now, then it will be that much easier to show students that the two applications are separate from each other, and not to be confused, for example through the use of Table 13.3.

Table 13.3 One way to illustrate the difference between small molecules and giant covalent substances

Type of substance	Bonding	Structure	Property
Giant covalent	Covalent bonds between atoms.	Many billions of atoms all bonded together.	High melting point (lots of energy required to break the bonds).
Small molecule	Covalent bonds between atoms.	A handful of atoms bond together to make molecules. Many billions of molecules are held together by intermolecular forces.	Low melting point (little energy required to 'break' the intermolecular forces).

To check for understanding here, a wrong answer approach can be very powerful. For example:

'A student says that water has a low melting point because the covalent bonds are weak and require little energy to break. Explain why the student is wrong.'

Sentence stems like because/but/therefore can also help. For example:

Diamond has a high melting point because…

Diamond has a high melting point but…

Diamond has a high melting point therefore…

With the final stem moving to what should be the next phase in this sequence, which relates properties to uses.

Tips and tricks

Sentence stem activities like these can be extremely powerful when used correctly. Because this topic situates content as part of a long chain (bonding → structure → properties [→ uses]) the activity is particularly conducive to hard thought.

Area 5: Metals

With any luck, by this point your students should have got the hang of the bonding → structure → properties chain, and applying it to metals should not be a particularly difficult jump.

Check for understanding

Because/but/therefore sentence stems like those below are excellent ways to check for understanding:

- Methane has a low melting point…
- Iron conducts electricity…
- Sodium chloride is brittle…
- Graphite has delocalised electrons…
- Diamond and graphite are both giant covalent substances…

Simple identification questions where students are asked to assign a type of substance to a statement can also be powerful, for example:

a. A brittle substance that is solid at room temperature.
b. A substance with strong covalent bonds, but a low boiling point.
c. A substance that does not conduct electricity, but has charged particles.

An additional benefit of questions like this is that it is very easy to do a whole class check on a question which has a one word answer using mini-whiteboards or the like.

14

THE MOLE

What students should know already

- Basic familiarity with the periodic table.
- Mass numbers and atomic numbers as representing subatomic particles (as a necessary simplification).
- The relative masses of the subatomic particles.

What students should know by the end

- What a mole is.
- How the periodic table can be used to calculate moles of substance from mass.
- How Avogadro's number can be used to calculate the number of items from the moles of a substance.

This is a classically difficult subject to broach with students as it is highly abstract in nature, relating to numbers we cannot fathom as well as concepts like 'relative mass'. As ever, there is a temptation to use manipulatives to teach moles, and routes using all sorts of physical objects are commonly found. The concern with such approaches is that students spend a lot of time manipulating the physical object with an eye to the surface detail, i.e. how it is properly manipulated, without attending to the deep structure, i.e. what the manipulation represents. The approach below does not use such methods and instead carefully structures the buildup of concepts to ensure that steps start as abstract, become concrete, and then serve as a building block for the next step.

Step 1: Relative Mass

It is likely that students will know that the 'mass' of a proton is 1, that of a neutron is 1 and that of an electron is 0. What is less likely is that they know that these numbers actually represent *relative* mass and what is meant by the term. Relative mass is a crucial concept underpinning the study of moles, so starting from how it relates to subatomic particles means that we can move from known to unknown more easily.

Draw four stick people on the board (Figure 14.1), taking the time to emphasise the differences in their appearances.

For each person, add their mass (Figure 14.2).

Figure 14.1   Stick people who will eventually represent relative mass

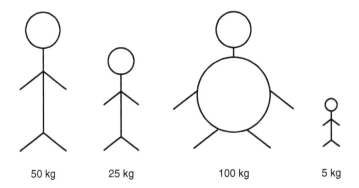

Figure 14.2 The stick people with their masses

Ask students to imagine that every person in the world was one of these stick people, that there were only four possibilities for a person's mass: it can only be 50 kg, 25 kg, 100 kg or 5 kg.

Tell students that in that case, it doesn't make sense to call them by their masses, as that takes a long time to say. Let's just call the first person 1, and the second person 0.5. Give students a second to think about why you did that, and invite them to suggest what to call the third person. Students should fairly rapidly register that the third person should be 2 and the fourth 0.1 (Figure 14.3).

Define the top row as the absolute mass: what their mass actually is. Define the bottom row as the relative mass: what their mass is relative to each other.

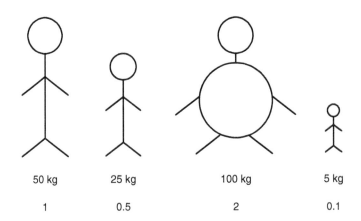

Figure 14.3 Absolute and relative masses

Chemistry

Figure 14.4   Demonstrating the effects of relative mass

Use a new whiteboard to draw a person 1 on a seesaw, and add a person 2 to the other side as in Figure 14.4.

Discuss with students what will occur, and what you would need to do in order to balance the seesaw. You can redraw the seesaw unbalanced and then balanced with two person 1s to support your explanation.

Tips and tricks

Having an extra whiteboard here means you can easily refer back to the different people's masses, without crowding your seesaw image.

Repeat the exercise with different combinations, showing each time that the relative masses allow us to predict how we could go about balancing the seesaw.

We are now ready to do the same with subatomic particles. Point out that the absolute mass of a proton is very small indeed ($1.6726219 \times 10^{-27}$) but the mass of a neutron is the same. We therefore say they are both '1', which is a lot easier than saying their actual mass each time. Draw a seesaw with a proton and a neutron on it to show that they are balanced (Figure 14.5).

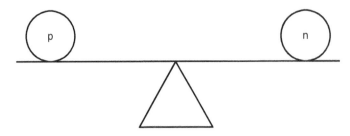

Figure 14.5 The relative mass of a proton and neutron is 1

The electron, however, has a much smaller mass. In fact, we would need to add around 1840 electrons to balance out just one proton or neutron. We therefore say that they have a relative mass of 0.

Step 2: To the Periodic Table

Have students locate helium on the periodic table. With students, note that helium has a relative mass of 4, with two protons and two neutrons. Again reiterate that electrons are so small that we pay them no notice (see Figure 14.6). An analogy you can use is of a person who is weighed by the doctor and then says 'the weight is inaccurate as I cut my nails last night' – it's such a small mass as to not be important or counted.

Next, draw out an atom of carbon in exactly the same way, highlighting its six neutrons and six protons.

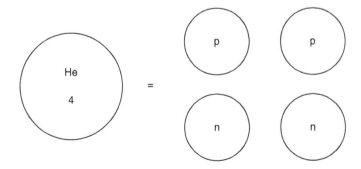

Figure 14.6 How the relative mass of helium relates to its subatomic particles

Some periodic tables have the mass number at the top and others at the bottom. When drawing the atoms on the board, ensure that you use the same convention as the students' periodic tables. This is crucial as a somewhat inevitable error at some point is mistaking the atomic number for the mass number, so any small steps you can take to pre-empt this error will help in the long term.

Finally, draw an atom of helium and an atom of carbon on a seesaw and ask students to explain what will occur. Discuss how you could get the seesaw to be balanced through the addition of two more helium atoms. The key learning point here is that three atoms of helium have the same mass as one atom of carbon – the mass changes depending on the atom involved.

Step 3: Relative Formula Mass

Draw out H_2O on the board, and ask students how many protons and neutrons it has in total. To scaffold this further if necessary, separate the molecule into three atoms (Figure 14.7).

Put that water molecule on a seesaw, and at the other end put an atom of beryllium. As before, ask students what will happen and how the seesaw can be balanced.

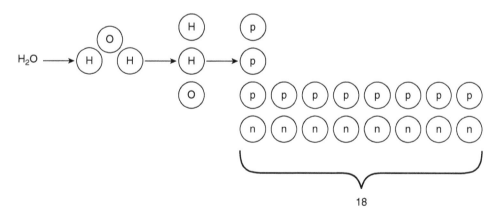

Figure 14.7 The relative formula mass of water

Calculating the relative mass for anything other than a single atom can therefore be done with ease by just combining the mass numbers of the atoms present.

Do a number of examples with the class and then give them plenty of opportunity to practise. Pause, check students' work, then add brackets as a factor increasing complexity, followed by more practice.

Step 4: The Mole

You have spent a lot of time with individual atoms and molecules, but explain to your students that chemists never use just one or two, and in fact we use vast numbers of atoms. To represent those numbers, we use a word called the mole.

Tips and tricks

Some things won't make sense to your students until further down the line. You are always within your rights to say things like 'I know that doesn't make sense right now, or it isn't clear how this relates to what we did just before. It will do eventually, and I need you to just bear with me for the minute.'

In order to make the above sensible, you have to now pivot to something that is already concrete and familiar: the use of words to represent numbers like dozen, baker's dozen, score and the like. Having students manipulate these words is a good way to remind them of them and also to demystify the process (e.g. How many eggs are in two dozen eggs? How many people are in four scores of people?).

Once students have familiarised themselves, introduce the word mole as a direct analogue, just representing a different number, as in Figure 14.8.

$$
\begin{aligned}
\text{A dozen} &= 12 \\
\text{A score} &= 20 \\
\text{A mole} &= 6.02 \times 10^{23}
\end{aligned}
$$

Figure 14.8 A comparison showing words that represent numbers

Give students plenty of practice using that number, and especially how the power works. Students who are unfamiliar with standard form conventions may really struggle here so it is crucial that you spend the time walking them through how to use the number. At some point, once students have gained familiarity with the number and how to manipulate it, tell students that it is called Avogadro's number (you can inject some hinterland at this point, provided it does not break up students' flow as they are practising).

Step 5: Tying the Two Together

Your students now have a good understanding of relative masses and associated calculations as well as Avogadro's number. It is now time to tie the two together to allow them to finally understand why you are doing all this.

Point out that the word/numbers you used earlier like 'dozen' are all used because they are sensible to the people that use them. Because of the way egg crates are designed, it's easy to get eggs into packs of six or twelve, so we use words like dozen. So why do we use Avogadro's number?

Go back to your drawing of water from earlier on. Draw out a beaker on a balance, and tell students that you have added one molecule of water. The balance still shows zero, as the mass of the molecule is incredibly tiny. Discuss how you could add more and more and more and eventually the reading would start increasing as you added millions and millions of molecules. You decide to stop adding molecules

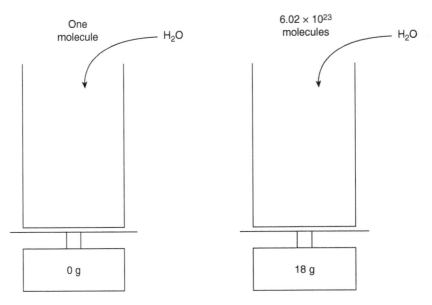

Figure 14.9 A diagram to help you show the connection between Avogadro's number and relative formula mass

when the balance gets to 18 g, and find that you have added 6.02×10^{23} molecules (see Figure 14.9). With any luck, the connection between the two halves of the learning sequence should now be clear to your students.

Repeat the process for another substance like sodium fluoride (don't worry too much about how NaF isn't molecular so directly comparable, the principle is the same).

Following this, go back to your water example ask students how many moles of water you would have if instead of showing 18 g, the balance showed 36 g? Repeat for 9 g and 1.8 g. Fill out a table like in Figure 14.10 slowly, using simple mathematical intuition, and then ask students how they could do it for a more complicated number like 86.4 g.

How many moles of water ...

18 g	1	moles
36 g	2	moles
9 g	0.5	moles
86.4 g	?	moles

Figure 14.10 A table showing relationships between masses and moles

How many moles of water ...

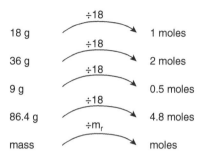

Figure 14.11 The completed table deriving the mole, mass and m_r equation

Your students may be able to tell you how to resolve this sum, or you can simply draw an arrow to illustrate the mathematical operation that moves from one column to the next. Add a final row at the bottom of your table, to show a generalised version of the operation which you can then turn into the mole equation with ease (Figure 14.11).

At this point, students should practise applying the equation following an I/we/you route.

Check for understanding

The 'final product' that students need is the ability to calculate relative formula mass, use Avogadro's number and calculate moles. Questions testing these will at all points be helpful. Of course, the explanation above aims for more conceptual understanding of the processes for which questions like the below may be helpful:

- How many atoms of hydrogen would be needed to have the same mass as one molecule of water?
- How many atoms of carbon would have the same mass as two molecules of water?
- A student suggests that two atoms of oxygen would have the same mass as one atom of germanium. What mistake has the student made?
- A student has 10 million oxygen atoms. Do these atoms have more or less mass than 8 million lithium atoms?
- A student says that a mole of atoms of oxygen has the same mass as a mole of ions of oxygen (oxide ions). Is the student correct? Explain your answer.

15

ELECTROLYSIS

What students should know already

- Elements and compounds.
- Ionic compounds are made of different ions with positive or negative charge.
- The conductivity of ionic compounds in solution or liquid form (molten).
- Opposite charges attract.
- How electrons are transferred in reactions involving ions.
- How to construct a half equation.
- Redox in terms of electrons.

What students should know by the end

- The process of electrolysis in solution and in liquids.
- The construction of half equations at anodes and cathodes.

The real art to explaining electrolysis is in an appreciation of the prior knowledge necessary to fully understand it. If your students have not fully grasped electron transfer, for example, then explaining that to them at the same time as introducing reactions at electrodes is going to be very tricky. The explanation below does recap the prior knowledge, but only in the sense of putting it in a new context, not in the sense of needing to solidify the basic understanding.

Sequencing is also a problem across the unit. There are three distinct parts of the unit in general:

a. Electrolysis of liquids.
b. Electrolysis of solutions.
c. Electrolysis of aluminium oxide.

The unit is often taught in that order, but it's probably better to do c before b as it is an example of a. It is also easier to understand the process in liquids so they should come first, therefore a strong sequence would be: liquids → aluminium oxide → solutions.

Step 1: Overview

Start with the purpose of electrolysis: the extraction of metals more reactive than carbon. It may be a good idea to start with an example like aluminium. As hinterland, state that it comes from aluminium ores like bauxite, also showing pictures and describing the uses of aluminium. It is definitely worth demonstrating electrolysis but picking an appropriate example is incredibly difficult. This is because:

a. You want to start with a liquid ionic compound.

b. Most liquid ionic compounds have very high melting points and effective electrolysis in the lab is complicated.

c. Zinc chloride is a common choice, but the charge on zinc is not immediately obvious to students so adds another level of complexity.

d. If using a solution, all metals more reactive than carbon are also more reactive than hydrogen so you wouldn't actually extract them.

As a compromise, you can use a copper chloride solution as demonstration, and only use the demonstration as a way of giving an overview. It is not part of the core instruction and makes it clear that you are just showing students the set-up and what is involved. You can use a low current so you and your students can smell the very small and non-dangerous amounts of chlorine coming off (using a fume cupboard will still allow for smelling the chlorine) and see the copper forming. Bring a mini-whiteboard while doing the demo to show the students the relevant word equation, emphasising the formation of elements from a compound. The major points to emphasise are therefore:

1. How it is set up (you do not need to detail terminology like anode and cathode at this point – it can come later).
2. That electricity is used to produce elements from a compound.

Tips and tricks

Doing the bleached litmus paper to test for chlorine is not a good idea at this point as it introduces too many new ideas. Unless, that is, your students know that test already.

This is a good opportunity to construct a diagram of the basic set-up as shown in Figure 15.1, and give students time to practise the various components – especially that metals are produced at the cathode and non-metals at the anode. Knowledge of the basic terminology and process is vital going forwards.

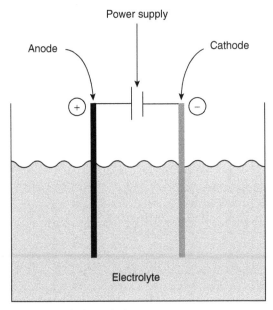

Figure 15.1 A simplified diagram of electrolysis

Step 2: Constructing the First Electrolysis Equation

After the demo, core instruction begins, and for this you can use liquid sodium chloride as a prime example. First, we recap the formation of sodium chloride from ions. Do this as independent questions for students to complete along the lines of:

1. Draw the full atomic structure/electronic configuration of sodium and chlorine.
2. Use arrows to show what happens when they bond ionically.
3. Draw both ions out.
4. Write the formulae for the ions.

Tips and tricks

Doing it this way rather than the common approach of starting from step 3 enables you to:

a. Test prerequisite knowledge.
b. Give your students the opportunity for retrieval practice.
c. Help your students see the connections between different topics.

Once that knowledge is assured (and if it isn't there is no point going ahead onto electrolysis), write on the board:

Sodium + chlorine → sodium chloride

And explain this is what you have been discussing. But sodium chloride is enormously abundant and easy to get hold of. What if you want to start from sodium chloride and produce sodium instead? Your students should by now know that you could not use reduction with carbon and that electrolysis is the correct route (even if they have no understanding of electrolysis).

As a class, construct the word equation:

Sodium chloride → sodium + chlorine

This is what happens in the electrolysis, and make reference back to your demo (how we used electricity to form elements from a compound).

Step 3: Redox

After review, go back to your word equation:

Sodium chloride → sodium + chlorine

Next, construct a symbol equation as:

$2NaCl \rightarrow 2Na + Cl_2$

Discuss the state symbol for NaCl. It cannot be (s) as it would not conduct electricity so must be (l) or (aq). Tell students you know that chlorine is a gas and just for the minute you will assume that Na comes off as a solid.

Tips and tricks

In reality sodium wouldn't come off as a solid but you don't want to let that get in the way of the explanation. As with using copper chloride as an example, sometimes we need to make compromises to keep the flow of an explanation. Once students are adept, you can always go back to the melting point of sodium later.

Next, break apart the sodium chloride into two ions, written as formulae. Refer students back to their previous work on this.

Isolate a sodium ion, and draw it next to a schematic representation of the cathode. Construct the diagram as shown in Figure 15.2, explaining as you go that sodium is *attracted* to the negative electrode, picks up an electron and becomes elemental sodium. Define this as reduction.

Directly below these images, align a half equation.

Repeat the process for the chloride ions. It may be helpful to draw the full ionic structure for chloride, so students can understand the need for two electrons to be transferred. Define this as oxidation.

Your key worked example is now complete. You will want to do more examples together as a class, gradually introducing changes one at a time and then allowing students to practise independently. A good sequence might be:

1. Sodium chloride.
2. Lithium chloride.
3. Lithium fluoride.
4. Lithium oxide.
5. Calcium oxide.
6. Aluminium oxide.

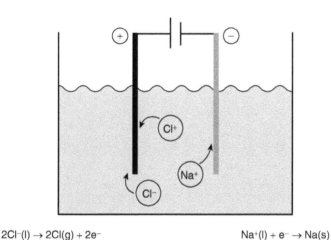

Sodium chloride $\rightarrow$ Sodium + Chlorine

$2NaCl\ (l) \rightarrow 2Na\ (s) + Cl_2\ (g)$

$2Na^+\ (l) + 2Cl^-\ (l) \rightarrow 2Na\ (s) + Cl_2\ (g)$

$2Cl^-(l) \rightarrow 2Cl(g) + 2e^-$ $Na^+(l) + e^- \rightarrow Na(s)$

Figure 15.2 A diagram giving an overview of the electrolysis of sodium chloride

Step 4: Electrolysis of Aluminium Oxide

Once students are proficient, introduce aluminium oxide as just another example of the above and explain the slightly different set-ups and additional points of:

- Cryolite to lower melting point of aluminium oxide.

- Reaction at anode with the oxygen produced. Emphasise to students that this is a two-step process.

Step 5: Electrolysis of Solutions

At this point, things become harder because there isn't a particularly good way at GCSE of explaining the products of electrolysis of solutions that will be accessible to the majority of students. It's generally good advice to be up front with students about that, and explain that if they continue to study chemistry to a higher level it will make more sense. Instead, you could demonstrate the electrolysis of a solution like sodium chloride and show students that sodium is most definitely not produced, and instead hydrogen is evolved (as above you do not need to test for it). You can then repeat the process for copper sulphate and state that the gas produced is oxygen, not 'sulphate' gas. Your next example sequence is important in terms of varying the conditions slightly for each question as well as including non-examples. A sequence like the below could be helpful. At first just ask students to predict products at each electrode. Following this and after review, show students the equation for water's electrolysis and the reduction and oxidation of hydrogen ions and hydroxide ions respectively. Then students can use the same sequence as you used already to construct equations for reactions at the electrodes.

NaCl(aq)

NaF(aq)

NaOH(aq)

CuOH(aq)

$CuSO_4$(aq)

$Na_2SO_4(aq)$

$CaSO_4(aq)$

$CaCl_2(aq)$

$CaCl_2(l)$

$CaCl_2(s)$

Followed by a mix of different substances and states.

Check for understanding

There are a number of ways to really check students' understanding throughout this topic, with the most challenging questions being around products of electrolysis. It is worth presenting students with a number of different substances, including:

- Ionic liquids.
- Ionic solutions (to include a range of anions and cations).
- Covalent liquids (other than water).

And ask students to predict the products at anodes and cathodes, along with the half equations occurring there.

16

ENERGY CHANGES

Relevant ages

14–16

What students should know already

- Fundamentals of chemical reactions including:
  - Word equations.
  - Identification of reactants and products.
  - Fundamental terms and concepts around energy.

What students should know by the end

- Energy is transferred in a chemical reaction.
- If energy is lost to the surroundings, the temperature of the surroundings increases and the reaction is termed exothermic.
- If energy is gained from the surroundings, the temperature of the surroundings decreases and the reaction is termed endothermic.
- How to draw a reaction profile.

In this sequence there is nothing that is particularly conceptually demanding but there are a number of occasions where students can come a cropper due to confusing language, especially when it relates to the interplay between energy and temperature. Many of the difficulties also come from a poor understanding of the term 'surroundings' with students not realising that the thermometer *is* the surroundings. We will elaborate on this misconception and how to tackle it later on in this chapter.

Step 1: Setting the Scene

The hinterland of energy changes in chemical reactions is fairly rich as all reactions involve a change of some sort. Demonstrations at this point are appropriate, with the only aim being to convey the idea that during a chemical reaction the temperature changes – up or down. Common demonstrations might include metals or metal hydroxides with acids, with more spectacular offerings coming from the extreme oxidation or combustion end of the scale, with methane bubbles or thermite bubbles conveying the point well. Common endothermic reactions tend to be less spectacular with weak acids and bases like sodium carbonate being fairly straightforward and illustrative.

Tips and tricks

At this point shy away from complications like thermal decompositions or cooking as they add the extra variable of the surroundings being actively heated by a source other than the reactants, leading to confusion about why they are labelled endothermic when the surroundings are very hot. These examples can – and should – come later.

The point of this is to put conflict at the heart of your learning sequence: why do some reactions get hot and others get cold?

Step 2: Energy

The end goal of this instruction is shown in Figure 16.1. As ever, it should be constructed slowly and step-by-step, with checks for understanding at each point.

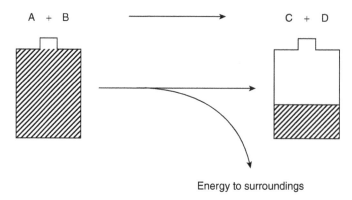

Exothermic reactions

A + B → C + D

Energy to surroundings

Figure 16.1   The battery model for energy change

First, draw out a simple reaction scheme of A + B → C + D. Explain that all chemicals store energy. Some more, some less. A good example might be glucose, which stores a lot of energy and is useful to us.

Tips and tricks

Mentioning glucose at this point helps ground something new in something more familiar. Remember that students do not need a detailed knowledge of respiration for this – all they need to be familiar with is the basic point: sugars and carbohydrates store lots of energy which we use. For this reason you don't need to extensively test this knowledge or spring-board into a retrieval opportunity about glucose and respiration as this will merely serve to break the narrative of your explanation.

You can use a qualitative bar model to illustrate what a chemical storing energy might look like. A battery can be used here as it is instantly familiar and easily interpretable. Say: A+B, the reactants, store loads of energy. This will be shown by shading the battery in up to the top. Then move on to C+D, saying that they have very little energy and show that by shading in only a part.

Point out that the energy must have gone somewhere – it can't just be created or destroyed (students should be familiar with this). That means that it must go to the surroundings. Explain explicitly that the surroundings are *anything which is not the reactant and product directly*. That includes the water a reaction might be taking part in but it also – and this is crucial – includes a thermometer. As such, if the thermometer gains all this energy, the temperature it shows will go up. This is called an exothermic reaction.

Step 3: Endothermic

Construct the inverse of the diagram in Figure 16.1, following the same steps and narrative structure, leading to an endothermic change.

Step 4: The Misconception

Show students a picture like the one in Figure 16.2. Tell them that there are two liquids reacting together on a piece of cotton wool. The thermometer is stuck into the wool and the temperature decreases as the reaction progresses. Ask if this is endo or exothermic.

Figure 16.2 Exposing misconceptions about the thermometer being part of the surroundings

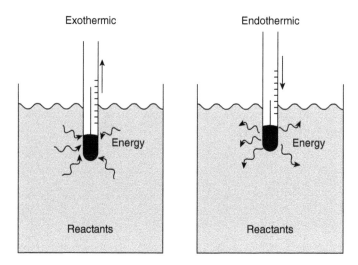

Exothermic   Endothermic

Energy

Energy

Reactants   Reactants

Figure 16.3   Showing exactly how the thermometer absorbs or loses energy

Normally, you will get a good spread of responses. Many students will assume it is exothermic as energy must be leaving the cotton wool for the thermometer to get so cold. Remind students that the *thermometer is part of the surroundings, not the reaction*. As such, if it is losing energy it means the reactants must be taking that energy in. A diagram like that shown in Figure 16.3 may help.

Step 5: Reaction Profiles

A second advantage of the battery model in Figure 16.1 is that it can easily be turned into a reaction profile. Construct the diagram again, and this time add a y axis that you can label 'energy'. Rub out the outline of the battery leaving you with just the top line showing the amount of energy stored. Identify the gap in energy and label it as the overall energy change (Figure 16.4). Repeat this for an endothermic reaction.

Tips and tricks

This may not be the best time to introduce activation energy, with it potentially being better placed once students have learnt collision theory as part of a kinetics/rates of reaction unit.

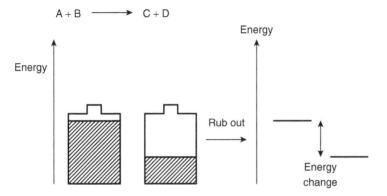

Figure 16.4 Turning the battery model into a reaction profile

Check for understanding

A range of reactions should be offered to students with temperature changes provided. Students should first identify whether the reaction is exothermic or endothermic, then explain how they know, then describe qualitatively the difference in energy stored between reactants and products. It is definitely worth doing the cotton wool example discussed earlier again, both from exo and endo perspectives.

17

RATES OF REACTION

Relevant ages

14–16

What students should know already

- Basic familiarity with chemical reactions.
- Understanding of an acid solution as 'acid particles' (hydrogen ions and an anion) in water.
- An understanding of 'concentration'.
- Fundamentals of rates – that some reactions are quicker than others and that we can calculate their rates from experimental data.

What students should know by the end

- The effect of surface area on rate of reaction.
- The effect of concentration on rate of reaction.
- The effect of pressure on rate of reaction.
- The effect of temperature on surface area.

Explanation

This explanation will focus on the different ways in which rate can be altered. In terms of introduction of new concepts, surface area is probably the most concrete and so starts the sequence. Concentration is also quite concrete, but introduces the additional factor of volume/mass of product increasing too so comes after this. Pressure comes next as it is quite abstract as we cannot directly change the pressure; we do this by changing other variables (volume of container, moles of gas, temperature). Temperature comes last as it contains two distinct ideas (increased motion and more particles with activation energy) and is therefore more complex.

All of the above follows the introduction to rate and how it is calculated. Without this foundational knowledge, the idea of 'increased' or 'decreased' rate will have to be taught at the same time as one of the four variables listed, which will make initial teaching more difficult.

Step 1: Surface Area

Surface area is one of the 'biggest' ideas in secondary science, underpinning and relating to topics including rates, transport, cell adaptation, animal adaptations, pressure, heat transfers, nanoparticles and more. Each of those areas requires its own model, and it is unlikely that novice students would be able to transfer their knowledge from one area to another. This means that students who have a good knowledge of how increased surface area increases rate of diffusion across a membrane will still struggle to transfer that knowledge to rates of reaction. It is therefore worth verbally signalling the similarity, but expecting to have to essentially teach it from scratch in this new area. Once students gain knowledge and mastery of all aspects of their course of studies, then activities could and should be designed to tease out the links between these different areas and how surface area relates to them.

Tips and tricks

The unifying idea that lies beneath all these variables is that for a reaction to take place 1) particles need to collide, and 2) that collision needs to have sufficient energy. Theoretically, a process of deduction should allow students to derive from these abstract principles how the different variables influence the rate of reaction. However, reality is far from theory and in truth students probably need to go from the variables up to the abstract principle and not the other way around.

Step 1a: Solid + Acid

Introduce the idea of a solid reacting with an acidic solution, potentially by a straightforward demonstration of a carbonate in acid. Use large marble chips first, then a powder, but there is no point at all referencing surface area now. Instead, frame it as a mystery – why is it that the powder reaction is so much quicker?

Tips and tricks

There is also probably little point taking student ideas as to why it is quicker when a powder. They will almost definitely not work out the answer due to the cognitive jump from 'smaller' to 'larger surface area' to 'more frequent collisions'.

Step 1b: What is an Acidic Solution?

At this point, you should assess student understanding of what an acid is on a particular level. Your students should be familiar with a diagram like Figure 17.1.

If they are familiar, then they should also know it is the H^+ that reacts and can be summarised as in Figure 17.2. If they are not familiar yet, then just refer to generic 'acid particles' and redraw your diagram as in Figure 17.2.

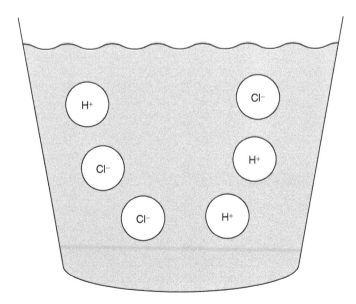

Figure 17.1 A representation of an acidic solution

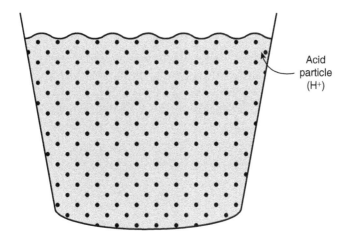

Figure 17.2 A simplified representation of an acidic solution

Step 1c: What is a Solid?

Next, use a model like in Figure 17.3 to illustrate what a solid looks like at a particular level.

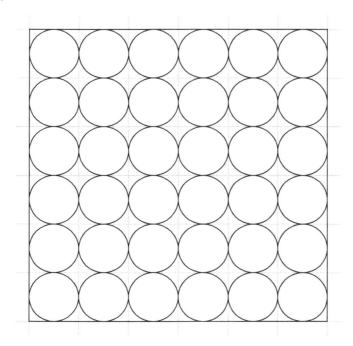

Figure 17.3 A model representing a solid

Step 1d: Collisions

Place the 'solid' in the 'solution' (Figure 17.4) and explain clearly that in order for a reaction to take place, the acid particles need to collide with the solid.

Count the number of particles that can actually collide – these are the ones around the edge. You may want to write it down at the side of your diagram too (as in Figure 17.5). In this case, there are 20 particles that can react.

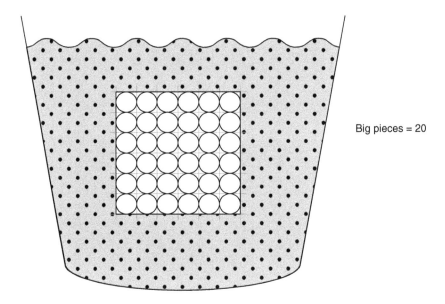

Big pieces = 20

Figure 17.4 The solid in the solution

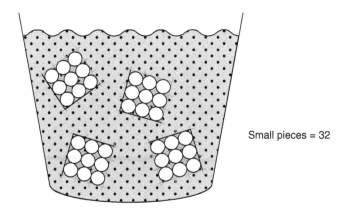

Small pieces = 32

Figure 17.5 The solid broken up into smaller pieces

Step 1e: Make Smaller Pieces

Cut up your model into four pieces. Lay these pieces on the diagram (Figure 17.5), and discuss/explain how there are now 32 particles available to collide. Because we are referencing collisions over time, it is important to stress the use of the word 'frequent' when describing how the collisions increase. If you left the solid in for the same amount of time as before, there would be more collisions now.

Step 1f: The Jump to Surface Area

The key point of error in student understanding of rates and surface area is the inverse relationship between size of piece and surface area. This is always difficult for students as linear relationships seem to be the default when it comes to recall. Therefore spend plenty of time on this and use multiple representations, for example including getting a ruler and measuring the area available around the perimeter of each object.

Check for understanding

Beyond questions that test the final product like 'explain why marble powder has a greater rate of reaction than marble chips', questions like the below may help:

1. A solid is broken into small pieces. Does this increase or decrease the surface area? Explain your answer.
2. A student takes a large solid that weighs 4 g. He breaks it into smaller pieces and notes that it still weighs 4 g. He concludes that the surface area has not changed. Explain why this is incorrect.
3. Draw a sketch graph showing the relationship between particle size (x axis) and surface area (y axis) (students will have to be familiar with sketch graphs for this to be effective).

Step 2a: Concentration

Now that we have covered surface area, many of the building blocks we need for concentration are already in place. Build up two diagrams as in Figure 17.6, but do not add the arrows yet.

These diagrams are also a good opportunity to check for understanding of concentration. Variations would include drawing them again but with the same number of particles, but a different level for the top of the solvent (i.e. changing the volume).

Step 2b: Adding the Solid

Add a solid to the diagram like you did earlier in Figure 17.4. It should be a fairly straightforward jump from this model to a description of the rate increasing due to increased frequency of collisions caused by an increased number of particles.

Step 2c: Increased Product

If the concentration is increased without a change in volume, provided the solid is in excess you will gain more product. Amending your diagrams from before as in Figure 17.6 should help here, where each arrow represents some gas formed. It is clear that more gas is formed when the concentration is higher. Once these concepts are solidified, you can make them more complex by discussing excess and limiting factors (whenever appropriate in your curriculum).

Step 3: Pressure

First, ensure students have a working understanding of pressure. This can be done through diagrams like Figure 17.8.

By this point, students should be getting the hang of applying the principle of 'increased frequency of collisions' and should easily note that box B in Figure 17.8 will have more frequent collisions.

Use other diagrams with a constant volume and a different number of particles to illustrate a further way to change the pressure (ignoring temperature for now). This of course will then tie back to the point made in step 2c which is that you could get increased product.

Tips and tricks

In Figure 17.8 it is vital that you emphasise the number of particles remains constant. One way to make that clear is by drawing out the particles in roughly the same arrangement, so students can see that the two boxes have the same number of particles. Counting them out loud will help as well.

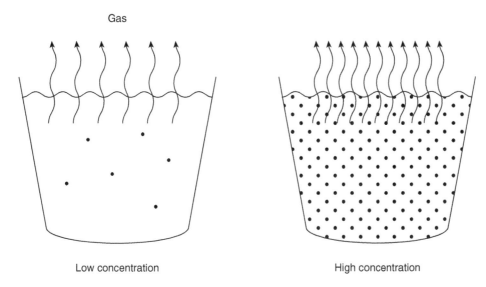

Gas

Low concentration

High concentration

Figure 17.6 Diagrammatic representation of increased product formed with increased concentration

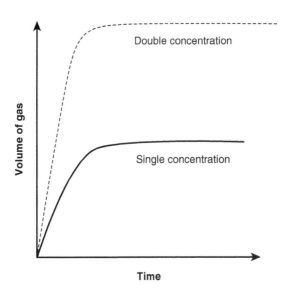

Figure 17.7 A graph you can use in a number of different ways to check for student understanding of concentration and rate

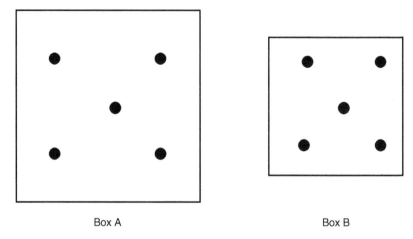

Box A   Box B

Figure 17.8   A simple representation of different pressures

Step 4: Temperature

Temperature has one major effect on the particles that results in two outcomes. The effect is that they move faster (increased kinetic energy/energy in their kinetic store). The two outcomes are that they collide more frequently *and* that more collisions are successful. It is crucial that these are presented as two different things.

Step 4a: Moving Faster

Students should know from lower down in school that heating particles up makes them move faster. As such by this point the jump from there to 'and therefore collide more frequently' should be very small.

Step 4b: Activation Energy

A simple analogy of two breaking eggs is a good start here – if two eggs roll into each other gently, they do not smash. The same applies to a chemical reaction – if two particles roll into each other gently, there is no reaction (obviously making clear that atoms do not 'smash' in a chemical reaction). That movement, that rolling, can be conceptualised as relating to kinetic energy. Rolling fast, lots of energy, more likely reaction. Rolling slow, little energy, less likely reaction.

How much energy though? We call this the activation energy, a threshold which the particles need to meet to react.

Step 4c: Activation Energy is Not a Property of This Particular Particle

Students often say that particles react when they have 'enough activation energy', which indicates they think of activation as a thing which can be possessed by that particle, rather than a threshold which that particle needs to meet. A useful analogy here is a height restriction at a theme park – you need to meet the restriction to go on the ride, but if you aren't tall enough we don't say 'you don't have enough height restriction', or the converse; we just say 'you don't have enough height'.

Step 4d: Tying it Back Together

A diagram like in Figure 17.9 is important here when it comes to separating the strands of the effect of temperature as discussed. Construct it slowly, overemphasising the difference between the two branches.

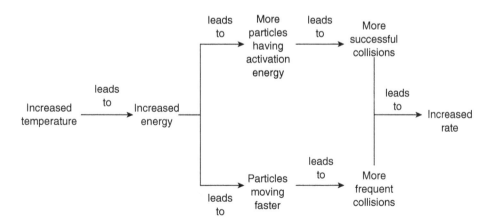

Figure 17.9   The two branches of temperature's effect on rate of reaction

After Figure 17.6:

As well as diagrams showing solutions of differing concentration and asking students to assign their relative concentrations, non-examples may help here too:

- A student has two identical solutions. In one she puts one lump of marble. In the other she puts two. Has she changed the concentration of the solution? Explain your answer.
- A solution has 100 particles in $50\,cm^3$ of water. Another solution has 200 particles in $100\,cm^3$ of water. Which one has a higher concentration? If a solid is added to each, in which one will the reaction have a higher rate?

To test knowledge of the second effect of increasing concentration on volume of product, graphical representations can be very helpful, with students having to predict the line for a reaction which featured a solution twice as concentrated (answer is dotted line in Figure 17.7). Having students explain every part of the graph is then a useful consolidation activity, as would be adding a line for the same mass of solid, but in bigger/smaller pieces.

After Figure 17.8:

Questions like the graphical ones in the previous two checks will work just as well here, as will wordier, more challenging questions like:

- A student has two boxes of equal volume. One has 1500 particles and the other has 2000. In which one will the rate of reaction be greater? Explain your answer.
- The student then doubles the number of particles in one of the boxes, but without changing the volume. What two effects will this have on the reaction?
- Very challenging: A student has a box with 100 particles of A and 100 particles of B, which can react together. The student then adds 100 particles of C, which does not take part in the reaction. The student says that this increases the pressure inside the box and therefore increases the rate of reaction. Explain why this is incorrect.

After Figure 17.9:

Here, you will want to highlight all the errors which you have discussed as part of your explanation, for example:

- A student says a cold reaction is slower because particles do not have enough activation energy. Explain why the student is wrong.
- Give two reasons as to why a hot reaction has a greater rate than a cold one.

18

DYNAMIC EQUILIBRIUM

What students should know already

- Basics of kinetic and collision theory.
- Rates of reaction.
- That some reactions are reversible.

What students should know by the end

- How dynamic equilibrium is reached.
- That rate and extent are distinct concepts.
- How adding or removing reactants/products affects extent.
- How external changes to the system (pressure, temperature) affect extent.
- What pressure is.

Dynamic equilibrium and Le Chatelier's principle are probably the hardest things in standard school chemistry courses to teach. The concepts are both highly abstract and complex, containing multiple parts tying together as well as a multi-step cause and effect process. The approach outlined in this chapter uses an imperfect analogy that acknowledges its imperfection. The goal is to give students a conceptual hook to hang their thoughts on, though it certainly does not map perfectly.

Tips and tricks

You may be tempted to use physical representations when teaching dynamic equilibriums like model atoms or beads or paper clips. You may think that these representations will help students understand the deep structure of the material, but all too often they are used as ways to make something more engaging or appealing, which does not necessarily lead to learning. Students will often be highly engaged with the technical process of putting beads on pipe cleaners or looping paper clips together, but failing to make the jump to the concepts at play. Partly because of this, the explanation below does not use manipulatives (physical representations) or demonstrations: as the concepts are so hard to get, there is a legitimate concern that students will be distracted by surface features and fail to see the ideas behind them. This is of course not to say 'never use manipulatives', but to use them judiciously.

Step 1: Moving Homes

This analogy uses migratory patterns in order to convey the idea of an equilibrium that is dynamic: a state where the overall quantities in two groups are not changing but movement is still happening between those groups.

Start with a person who lives in a large country. Point out that if she wanted to, she could move to another country, which was a lot smaller (Figure 18.1). Likewise, if she lived in the small country, she could move to the big one (Figure 18.2).

Increase complexity, and point out that there would never be only one person, and we might have three people instead. Each of those could move backwards or forwards at will (Figure 18.3).

Now expand even further and point out that there are never just three people, but a great many, and you will draw them as just lines, where each line represents a person (Figure 18.4).

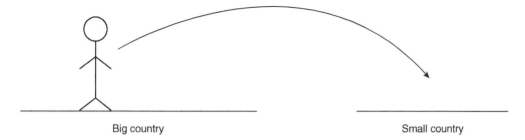

Figure 18.1   Simple representation of one person moving countries

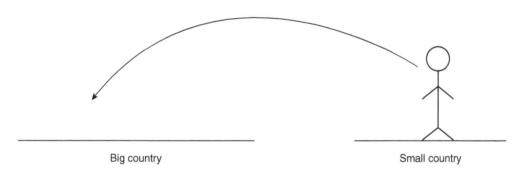

Figure 18.2   How that person could move back

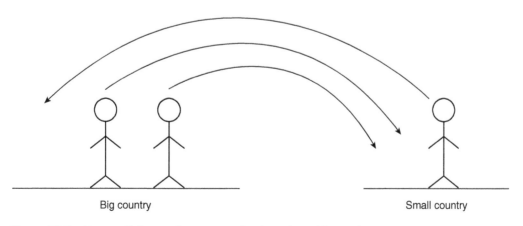

Figure 18.3   How multiple people can move backwards and forwards

Big country   Small country

Figure 18.4   Representing multiple people as vertical lines

Tips and tricks

Using a line as a person is a sensible way to represent something that would be laborious to draw. But this approach where you use stick people first allows you to move from familiar to unfamiliar in incremental steps, without changing or introducing too much at once.

If these people all lived in the big country, you would expect a lot of them to move to the smaller country to get some space.

However, once the small country starts to fill up, some people might think that actually they were better off beforehand and should return to the big country. There would still be some people moving from big to small, but there would also now be people moving small to big (Figure 18.5).

It is now time to introduce rates of movement. Slowly build up to the diagram in Figure 18.6, starting at the top – showing it as a process.

As we build the abstractness of the model, it may be time to add some arbitrary values in units of people per hour (Figure 18.7).

In Figure 18.7, you want to emphasise that because the rate at which people move backwards and forwards is the same, the total number of people on each side does not change. People are still moving, but the population size is not changing. Call this point 'dynamic equilibrium' and explain those two words fully as in Figure 18.8.

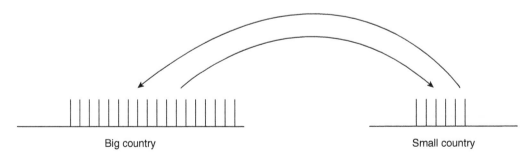

Big country   Small country

Figure 18.5   Many people moving backwards and forwards between the countries

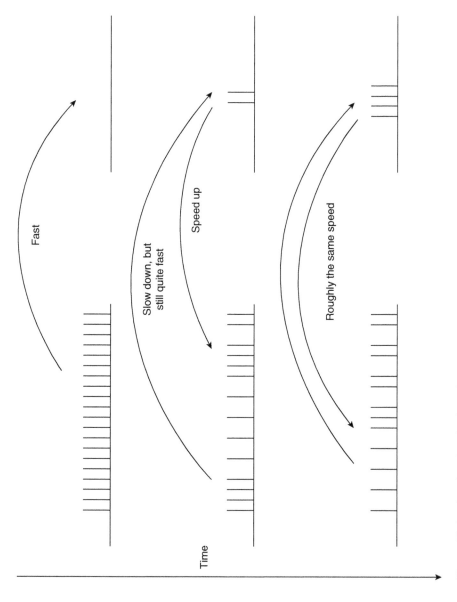

Fast

Slow down, but
still quite fast

Speed up

Roughly the same speed

Time

Figure 18.6 A series showing how the rate of movement changes with time

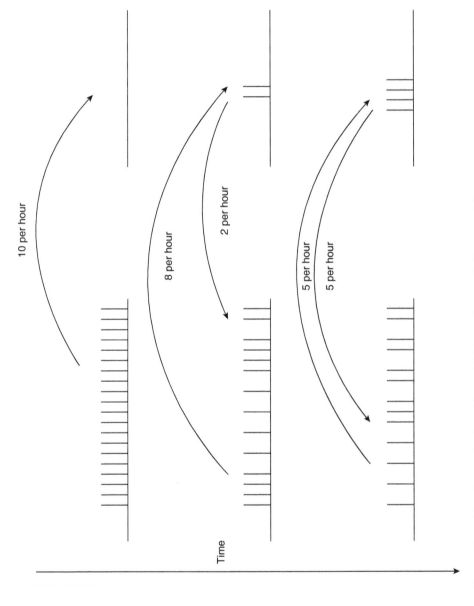

10 per hour

8 per hour

2 per hour

5 per hour

5 per hour

Time

Figure 18.7 The time series from Figure 18.6 but with quantitative description

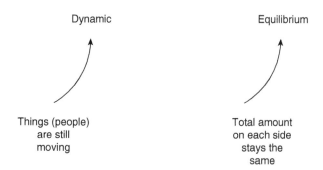

Figure 18.8 Breaking apart dynamic equilibrium

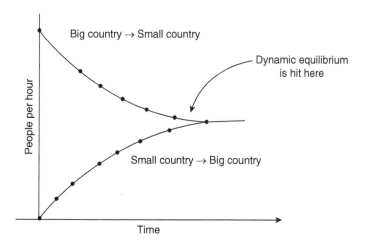

Figure 18.9 A sketch graph showing how dynamic equilibrium is reached

You could even live draw a graph at this point to represent how dynamic equilibrium is reached (Figure 18.9).

Tips and tricks

Using multiple mini-whiteboards under a visualiser will really help here as when constructing the graph you can go back to your previous image showing how the 'people per hour' measure changes with time and that your graph is just a representation of that.

Step 2: A Reaction

You can now repeat the analogy – every step of it – but for a chemical reaction. Using molecules as shown in Figure 18.10 is a simple way to do it.

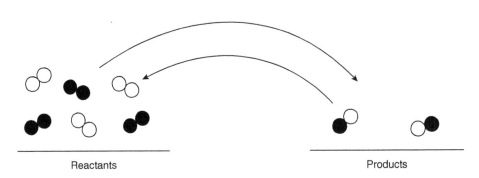

Figure 18.10   Molecules turning from reactants to products

As above, build up from using just a few molecules to using a great number (you can just use dots to represent both reactants and products at this stage), then start adding in a time dimension, then add the 'rate of reaction' (which students should know as prerequisite knowledge) and then draw the graph. Emphasise again that the amounts on each side are not changing, even though reactants are being turned into products and products are being turned into reactants.

Tips and tricks

There is a potential teacher-caused misconception here, which is that in a reaction the reactants move from one *place* to another *place* as in the physical movement of the migration analogy. You should tackle this head on and say it's just you showing reactants and products, but in reality they are all distributed randomly throughout the reaction vessel. You can illustrate this by rubbing out the horizontal lines in Figure 18.10 and drawing a large box around the whole thing.

Step 3: Conditions

Point out that when discussing migration, there were not equal numbers of people in the big and small country at equilibrium. There were more in the big country, and this stands to reason. More people in a big country have as much space as a few people in a small country. The same is true in a chemical reaction: the amount of reactant and product will be different even at equilibrium.

In migration the reason for that is obvious, but in reactions the reason is less so. Discuss how chemists call this the *extent* of a reaction or the *position of the equilibrium* and it depends on the *conditions* under which the reaction is carried out. So tying back to the migration example: one condition is the amount of space in the countries.

Step 4: Changing Conditions

We now return to the migration analogy. Imagine that instead of just watching these people moving backwards and forwards, you are god and have some kind of control over what goes on. You decide to wait until equilibrium, and then add a whole load of people into the small country. Inevitably, this would increase the rate at which people moved small → large, eventually a new equilibrium point would be reached and the *extent* of the population would change. The reverse would happen if you made the land in the big country less habitable, or subject to extreme weather or famine or war. By changing the *conditions* you change the equilibrium (see Figure 18.11).

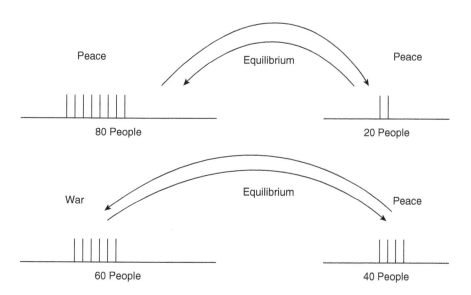

Figure 18.11   Changing the conditions of the equilibrium

At this point, the analogy has served its useful purpose. It cannot really account for the interplay between externally changing the conditions and the reaction system opposing them (Le Chatelier's principle) so we will not use it any more. It has conveyed for us the principle that you can have movement from one 'place' to another and that the rate of that movement can be influenced by external changes.

Step 5: Le Chatelier

The simplest place to start with Le Chatelier is off the back of our last example. When you were god and you removed people from one side, the 'system' (and you will need to explicitly teach this word as tier 3 vocabulary) increased the flow to that side, i.e. it tried to oppose your change. Le Chatelier's principle is just that: whatever change is made externally (to the system) is opposed by an internal change (the system). If you do X – whatever X is – the system will do the opposite of X.

It is helpful to use a kind of template or writing frame here which will allow students to make causative statements (Figure 18.12).

if I ___ _____

the system ___ _____

Figure 18.12   The start of a writing frame

Which could become Figure 18.13.

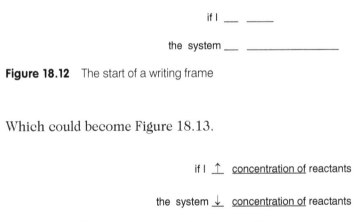

if I ↑ <u>concentration</u> of reactants

the system ↓ <u>concentration</u> of reactants

Figure 18.13   The writing frame beginning to be filled in

Step 6: The Right Language

Chemists use specific language here, to do with shifting the position of the equilibrium or favouring one side. It's probably best when explaining to stick with one term. Shifting the position to the left or right is probably best and can be demonstrated by increasing the size of one of the half arrows as in Figure 18.14.

Figure 18.14 'Shifting' the equilibrium

if I __ _____ reactants

the system __ _____ reactants

by shifting the equilibrium _____

Figure 18.15 The complete writing frame

if I ↑ <u>concentration of</u> reactants

the system ↓ <u>concentration of</u> reactants

by shifting the equilibrium <u>to the right</u>

Figure 18.16 A filled in writing frame

You can then add a third clause to your writing frame (Figure 18.15).

Which when filled out looks something like the one shown in Figure 18.16.

This frame is useful as it can apply to external changes to temperature and pressure as well.

Tips and tricks

You can make reference to your earlier analogy here, reminding students that this is similar to when god removed some people from one country, and the number of people in each country shifted and then reached a new equilibrium. The point here is that shifting the position of equilibrium affects the composition of substances: shift to the right and you get more product and less reactant. Shift to the left and you get less product and more reactant. A big misconception that students have is that at equilibrium there is a 50:50 ratio, and it is important you tackle that head on through your analogy and examples.

As discussed in the Introduction to this book, no analogy will ever be perfect, and there is little further use now for this analogy. It is important to acknowledge the limitations in your explanations and be explicit with your students that 'we used that analogy because I wanted you to get the basic idea. However, the analogy deals with people, and we are dealing with atoms so we are now going to look at the reaction in more detail and leave the analogy behind.'

Step 7: Temperature

This step is a lot easier if your students' understanding of energy changes (see Chapter 16 'Energy changes') is already secure. Without this security, they are likely to become very confused as issues around energy and temperature will become conflated.

Students should have been taught earlier that in a reversible reaction, one direction is endothermic and the other is exothermic. Getting your head around what are the surroundings and what is the system can be a bit tricky, so describing a reaction in a box, which you then put in an oven is a good place to start. Remind students of the writing frame, and say that if the reaction is in the oven, the temperature *of the surroundings* must be increasing. Therefore, the system has to decrease the temperature *of the surroundings*. The way it does that is by 'pulling' energy out of the surroundings through an endothermic reaction. Slowly constructing diagrams like the one shown in Figure 18.17 should help, and you should cover four examples: 1) Forward = exo, placed in oven; 2) Forward = exo, placed in fridge; 3) Forward = endo, placed in oven; 4) Forward = endo, placed in fridge. Putting these diagrams on a board side by side can be very helpful too as it encourages students to compare the different cases.

Some methods involve adding 'heat' into the equation, so something like A + B C + D + heat, which makes the case directly comparable to a change in concentration (as above). Conceptually, this will certainly help students understand, but runs the risk of students thinking of 'heat' as an object made of matter in the same way that A, B, C and D are. This will then cause problems if there are questions about mass, with students potentially thinking that A and B lose mass when they turn to C and D because the energy is being lost.

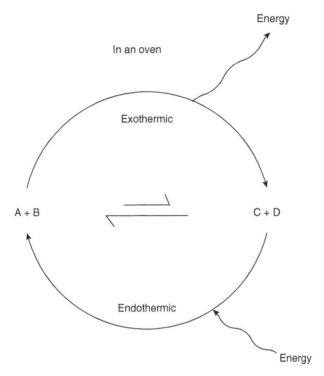

Figure 18.17   The effect of changing temperature on the position of equilibrium

Step 8: Pressure

Knowledge of pressure as the collision of particles with the sides of a container is prerequisite to this step. If you try teaching both pressure and the effect of pressure on position of equilibrium, your students will not understand you at all. It is worth doing some examples of different systems and asking students to identify which will have a higher pressure, for example as shown in Figure 18.18.

The Haber process is a good example to use when tying pressure to equilibrium. Start with just three molecules of hydrogen and one molecule of nitrogen in one box, then two molecules of ammonia in another and ask students which one is at higher pressure (Figure 18.19).

You can now put those boxes together and show how the pressure is affected by this change (Figure 18.20).

You are now ready to go back to your writing frame and fill it out for pressure.

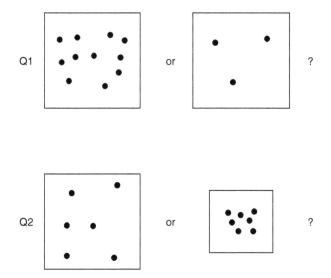

Figure 18.18 A simple question set to test student understanding of pressure

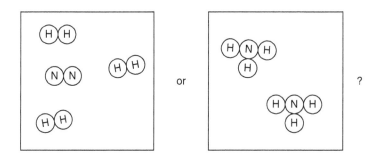

Figure 18.19 Demonstrating that the reactants in the Haber process have a higher pressure than the products (when in stoichiometric amounts)

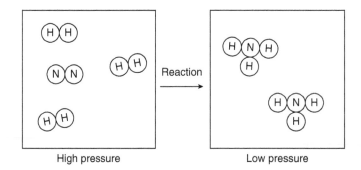

Figure 18.20 Adding to Figure 18.19 to show the process of changing pressure as the reaction progresses

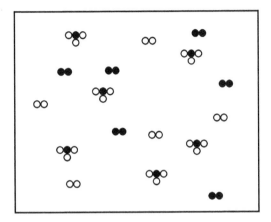

Figure 18.21 A simple diagram that allows for checking for understanding of the effect of pressure on equilibrium

Make sure to also do an example where the number of molecules on each side are equal like $H_2(g) + I_2(g) \rightleftharpoons 2HI(g)$ as well as examples involving a solid like $H_2O(g) + C(s) \rightleftharpoons CO(g) + H_2(g)$.

An image like the one shown in Figure 18.21 can be helpful as another route to student understanding (black circles are nitrogen, white ones are hydrogen).

You can then ask a battery of questions like:

1. How many hydrogen molecules are there in the box?
2. How many nitrogen molecules are there in the box?
3. How many ammonia molecules are there in the box?
4. How many molecules are there in total in the box?
5. Draw out two molecules of hydrogen and one of nitrogen.
6. If they react together, how many molecules of ammonia are formed?
7. Is this more or less than there were before?
8. Looking back at the box, if a student reacts four hydrogen molecules with two nitrogen molecules, how many molecules *in total* would there be in the box?
9. Looking back at question 4, how would the pressure be different after the student carried out this reaction?

And so on.

Check for understanding

There is no single issue that represents the biggest hurdle in this unit and there is no alternative but for students to be exposed to a huge number of applications and be expected to identify how the equilibrium shifts in each one. A table like the one shown in Table 18.1 can quickly and easily give students a lot of practice.

Going over the table and asking students to shade or box the ones they got wrong also means you can rapidly assess if there are any common issues. Of course, students will need to move beyond the formulaic boxes as soon as possible into more probing and complex questions that rely on deeper understanding.

Table 18.1 Two rows from a table which can be used to check for understanding of Le Chatelier's principle

Reaction	Forward reaction is...	Change applied	The system opposes this by...	The equilibrium shifts to the...
$A(g) + 2B(g) \rightleftharpoons AB_2(g)$	Exothermic	Temperature of surroundings is increased	Decreasing temperature of surroundings	Left, favouring the endothermic reaction
$A(g) + 2B(g) \rightleftharpoons AB_2(g)$	Exothermic	Pressure is decreased	Increasing pressure	Right, because there are fewer molecules on the product side

19

FRACTIONAL DISTILLATION

Relevant ages

14–16

What students should know already

- Definition of a mixture.
- Basic concepts surrounding molecules and molecular substances.

What students should know by the end

- The process of fractional distillation and how it separates molecules based on boiling points.

Fractional distillation is a process, which means when you teach it you don't necessarily want to break the process up into smaller chunks in order to retain the narrative flow. In order to offset the increased load of a longer explanation, you must make sure that as much prerequisite knowledge as possible is fully consolidated before starting the explanation. The steps below bring those building blocks to bear so that when it comes to tying them together in the process of fractional distillation, students can follow your narrative without becoming overloaded.

Step 1: Formation of Crude Oil

The formation of crude oil and its importance as an energy store is not necessarily prerequisite knowledge for fractional distillation (more so for combustion, which often comes later). However, it does set the scene, and it's worth giving students an overview so that they are at least familiar with the idea of it first. When explaining the formation of crude oil, it's a good idea to start with a familiar energy source (like a log), trace the energy stored in it back to the sun which is then stored by the tree, and then describe how that energy can be locked up in the tree if buried underground. If the conditions are right, over millions of years the tree might turn into coal, but the energy is still stored in it. The same could be applied to algae and plankton and other sources of ancient biomass.

Step 2: What is Crude Oil? Starting with the Familiar

As a mixture of different hydrocarbons, there are essentially three important pieces of information to teach here: 'mixture', 'hydrocarbon' and 'different'. Students will probably not have a well-developed mental model of what a molecular mixture looks like, so it is worth starting from something concrete and familiar. In this case, you might want to start with water as it is more familiar to students both in its simple form as a liquid, but also its molecular description as H_2O.

Modelling is crucial here. You want to emphasise that each molecule is one unit, but is made of three atoms. Drawing this out on a board is difficult, because it is hard to emphasise the fact that the molecule is one discrete unit. Often, teachers use molecular modelling kits to help here, but remember that this involves an additional cognitive step as well – substituting the physical model for a specific atom, i.e. that a red ball represents an oxygen atom. To get around this, you may want to draw out the conventional representation of a water molecule (H-O-H) on a piece of paper and cut around it (using pastel coloured paper will help distinguish it from a whiteboard). If you had enough of these you could easily show students how water is made from molecules which are all discrete, self-enclosed units.

Tips and tricks

Whichever physical representation you go with, stick with that one throughout. So in the fractional distillation step later on you will need a physical representation; using the same type as you used earlier will eliminate another level of undesirable processing: your students will be familiar with it already so will not need to devote thought to that particular aspect.

Step 3: What is Crude Oil? Moving to the Unfamiliar

The slow move from familiar (water) to unfamiliar (different hydrocarbons) requires a bridge, and using hexane for that bridge is sensible as it is an alkane which is liquid at room temperature, readily available and not such a large molecule as to make drawing and representing it cumbersome. If you don't have a sample of hexane to show then use paraffin, but make sure to say it is hexane as you don't want to introduce the idea of a 'mixture of hydrocarbons' yet.

Introduce the hexane, perhaps combusting a little in an evaporating dish to demonstrate its difference to water. Next draw it out on a piece of paper as above, and show students a number of them mixed together to emphasise the similarity to water in that they are both made of millions of discrete molecules.

Then you can move on to calling it a hydrocarbon. Start by naming it on the board, writing its formula underneath it and then the displayed formula. Use this convention for each new alkane you introduce to allow for some consistency.

Next to it, draw a molecule of ethane with the same layout. Show that they are both hydrocarbons because they have carbon and hydrogen only.

At this point you are introducing an organised hierarchy, that alkane is a type of hydro-carbon, which is a type of molecule, which is a type of substance. When doing this it's always best to have another item within each level to serve as a bridge and way to clarify that an extra level is actually necessary. So here, if you don't talk about other families within 'hydrocarbon', students will not understand why you need both the words 'alkane' and 'hydrocarbon' and why one wouldn't suffice. It is therefore worthwhile just naming 'alkene' and 'cycloalkane' and saying that 'you don't need to know anything about them yet, I just want to show you that there are other groups within this big hydrocarbon family'.

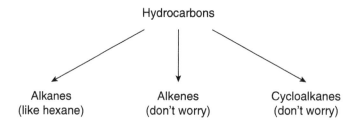

Figure 19.1 The hydrocarbon family

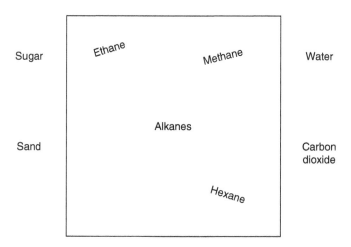

Figure 19.2 Showing a definition in a way that visually distinguishes between examples and non-examples

Diagrams like the ones shown in Figures 19.1 and 19.2 are also a good way of introducing non-examples to clarify to students that there are some things which are 'in' and other things which are 'out'. This can often be the best way of really showing students how a bounded definition works (i.e. a definition where it is clear that some things count and other things do not). Reciting that a hydrocarbon is made of carbon and hydrogen atoms only is concretised by looking at things which are explicitly not hydrocarbons. You can start with one for 'alkanes' and then do one for 'hydrocarbons' to fully ram home the bounded nature of the definition.

Step 4: What is Crude Oil? Different Alkanes Mixed Together

At this point introduce the four alkanes that they need to know (methane, ethane, propane, butane) and emphasise that there are many more, but students do not need to know their names and structures off by heart.

Tips and tricks

You can do the general formula for alkanes now, but it isn't prerequisite knowledge for fractional distillation so you could come back to it later and use it as an opportunity to space out your students' practice of the content covered so far.

On pieces of paper as above, draw out a number of different alkanes and mix them together in front of the students. Explain that this is what crude oil is, a collection of all these different alkanes mixed together. Some are short, some are long, but they are all alkanes.

Tips and tricks

When comparing items, a because/but can be a helpful check for understanding, for example asking students to complete the sentence stems:

Methane and ethane are hydrocarbons because…

Methane and ethane are hydrocarbons but…

Step 5: Properties of Alkanes

Your students now know what an alkane is, the names of the first few and that they are mixed together in crude oil. Using your jumble of paper alkanes, separate them into piles in front of your students (one pile for methane, one for ethane, etc.). Explain that these different piles have different properties depending on their chain length. If you have the capacity to do so, you can soak mineral wool in different alkanes to demonstrate flammability and boiling points, as well as viscosity using the pure liquids and a ramp.

Step 6: Using a Question Set to Lay the Foundations for Fractional Distillation

Give students a range of alkanes with different chain lengths and ask a series of questions based on them like 'which will have the highest boiling point?' or 'between alkane C and alkane E, which one will be more viscous?'

Then give those alkanes (or a new set) their boiling points as well. For example, alkane A might boil at 50°C and alkane B at 75°C. Ask a series of questions like the below:

1. Which has a higher boiling point?
2. At 25°C, what state is A?
3. At 25°C what state is B?
4. The temperature is increased to 55°C. What state is A? Explain your answer.
5. At this temperature, what state is B? Explain your answer.
6. The temperature is increased to 80°C. What state is A? Explain your answer.
7. At this temperature, what state is B? Explain your answer.

These questions are completely non-threatening and relative easy to solve, but lay the groundwork well for fractional distillation. Pause your class, review the answers, and then do the reverse, i.e. asking questions like 'A and B are at 80°C. They are cooled to 70°C. What state is A? What state is B?' etc.

Tips and tricks

Most students know that a boiling point is the temperature at which a liquid will turn to a gas, but they don't realise that it works the other way too and you can cool a gas to that point and it will turn to a liquid. Therefore explicitly teach condensation, then ask questions like 1–7 above but from the perspective of two substances which are above their boiling points.

Step 7: Putting it All Together

By this point, your students are ready to tackle fractional distillation as their knowledge of alkanes, mixtures and boiling points is now strong. You can now give the extended narrative explanation of fractional distillation without having to introduce lots of new material at once.

Use paper cut-outs of three alkanes, which at this point you can just name A, B and C. On each one add a boiling point, 20°C, 150°C and 475°C to the front and back. Then on one side write 'liquid' (or (l)) and on the other write 'gas' (or (g)).

Your eventual diagram looks like the one shown in Figure 19.3.

Begin by slowly drawing it without making reference to any of your molecules, just by describing what the column is like. Then take molecule B (b.p. 150°C) and feed it into the system. At 500°C it will be a gas, so make sure you point out to students that you are flipping it to show that side of the paper cut-out. Then move it into the column, and discuss how at 350°C it is still a gas. Explain that because it is hot it rises up (this may be new knowledge but you don't need to go into detail with it) and cools down. As it hits 250°C, it is still a gas. It continues to rise until it hits 150°C, at which point it condenses and you can flip the card to show the other side and remove it from the column. Then repeat the process with the two extremes (A and C) to demonstrate the boundaries of the process and at this point your students should now be able to describe the extraction of any given alkane through fractional distillation.

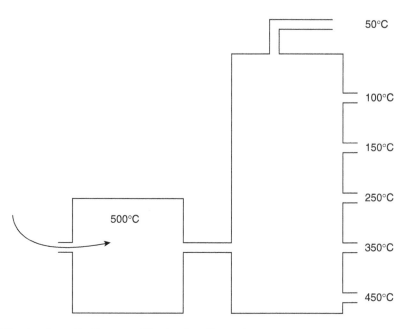

Figure 19.3 A schematic diagram of the fractionating column

Check for understanding

You can use different molecules to ensure your students can describe the process well. You have verbally done three examples, it may be worth doing a fourth example together as a class and writing down in bullet points what happens at every stage, then allowing students to do something very similar for a fifth molecule (i.e. following an I/we/you process).

Responding to fractional distillation can be a number of sentences, so giving students wrong answers to correct can be powerful, as can a 'sensitivity analysis', which works by providing two texts, for example:

'As the octane rises up the fractionating column it cools down until it reaches its boiling point of 126°C at which point it condenses and can be removed from the column.'

'As the octane goes through the fractionating column it cools down until it reaches its boiling point at which point it can be removed from the column.'

Followed by questions asking students to identify the differences in the two texts and explain how each difference affects the overall quality of the answer.

20

LIFE CYCLE ASSESSMENT (LCA)

Relevant ages

14–16

What students should know already

- The use of fossil fuels in the release of energy.
- Problems associated with fossil fuels including renewability and carbon dioxide release.
- The terms renewable and non-renewable.
- Definition and use of sustainable development.

- The purpose of an LCA.
- The major stages of an LCA.
- Common context-specific factors affecting the stages of an LCA.

Explanation

Constructing an LCA may be new to many teachers of chemistry, though issues of sustainability have been part of the curriculum for a long time. There is a temptation to jump straight into extended responses of the format:

1. Provide data on two products.
2. Evaluate which product has a larger environmental impact.

or the like. However, an LCA properly constructed has distinct stages, and each stage has recurring themes and concepts so it is much wiser to break the LCA into its component parts, practise each part individually and then start constructing the complete LCA. The four component parts are:

1. Extracting and processing raw materials.
2. Manufacturing, packaging and transport.
3. Use and operation during its lifetime.
4. Disposal at the end of lifetime (including transport and distribution).

Transport could be considered as a factor at every stage in the process rather than just stage 2, but that may over-complicate matters.

The route below therefore chunks each part of the process and is split up into different steps which cover the different stages of an LCA as well as additional guidance on appropriate language and data analysis. Within each stage there are a number of potential scenarios. For example, within the 'extraction and processing of raw materials' stage of the LCA, scenarios could include raw materials as diverse as wood, plastic, fabric, metal and so on. Each of those in turn can have further subdivision, for example the extraction of gold and the extraction of aluminium are very different processes, though they are both metals. A number of these scenarios will be referenced throughout the explanation, and you should endeavour to give your students as many as possible when they are practising, though it is of course not feasible to attempt to expose them to *all* possible scenarios and subdivisions. In general, the more detailed a student's knowledge of chemistry, the richer their LCAs will be.

Step 1: Introduction to LCA

As with many other concepts, breaking them down into constituent parts runs the risk of failing to see the wood for the trees. Students need to understand what you are trying to achieve and why in order to be able to anchor the constituent parts and see them as part of a cohesive whole, rather than a series of seemingly arbitrary and unconnected ideas.

As 'setting the scene' counts as hinterland, taking a discursive approach with a class can be very fruitful at this point. A fairly straightforward place to start might be a comparison of plastic bags with paper bags, as these are both products students should be familiar with. Ask students to vote on which they think is 'better' for the environment. Probe students' opinions on this and most will probably go with 'paper as it breaks down' or some equivalent. Point out that paper comes from wood which means deforestation, and potentially take another vote. Point out that the paper ones require much more energy to produce which results in more carbon dioxide emissions, and potentially take another vote. Continue along the same vein but with transport costs (less energy to transport plastic), water usage, general waste in production as well as reusability, and many of your students may change their minds. Explain that this is why we need an LCA: to be able to look at the impact across a life cycle and not just the most obvious factors.

Step 2: Extracting and Processing Raw Materials

In terms of specific scenarios for extraction and processing, some common materials and associated considerations are listed in Table 20.1.

Table 20.1 Some common materials for LCA

Material	How it is extracted and processed	Environmental impact	Example uses
Plastic	From crude oil	Non-renewable source. Problems associated with drilling for oil.	Plastic bags, polystyrene cups, fabrics like polyester
Wood	From trees	Deforestation and associated issues like habitat loss, changing weather patterns in extreme cases, removal of a carbon sink. Renewable.	Construction

(Continued)

Table 20.1 (Continued)

Material	How it is extracted and processed	Environmental impact	Example uses
Paper	From wood as above	As well as deforestation issues, paper requires a large amount of water and energy to produce from wood. White paper manufacture can use chlorine for bleaching and the chlorine compounds formed must be disposed of carefully.	Paper bags, paper cups
Iron (or steel)	Mining followed by reduction with carbon in a blast furnace	Mining can cause habitat loss, noise pollution as well as emissions from heavy machinery. Reduction with carbon produces carbon dioxide and requires a lot of energy. Non-renewable.	Extensive uses in construction
Aluminium	Mining followed by electrolysis	Mining as above, electrolysis requires a lot of energy to conduct as well as to melt the aluminium ore. Constant replacement of graphite anodes requires further energy. Non-renewable.	Extensive uses in construction and in vehicle production
Concrete	Quarrying and processing of limestone	Quarrying has similar issues to mining. Non-renewable (though we have lots of it).	Extensive uses in construction

As discussed in the introduction, it should be clear that students will be better able to assimilate and manipulate the information in Table 20.1 if they have a greater general knowledge. If students for example are already well-acquainted with the electrolysis of aluminium oxide, then the problems associated with it should be easy to understand and integrate into a broadening schema of LCAs.

Step 3: Appropriate Language

The phrase 'environmental impact' has been used so far deliberately, as phrases like 'environmentally friendly' or 'eco friendly' or 'good for the environment' are probably not technical enough and best avoided. It is also a useful phrase for students to bolt on to any given statement, for example:

'Paper requires lots of wood in its manufacture, which has a large environmental impact due to deforestation.'

In general students do not need to go into a huge amount of detail, but providing sentence structures of the kind above can be helpful:

'_____ requires _____ in its extraction/manufacture, which has a large environmental impact due to _____.'

Table 20.1 is an example of a support and should be provided to students early on in the learning sequence, but by the end they should be able to work without it. Sample questions to check for understanding at this point might include:

1. In terms of extraction and processing, explain why the environmental impact of using plastic bottles is high.
2. Assess the environmental impact of the extraction and processing of paper.
3. A student suggests that the environmental impact of the extraction by electrolysis is low. Explain why the student is wrong.

Step 4: Manufacturing, Packaging and Transport

Ordinarily there will be data provided for this stage in the process, with interpretation required (see further information on data interpretation below). Often the key factors here are mass and volume. If an item has a large mass, then it requires a lot of energy to transport. If an object has a large volume and cannot be easily stacked, then it also requires a lot of energy to transport as you need larger vehicles in order to be able to fit the units in. You can give students sample calculations and data to check for understanding, for example as below:

1. A lorry can fit 10,000 paper cups or 8,000 plastic cups. Which has a greater environmental impact during transport?

2. Delivery of 1,000 coffee mugs requires 50 kg of plastic packaging to protect the mugs. Discuss the environmental impact of the transport of mugs.

3. A shed can be built using aluminium or steel. Steel has a much larger mass than aluminium. Explain which of aluminium or steel has a higher environmental impact during transport.

4. The manufacture of paper bags from paper requires about four times as much energy as plastic bags from plastic. Which one has a greater environmental impact in its manufacturing?

Step 5: Use and Operation During its Lifetime

This is the stage that students will be most familiar with, and in general the key variable to consider is how long it will last for or how many times it can be reused. For example, plastic bags can be reused whilst paper bags cannot, but even within plastic bags some bags are made from more durable plastic and so last longer.

When dealing with vehicles, energy efficiency in use is also important. Some cars have more efficient engines than others or have a lower mass thereby increasing overall efficiency and decreasing environmental impact as a result of carbon emissions. Indicative questions therefore might be:

1. Explain why a car which can drive 45 miles per gallon of petrol has a lower environmental impact while being used than one which drives 35 miles per gallon.

2. Two cars have an identical engine, but the first car has a mass of 580 kg and the second has a mass of 500 kg. While they are being used, which one will have a lower environmental impact? Explain your answer.

3. A bag for life produces about four times as much carbon dioxide as a normal plastic bag when being produced. However, it can be used about ten times more than a normal plastic bag before breaking. In terms of its use, which plastic bag has a smaller environmental impact? Explain your answer.

4. A gardener is looking to buy a wheelbarrow, and can choose one made of plastic or one made of steel. In terms of use and operation during its lifetime, what should the gardener base her decision on?

Step 6: Disposal

This step is surprisingly complicated, as there are a number of factors to consider due to a number of different disposal routes as in Table 20.2.

Table 20.2 Common disposal methods

Route	Environmental impact	Examples
Recycle	Energy costs involved in separating materials and then in actually recycling them into a new product. Lowers the environmental impact of the 'extraction and processing' stage of the new product. Conserves non-renewable resources.	Glass, plastic, cardboard, steel
Landfill	Uses a large amount of space (habitat loss). Can produce leachates, which are toxic solutions which can enter the local ecosystems. Often materials in landfill are non-biodegradable so the landfill can last (persist for) hundreds of years.	Mixed products that cannot be easily recycled as they are made of many different materials together
Incineration	Production of carbon dioxide from incineration. Energy released can be used for other processes (e.g. energy from incineration of sugar cane stalks is used to speed up the fermenting of the sugar).	Paper or card-based products

It is worth noting that converse arguments are perfectly acceptable, so arguing for example that recycling might have a low impact because it does not result in material going to landfill is legitimate.

Examples of questions to check for understanding:

1. Used paper cups can either be incinerated or recycled. Describe the environmental impact of each disposal route.
2. Explain why we should try to avoid sending items to a landfill.
3. In terms of their disposal, explain why it is better to send paper bags to a landfill than plastic ones.

Step 7: Interpreting and Using Data: Specifying, Magnitudes and 'So it…'

A data table will almost inevitably be provided in LCA questions, and though analysing them is not particularly complicated, students often make errors of omission. It is worth looking at sample answers and modelling what a poor, good and excellent response looks like, for example by using comparison data like in Table 20.3.

Table 20.3 A comparison of two materials used for bags

	Plastic bag	Paper bag
Raw materials	Crude oil	Wood
Mass of solid waste (g)	11	45

If a student is asked about the waste involved, they could write:

'Paper bags produce 45 g of waste.'

This is not creditworthy, as it is just copying from the table, and does not compare the two. Changing this to the common response below does not help much either:

'Paper bags produce 45 g of waste. Plastic bags produce 11 g of waste.'

Even though both are included, there are no comparisons made.

'Paper bags produce more waste.'

Is an improvement, but though correct, does not draw much credit. We could improve this answer to:

'Paper bags produce 45 g of waste, but plastic bags only produce 11 g.'

This is a stronger comparison and it uses specific data to back up the argument. An even better response would be:

'Paper bags produce around four times as much waste as plastic bags.'

This answer gives us a much better sense of scale by tying the data together and by using a statement that refers to the magnitude of the difference.

Modelling these sentences as a class can be extremely powerful. Write each one in turn and as a class discuss how to incrementally improve them. Ensure that students write down a final model so they have an understanding of what you are looking for. It may be worth repeating the exercise for another row of data but with less guidance, so starting with a poor sentence and asking students to write down why it is poor. Then move on to a better one and repeat the process, finally asking students to write down an excellent sentence themselves.

Another common error is not explaining a comparison adequately. For example, Table 20.4 shows data regarding two materials used for wiring.

Table 20.4   A comparison of two metals used for wiring

Metal	Density in g/cm³
copper	8.9
aluminium	2.7

Let us assume the students are asked: 'in terms of their transport, explain which metal has a larger environmental impact?'

Commonly, students will write something like:

'Aluminium has a lower environmental impact because it has a lower density.'

Which is only part of the answer as it does not explain how density relates to environmental impact. A better answer is:

'Aluminium has a lower environmental impact because it has a lower density *so it* requires less energy to transport.'

The addition of the phrase *so it* can be applied in a range of data analysis questions to ensure that students are fully fleshing out their explanations. As above, an even better answer to this question would be:

'Aluminium has a lower environmental impact because its density is around a third of copper's density *so it* requires less energy to transport.'

Check for understanding

There have been questions checking for understanding at each stage in the process, and you should interleave questions once you have finished each stage, so after stage 2, ask questions on stage 1 and 2, after stage 3 on stages 1, 2 and 3 and so on. You can also combine questions, so ask to compare the extraction and transport of two materials or the like. By the end, students should be ready to move onto more extended response questions for which you will have to use published data tables, obtained from exam boards or textbooks.

PART 3: PHYSICS

21

INTRODUCING ENERGY STORES AND PATHWAYS

Relevant ages

11–14

What students should know already

- That animals cannot make their own food and need the right types and amount of nutrition. They may also have encountered the energy values of foods in 'kilojoules' or 'calories' in this context.
- That many common devices (e.g. TVs, toasters, mobile phones) run on electricity. They may also associate 'electricity' as a source of 'energy' or 'power' in this context.

- Energy is a quantity that can be quantified and calculated.
- Energy is transferred and stored in many physical processes, e.g. heating and cooling; speeding up and slowing down; stretching and squashing elastic objects; and changing position in a gravitational or magnetic field.
- Energy is measured in joules and power is measured in joules per second.

Explanation

Energy is an abstract scientific concept that is very difficult to explain in simple language. Firstly, energy is *not* 'needed to make things happen' and energy is not a 'cause of events'. These are common misconceptions. Many dynamic processes happen without any transfer of energy; for example, diffusion (e.g. perfume spreading through the air in a room) or a satellite in a circular orbit.

It is more helpful to think of energy as a quantity that places a limit on what *can* happen. Energy is a 'universal accounting system' that has been found to be extremely useful. Just as the money in a bank account places a limit on what the person's next purchase will be but is not the cause of any transaction, so the amount of energy a ball has will place a limit on how far up the slope it can roll but is not the cause of the event.

As mentioned earlier, energy is hard to describe in simple language. However, 'energy is the capacity to do work' is a useful starting definition, but will remain circular until students have encountered the scientific definition of 'work' (see Table 21.1).

Table 21.1 An analogy to support teaching the definition of energy

Definition	Meaning	Unit	Comment
Money is the capacity to buy things	A person with a lot of money can buy a lot of things.	GBP, £	'Buying' involves transferring money between people, e.g. coins and notes.
Energy is the capacity to do work.	An object with a lot of energy can do a lot of work.	joules, J	'Work' involves transferring energy between objects, e.g. using forces to push or pull. (Note: the definition of 'work' will be taught later.)

Step 1: Introducing Energy Stores

We will be using the Energy Stores and Pathways model developed by the UK's Institute of Physics (see Table 21.2).

There are five energy stores which students up to the age of 14 need to know. They are: chemical energy stores, kinetic energy stores, gravitational potential energy stores, elastic energy stores and thermal energy stores (see Institute of Physics 2014b).

It is a good idea to demonstrate these stores so that students can associate them with concrete examples.

The energy within a store can be modelled by the amount of liquid in a beaker or measuring cylinder as a bridging analogy between concrete and abstract concepts and encourages quantitative thinking. Although energy is not a material substance, it is helpful to model it as one (a 'quasi-material entity' if you will) for novice learners.

Tips and tricks

The first lesson in many energy schemes of work is the 'energy circus'. The sequencing and suggested experiments in the 'circus' should be looked at critically since they were often developed to support the Forms and Transfers model rather than the current Stores and Pathways model. The focus in the first part of teaching about energy should be on *stores* of energy rather than *transfers* of energy. Many energy transfers involve 'busy' and complex situations and encourage a focus on extraneous surface detail rather than the deep structure.

- Show a beaker or measuring cylinder filled with water (optionally dyed orange for visibility) and labelled 'Chemical energy store'. Ask students if this represents their mobile phone battery at the start of the day or at the end of the day. (Start of the day, as it contains a lot of energy.)

- Ask 'You text your friend to tell them you're running late. What happens to the chemical energy store?' (It decreases.) Demonstrate the decrease by pouring some of the energy down the sink and repeat with other examples of tasks performed by smartphones.

- Next discuss the kinetic energy store of a car moving at 70 mph. Use the same measuring cylinder as previously but stick on a 'Kinetic energy store' label. This is important to show that there aren't different forms of energy, but simply different labels.

- Ask questions such as 'The car slows down because of heavy traffic. What happens to the kinetic energy store?' (It decreases.)

Table 21.2 A comparison of energy models

pre-2014 Energy Forms and Transfers model	post-2014 Energy Stores and Pathways model
✗ Encourages too great a focus on the energy *labels* rather than the physical processes and quantitative calculations. ✗ Allows long 'daisy chains' of energy transfers such as this one for an electric torch: 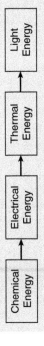 ✗ The 'daisy chains' often lead to superficial explanations; deeper explanations rely on detailed understanding of physical processes. ✗ The 'start' and 'end' points of the 'daisy chains' are often arbitrary and depend on personal preference. ✗ Includes 'electrical energy', 'light energy' and 'sound energy'. These are problematic in that they: • Do not persist over a significant time (e.g. what happens to the 'electrical energy' in a circuit when the switch is opened?). • Do not have a well-defined location (e.g. if 10 J is transferred as 'light energy', where exactly is it located? In the room? Travelling through the window? Absorbed by the observer's eyes?). Persuasive criticisms of the 'Forms and Transfers' model can be found in Millar (2014) and Boohan (2014).	✓ Encourages quantitative thinking about energy as a more accurate approximation of the way that professional physicists and scientists use energy concepts. ✓ Descriptions of energy transfers are simplified to 'before' and 'after' snapshots. The making of long 'daisy chains' is discouraged. ✓ The 'start' and 'end' points are selected with a view to the calculations that could be usefully carried out at that point. So, for an electric torch: 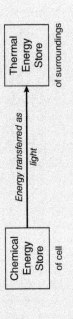 e.g. we could calculate the amount of energy in the chemical store of the battery and hence calculate by how much the thermal energy store will increase. ✓ Previously recognised forms of energy such as 'light energy' are now classed as *energy carriers* or *pathways*. That is to say they are the means by which energy is transferred rather than stores of energy which: • Persist over a significant period of time. • Have a well-defined location. As a rule of thumb, stores are measured in joules and pathways in watts. The Stores and Pathways model is introduced in Institute of Physics (2014a) and Tracy (2014).

Step 2: Modelling Energy Transfers

When work is done *on* an object, the energy store is increased. When work is done *by* an object, the energy level decreases. An example of this is shown in Figure 21.1.

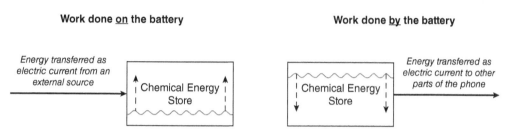

Figure 21.1 Work done on and by an object

Figure 21.2 shows how we could represent the energy transfers associated with a trolley rolling down a slope.

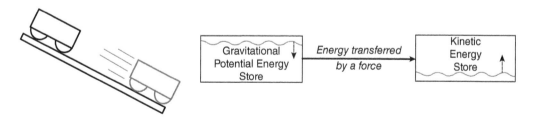

Figure 21.2 Representing an energy transfer

One of the reasons the Stores and Pathways model focuses on 'Before' and 'After' snapshots is to limit discussions about energy to situations where an energy calculation would give a useful result. This approximates the way professional physicists and engineers actually use the concept of energy. The aim is to lay the conceptual groundwork for a later rigorous and quantitative understanding of energy.

Step 3: The Principle of Conservation of Energy

The principle of conservation of energy states that energy cannot be created or destroyed. This means that the total energy before an event is equal to the total energy after an event.

Let's consider a tennis ball thrown vertically upwards as shown in Figure 21.3.

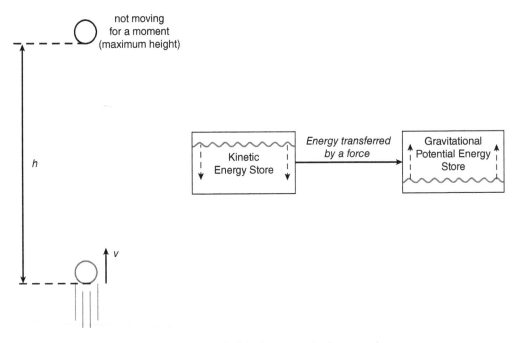

Figure 21.3 The energy transfers when a ball is thrown vertically upwards

- If the ball has a kinetic energy store of 6.0 joules at the start then it will have a gravitational potential energy store of 6.0 joules at the end (assuming, of course, that the frictional forces are small enough to be ignored).
- (For older students) We could find the kinetic energy of the ball by using $E_k = 0.5mv^2$.
- (For older students) We could then find the height the ball reaches by using $h = \dfrac{E_g}{mg}$ where the gravitational potential energy store is 6.0 J and the mass is 0.06 kg. (Answer = 10.0 m.)

Step 4: Efficiency

We can model an efficient process and an inefficient process as shown in Figure 21.4.

- Process A is more efficient than Process B because only 200 ml of water ('energy') is wasted compared with 400 ml wasted in B. More water ends up where it was meant to go in A.
- Note that the energy (water) does not disappear or vanish. The wasted water is just not easily recoverable.

Efficiency is the ratio of the energy that is transferred usefully to the total energy transferred. So the efficiency of A is 300/500 = 0.60 and the efficiency of B is a paltry 100/500 = 0.20.

Modelling our thinking while working through an example problem can be hugely beneficial for developing students' understanding.

Example: An electric fan is supplied with 2500 J of energy. 900 J of that energy is transferred to the thermal energy store of the surroundings. Calculate its efficiency.

Firstly, use the principle of conservation of energy to calculate the amount of energy transferred usefully. In this case it will be 2500 J – 900 J = 1600 J.

Secondly, work out the ratio of useful energy to total energy supplied. In this case it will be 1600/2500 = 0.64.

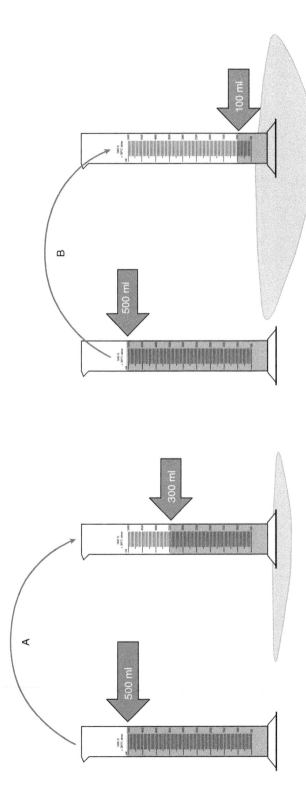

Figure 21.4 Modelling efficient and inefficient processes

Step 5: Distinguishing Between Energy and Power

'Energy' and 'power' are almost synonymous in everyday language. However, they must be carefully distinguished in scientific discourse.

We suggest that you begin with 'power is how quickly energy is transferred'.

Tips and tricks

- Textbooks often define power as the *rate of transfer* of energy.
- Beware of the 'curse of knowledge' when teaching novice learners: defining an unfamiliar concept (power) by using another unfamiliar concept (rate of transfer) is unhelpful and likely to induce cognitive overload.
- Using a familiar concept like 'quickly' (with a view to developing it into 'rate of transfer' later on) is useful.

The power rating of an appliance tells us how much energy is transferred each second. Figure 21.5 outlines a possible teaching sequence based on a concrete example of a toaster.

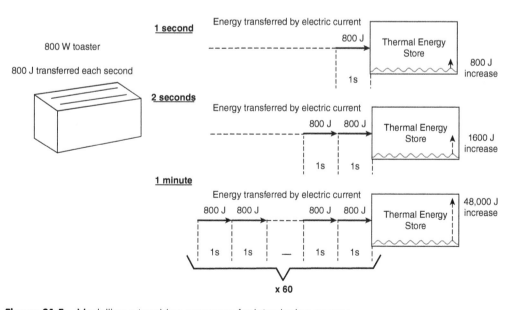

Figure 21.5 Modelling a teaching sequence for introducing energy

Check for understanding

Ask questions such as:

- You wind up a clockwork toy. Has work been done *on* the toy or is work being done *by* the toy? (On the toy since its elastic energy store has increased.)
- A girl does 1500 J of work walking up a flight of stairs. Draw a labelled diagram to show the energy transfer. (See Figure 21.6 for answer.)

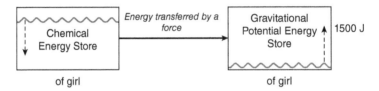

Figure 21.6   Energy transfer diagram for a girl climbing stairs

- 900 J of energy is supplied to a TV set. 300 J is transferred to the surroundings by light and 120 J by sound. Calculate the useful energy transferred, the wasted energy and the efficiency. (420 J, 480 J and 0.47.)
- A kettle transfers 180 kJ in 1 minute. Calculate the power. (180,000 / 60 = 3000 W.)

References

Boohan, R. (2014) Making sense of energy. *School Science Review*, 96 (354): 33–43.

Institute of Physics (2014a) Helpful language for energy talk. Available at: https://spark.iop.org/helpful-language-energy-talk#gref [Accessed 1 August 2020].

Institute of Physics (2014b) What stores do we need? Available at: https://spark.iop.org/what-stores-do-we-need [Accessed 1 August 2020].

Millar, R. (2014) Teaching about energy: From everyday to scientific understandings. *School Science Review*, 96 (354): 45–50.

Tracy, C. (2014) Energy in the new curriculum: An opportunity for change. *School Science Review*, 96 (354): 51–61.

22

ELECTRIC CURRENT

What students should know already

- Identify devices that run on electricity and list common electrical insulators and conductors.
- Associate metals with being good conductors.
- Understand operation of a switch in a simple series circuit featuring bulbs and buzzers and draw their circuit symbols.
- Associate the brightness of a bulb or loudness of a buzzer with the number of cells (batteries) in the circuit.

(Continued)

What students should know by the end

- Electric current I as a flow of electric charge measured in amps.
- Potential difference V measured in volts and a qualitative understanding of resistance R measured in ohms.

Explanation

Electrical circuits are best introduced in a structured and teacher-led sequence that attempts to minimise the risk of students making incorrect inferences.

There is, of course, enormous scope for students to carry out useful and effective practical work in this topic *as long as the foundational concepts have been introduced and understood first*. It is recommended that these are first introduced as demonstrations rather than class practicals to minimise student cognitive load.

The sequence outlined below follows the 'parallel circuit first' convention as parallel circuits offer a more direct inroad into the important idea of conservation of electric current.

In this chapter the focus will be primarily on the concept of electric current and potential difference is left somewhat vaguely defined as 'electrical push'. We will also be agnostic on the vexed question of the direction of electric current flow, i.e. whether current flows from positive to negative (positive charge carriers) or negative to positive (negative charge carriers). The arguments for and against both conventions are summarised in Table 22.1, but the plain fact of the matter is that since current is conserved there will be *no direct experimental evidence* in favour of either convention until students encounter the Hall effect in A-level physics or beyond. However, it is beneficial if all the science teachers within a department agree on a common approach.

Table 22.1 Comparing different models of current flow

Convention	Majority charge carrier	Advantages	Disadvantages
Electron flow (from negative to positive)	Negative	• Electrons are the majority charge carriers in metals. • Useful potential links with the structure of the atom and static electricity. • Excellent for explaining the effect on resistance of increasing the length of a metal wire in a circuit.	• Arguably it has too narrow a focus on charge flow in metallic conductors which could lead to misconceptions in situations where majority charge carriers are not electrons, e.g. flow of current in electrolytes and semiconductors. • Inconsistent with many magnetic field rules at GCSE such as the Right Hand Grip Rule.
Conventional current (from positive to negative)	Positive	• Consistent with the direction of electric current as shown on most formal circuit diagrams. • Consistent with magnetic field rules such as Fleming's Left Hand Rule studied at GCSE.	• Difficult to explain increase of resistance due to changing the length of a metal wire in a circuit.

Step 1: Making and Breaking Circuits

Start with Figure 22.1 on the board and this circuit set up as a demo and ask why the bulb is not lit and why the reading on both ammeters is zero. The answer is, of course, that there is not a complete circuit.

It can be a very useful exercise to test students' understanding of what a 'broken' (in the sense of incomplete rather than stopped working) circuit is at this point by alterations in both the demo circuit and the drawn circuit on the board. It is really surprising how many students will incorrectly believe that the bulb will be lit in the circuit in Figure 22.2 because it is connected to the 'plus' side of the battery.

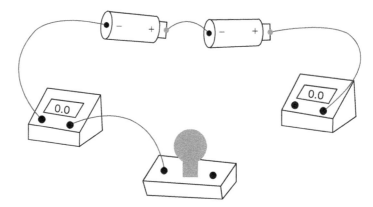

Figure 22.1 A 'broken' circuit

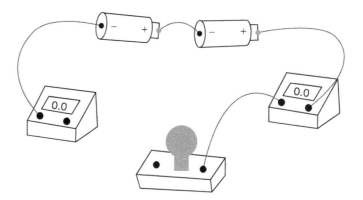

Figure 22.2 Another 'broken' circuit

Note that the suggested default representation of electrical circuits should be the rudimentary 3D drawings as shown above. Some students may already be familiar with circuit diagrams, but others may well not be. The teacher should seek to assess this by questioning how comfortable the students in front of her are with circuit diagrams, perhaps by asking students to draw a circuit diagram of the circuits shown on the board on student whiteboards or scrap paper and checking a random selection of examples. Good and bad examples can be shared on a visualiser if there is one available.

If students are indeed adept at using circuit diagram conventions, then the teacher and students can switch to the more time-efficient and parsimonious circuit diagram representations (e.g. Figure 22.3) without fear of overloading students' limited working memory. If not, then the teacher should continue with the 3D representation for the short term.

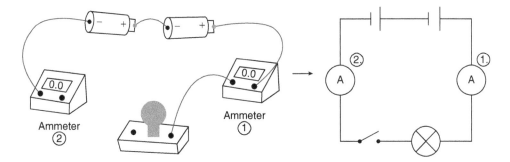

Figure 22.3 Moving from a 3D representation of a circuit to a more formal circuit diagram

Step 2: Discussion of Conservation of Current

The next vital question is then for students to predict which ammeter will have the largest reading when the gap in the circuit is closed: ammeter 1 or ammeter 2? Often this question is better presented in a focused way, e.g. 'The possible readings are 0.0 or 0.3 amps. Decide which ammeter will have which reading and give a reason for your answer'. (Ideally, the teacher should give the value of the ammeter reading in the demo circuit here, if it is not 0.3 A.)

Students will often give a number of answers to this question which the teacher can use to assess the proportion of students that hold a particular misconception and whether to spend valuable teaching time addressing them or to move on to the next part of the teaching sequence (see the check for understanding section at the ·end of the chapter).

Step 3: Demonstrating that Current is Conserved

Use the demonstration circuit to demonstrate conclusively that the pattern of ammeter readings is as shown in Figure 22.4. I would recommend that the current readings should be written in 'live' as the demonstration is carried out.

If time and resources allow, it is excellent practice to run the demo before it is done in front of the class. Please note that the current readings are written to 1 decimal place (d.p.) even though most digital ammeters read to 2 d.p. The reason for this is that the precision of most ammeters available in schools is ±2% or similar, so this can often lead to a discrepancy in the final decimal place

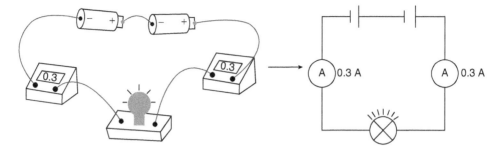

Figure 22.4 A demonstration of the conservation of current

between two ammeters. To avoid misunderstandings as a result of this, either 1) write down the current to 1 d.p. as shown; or 2) select two digital ammeters that will give two identical readings to 2 d.p.

Step 4: Using the Rope Model to Explain Conservation of Current

Using a continuous loop of rope to represent current flow in an electrical circuit is a common and well-established technique. However, used incorrectly it can reinforce misconceptions rather than eliminate them. For example, if a large proportion of the class is holding on to the rope at any one time, then it is being used incorrectly.

For best use, the rule should be that *one student represents one component*.

For example, two students should represent each cell and push the rope in a clockwise (or anticlockwise) direction. The ammeters are cardboard tubes with a large enough internal diameter so that the rope slides easily through them. They can be held in position by students. The bulb is represented by a student who grips the rope with a high enough pressure to provide a resistance to the 'flow' of the rope. This is shown in Figure 22.5.

To summarise:

- The number of cells is modelled by the number of students pushing the rope. The amount of 'push' is equivalent to the potential difference produced by the cells.

- The current is the speed of the rope.

- The ammeters are modelled as loose cardboard tubes.

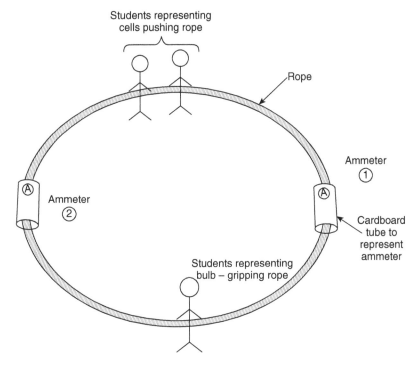

Students representing
cells pushing rope

Rope

Ammeter
①

Ammeter
②

Cardboard
tube to
represent
ammeter

Students representing
bulb – gripping rope

Figure 22.5   Using the rope model to represent a simple circuit

Tips and tricks

Remember the golden rule for effective use of the rope model – ONE student represents ONE component.

There is an opportunity here to use the rope analogy to model how to use a conceptual framework to 'think through' answers to questions such as:

- What happens to the current if we remove one of the cells? (There will be a smaller current as there will be a smaller 'push'.)

- What happens to the current if we replace the bulb with one that has a bigger resistance (i.e. one where the rope is gripped with a higher pressure)? (There will be a smaller current as the rope will move more slowly. NB Don't introduce adding bulbs in series – yet.)

- Do the two ammeters give us any information on whether the current flows clockwise or anticlockwise? (No, we need more information from another source before we can tackle this one.)

One note of caution: remember that this is part of a planned sequence for teaching electric circuits. The temptation is there to cover the whole of current electricity in the first 17 minutes: don't, just don't.

Be especially resistant to the 'curse of knowledge'. Current, amps, potential difference, volts, resistance and ohms may be 'familiar in your mouth as household words', but avoid unleashing a blizzard of unfamiliar technical terms onto the heads of your students. In the first instance, focus on current, and just on current.

Step 5: Current Readings in a Parallel Circuit

Set up the demonstration circuit as shown in Figure 22.6 and ask students to predict the current readings on ammeter 1 and ammeter 2 when:

a. The first flying lead is connected to X. (Both ammeter readings should increase to 0.60 A – assuming the bulbs are identical.)

b. The first flying lead is disconnected from X. (Both ammeter readings should decrease back to 0.30 A.)

c. The second flying lead is connected to Y. (The ammeter readings should stay at 0.30 A as the second and third bulbs are not part of a complete circuit.)

d. The first flying lead is reconnected to X. (The ammeter readings should both be at 0.90 A.)

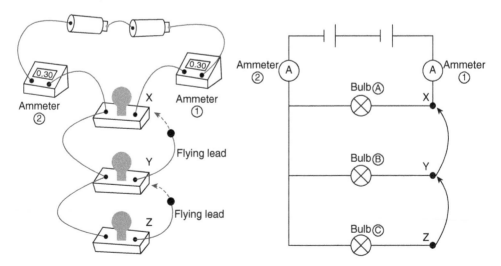

Figure 22.6 Parallel circuits by continuous conversion

Note that this demonstration uses the powerful idea of the *continuous conversion of examples*: students are not being asked to hold results in their head and then compare and contrast; rather, any changes are modelled 'live' and the results are instantly observable and verifiable. Again, this is to minimise students' cognitive load.

The technique can work well with students writing their predicted answers on student whiteboards which allows the teacher to ask individual students to justify and explain their answers.

Step 6: Using the Rope Model to Explain the Current Readings in a Parallel Circuit

The rope model can be really useful to explain the pattern of current readings in a parallel circuit (see step 4 and Figure 22.7 for more detail).

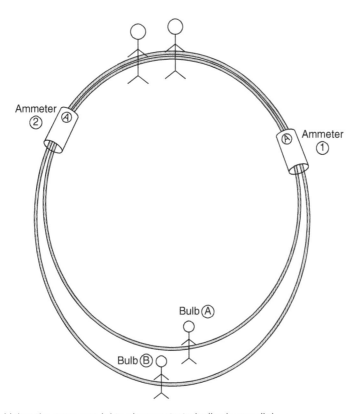

Figure 22.7   Using the rope model to demonstrate bulbs in parallel

To set the scene for series circuits, it is immensely helpful at this point to discuss the brightness of each bulb in terms of the amount of 'push' or potential difference 'transmitted' to each bulb from the cells by the rope or flow of current.

Each bulb gets the full 'push' or potential difference in a parallel arrangement.

Step 7: Series Circuits by Continuous Conversion of Examples

Set up the demonstration circuit shown in Figure 22.8.

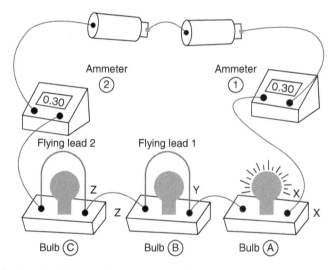

Figure 22.8a Series circuits by continuous conversion

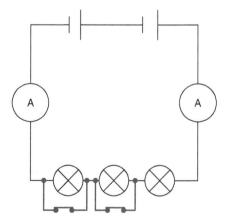

Figure 22.8b Series circuits by continuous conversion

- Always have a minimum of one bulb in the circuit that has not been 'shorted out'. If all three bulbs are shorted out simultaneously then there is a risk of very large current flow and overheating.
- This may be a good time to talk about resistance, e.g. 'The flying lead provides a *low resistance path* so very little current goes through the bulb.'

Ask students why only Bulb A is lit initially. (Answer: Bulb B and Bulb C are 'short circuited' by the flying leads. In other words, the flying lead provides a low resistance path for electric current so that, in effect, Bulb B and Bulb C are not part of the circuit.)

Next, unshort B. Both bulbs A and B will now be lit, but much dimmer than bulb A alone, and the current reading will be smaller. The power of this sequence is the fact that it uses the *continuous conversion of examples*: students are not comparing the brightness of a particular bulb with a bulb they saw five minutes ago. Instead, changes are immediate and directly observable.

Students' understanding can be checked by (for example) disconnecting the flying lead from Z and reconnecting the flying lead to Y.

Step 8: Using the Rope Model to Explain Series Circuits

The rope model (see step 4 and Figure 22.9) can be used to explain series circuits. Initially, students B and C are not touching the rope.

This is a good point to show that when Bulb B is added into the circuit, the decrease in the brightness of both bulbs can be explained in two ways.

- The current (the speed of the rope) decreases because of the increased total resistance of the circuit.

- The potential difference ('push') supplied by the cells is now shared between two bulbs.

Student understanding can be checked by questioning what will happen when bulbs are added into and removed from the circuit.

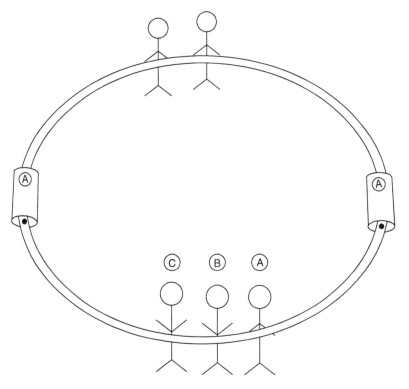

Figure 22.9 Using the rope model to explain conservation of current

Check for understanding

Multiple choice questions such as those below can be very revealing about students' thinking (see Table 22.2).

Which of the following statements could be true about the circuit in Figure 22.10 when the bulb is lit?

A. Ammeter 1 reads 0.00 A.

B. Ammeter 1 reads 0.30 A.

C. Ammeter 2 reads 0.00 A.

D. Ammeter 2 reads 0.30 A.

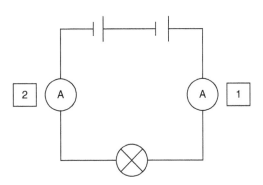

Figure 22.10 A simple circuit

Table 22.2 A diagnostic approach to student ideas about current

Possible student response	Correct or incorrect	Diagnostic inference about student mental schema
A and D are true	Incorrect	• Students believe that current originates at the negative side of the cell and circulates anticlockwise on the diagram. • Students also have a 'current consumed' mental model of the operation of a circuit.
B and C are true	Incorrect	• Students believe that current originates at the positive side of the cell and circulates clockwise on the diagram. • Students also have a 'current consumed' mental model of the operation of a circuit.
B and D are true	Correct	• Students understand that current is not consumed. • It will be unclear at this stage if students giving this answer believe that electric current flows in a clockwise direction (i.e. positive charge carriers) or in an anticlockwise direction (i.e. negative charge carriers, e.g. electrons).

23

INTRODUCTION TO FORCES

Relevant ages

11–14

What students should know already

- Compare how things move on different surfaces.
- Notice that some forces need contact between two objects, but magnetic forces can act at a distance.
- Explain that unsupported objects fall towards the Earth because of the force of gravity acting between the Earth and the falling object.
- Identify the effects of air resistance, water resistance and friction that act between moving surfaces.
- Recognise that some mechanisms including levers, pulleys and gears allow a smaller force to have a greater effect.

- Forces such as pushes or pulls, arising from the interaction between two objects.
- Using force arrows in diagrams, adding forces in one dimension.
- Moment as the turning effect of a force.
- Forces associated with: deforming objects; stretching and squashing – springs; rubbing and friction between surfaces; pushing things out of the way; resistance to motion of air and water.

Explanation

Many of the myriad misconceptions and confusions associated with forces can be avoided if we are crystal clear about three things:

1. The magnitude (size) and direction of the forces.
2. Which object the force is acting on.
3. The total force (or resultant force) acting on the object.

Sadly, many force diagrams, although well-intentioned, cause confusion rather than clarifying the issues. Figure 23.1 shows an example of a bad force diagram.

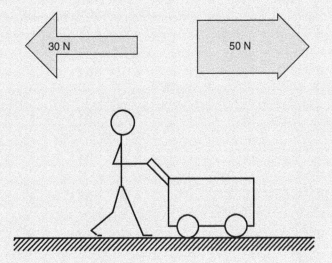

Figure 23.1   A bad force diagram

Considering the three criteria outlined above, Figure 23.1 is an unhelpful diagram because:

- Although the arrows show the direction of the forces, their magnitude is represented by the thickness rather than the length of the arrows: this is unhelpful because techniques such as the parallelogram of forces rely on the magnitude being directly proportional to the length.
- It is unclear which force is acting on which object; for example, is the trolley pulling the human with a force of 50 N or is the human pushing on the trolley with a force of 50 N? Is the human pulling back the trolley with a force of 30 N or is that the frictional force exerted by the ground on the trolley or the human?
- And without clarity on the points above, we cannot begin to calculate the total (resultant) force acting on any of the objects in this situation.

Note also that we are using the term *resultant force* rather than *unbalanced force* and *balanced forces*. The reason for this is that students often have the misconception that certain types of object will *always* have balanced forces and that the forces acting on them can never be unbalanced. 'Resultant force' implies that the quantity is the result of a calculation that can change from instant to instant. To encourage a strong association between the length of a force arrow and its magnitude, using centimetre squared paper is very helpful as in Figure 23.2.

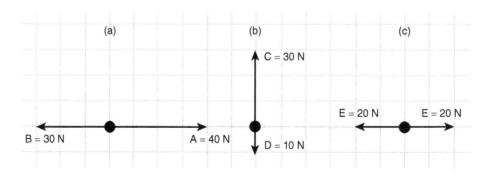

Figure 23.2 Calculating resultant (total) force

- The resultant force on object (a) is 10 N to the right (don't forget to specify the direction of the resultant force).
- The resultant force on object (b) is 20 N upwards.
- The resultant force on object (c) is zero.

Step 1: Draw Free Body Diagrams

The above problems with force diagrams can be solved if we use the physicists' technique of drawing what are called *free body diagrams* (FBD). Essentially, these are a collection of separate diagrams drawn in turn showing the forces acting on each object in the situation under consideration. An example of this is shown in Figure 23.3.

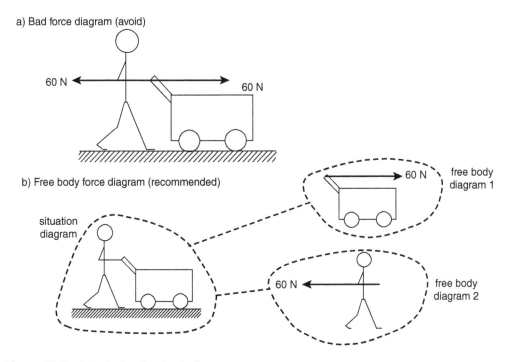

Figure 23.3   Introducing free body diagrams

Step 2: Understanding the Responsive Nature of Friction

Friction is a contact force that opposes the relative motion of two surfaces that are touching each other. It arises because even apparently smooth surfaces have microscopic irregularities which cause the surfaces to 'lock' together, as shown in Figure 23.4.

However, the frictional force in Figure 23.4 is zero since there is no relative movement between the surfaces, or even a tendency for relative movement.

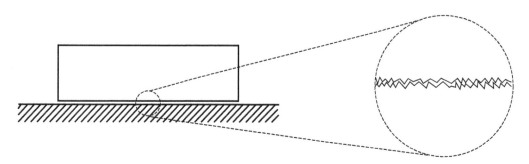

Figure 23.4 An example of static friction (no relative movement between surfaces)

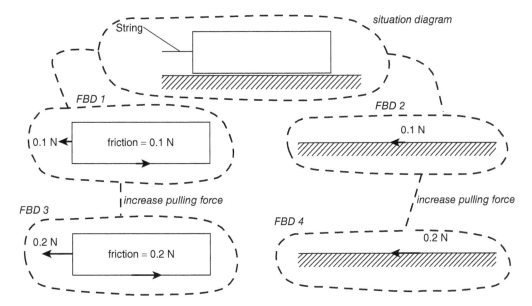

Figure 23.5 Illustrating the responsive nature of static friction

Now let's pull the block with a force of, for example, 0.1 N. The effect of this force and the effect of increasing it to 0.2 N is shown in Figure 23.5.

Tips and tricks

- Where possible, use concrete numerical examples like 'increase the force to 0.2 N' rather than vaguer descriptions such as 'increase the force'.
- Begin by just drawing the situation diagram and free body diagram (FBD) 1 and (optionally) FBD 2.
- Extend the analysis by drawing FBD 3 and (optionally) FBD 4.
- FBD 2 and FBD 4 could be omitted at the discretion of the teacher if, in their judgement, they might be confusing to some students in the class.

In free body diagram 1 on Figure 23.5, we can see that there is zero resultant force on the block due to the frictional force created by microscopic bumps and hollows as shown in Figure 23.4. (It is always essential to *explicitly* relate any discussion of friction to a diagram similar to Figure 23.4.)

When we increase the pulling force to 0.2 N then the frictional force also increases to 0.2 N as the microscopic bumps and hollows change shape to produce the increased force. The same would happen if the pulling force was increased to (say) 0.3 N and 0.4 N also. This is what we mean when we say that friction is a 'responsive' force.

However, there is an upper limit to the frictional force that the microscopic bumps and hollows can supply when the surfaces are locked together. At a certain value, 0.5 N let's say, the pulling force is large enough to begin partially smoothing out the bumps and hollows. The surfaces begin to slide past each other at this point. The smoothed out bumps and hollows still momentarily 'lock' together from time to time and produce a frictional force which opposes the relative motion, but this is always smaller than the maximum value achievable when the two surfaces are stationary.

The maximum possible value of static friction will depend on the nature of the surfaces and a number of other factors: in general, the rougher the surfaces, the greater the maximum value of the static friction.

Steps 3/4: The Vital Role of Friction

Friction is a vital part of our normal world: without friction we couldn't take a single step forward and self-propelled wheeled vehicles like cars wouldn't work.

Free body diagram analyses can help us see why this is the case (see Figures 23.6–7).

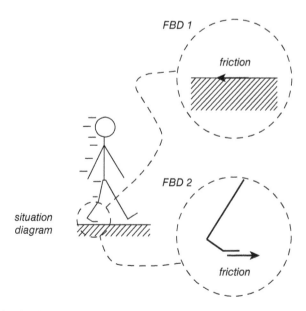

Figure 23.6 Free body diagram analysis of a person taking a step forward

Free body diagrams are so much clearer than other force diagrams on *which* force is acting on *which* object and in *which* direction.

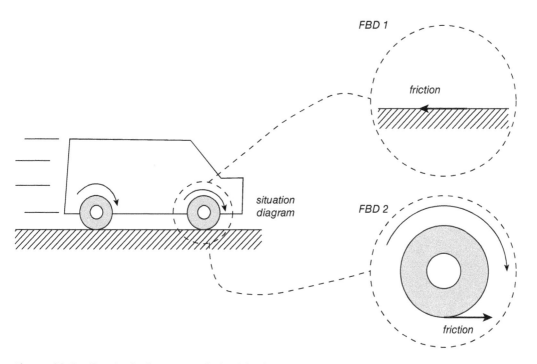

Figure 23.7   Free body diagram analysis of the force on a car tyre

Step 5: Weight and Reaction Force

Any object within another object's gravitational field will experience a non-contact force. For objects within the Earth's gravitational field, this action-at-a-distance force is called its weight. To illustrate this, consider an apple in the process of falling out of a tree as shown in Figure 23.8.

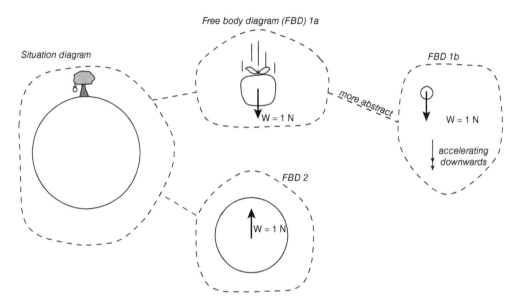

Figure 23.8 A free body diagram analysis of an apple in free fall

Tips and tricks

- Free body diagram 2 (FBD 2) is included for completeness here. However in practice it can be omitted unless one of the learning points is the idea that 'forces come in pairs' or Newton's Third Law of Motion.
- The fact that a typical apple, by happy chance, has a weight of almost exactly one newton can be taken as an opportunity to explore the hinterland of science and discuss the famous story of Sir Isaac Newton and the apple.
- FBD 1b shows a more abstract version of FBD 1a and shows the apple as a particle rather than as an extended object. This follows the concrete abstract progression argued for in this book. Presenting both versions to students as shown is a powerful way of ensuring that the link with the more concrete version is not lost.

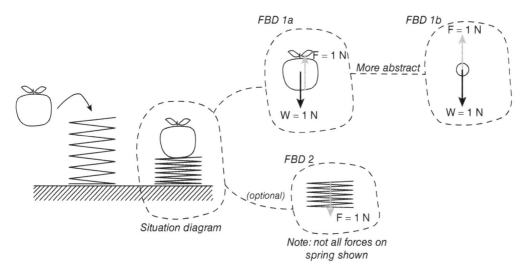

Figure 23.9 The forces acting on a stationary apple on a spring

What would happen if we placed the apple on a spring as shown in Figure 23.9?

Tips and tricks

- FBD 2 is optional. The arrow F shows the apple pushing down on the spring which compresses it.
- FBD 1b is a more abstract version of FBD 1a which shows the apple as a particle. We can see that there is zero resultant force on the object.

Why include the highly artificial situation of an apple resting on spring in the teaching sequence?

It is to circumvent the common misconception that an object such as a table 'blocks' the action of gravity. Having accepted that the apple is stationary in Figure 23.9 because the spring generates an upward force, students are much more likely to accept that an apple placed on a table (as in Figure 23.10) will be stationary because the table generates an upward force called the reaction force. Figure 23.10 shows what is sometimes called a 'bridging analogy' (see Hammer 2000: S54–5).

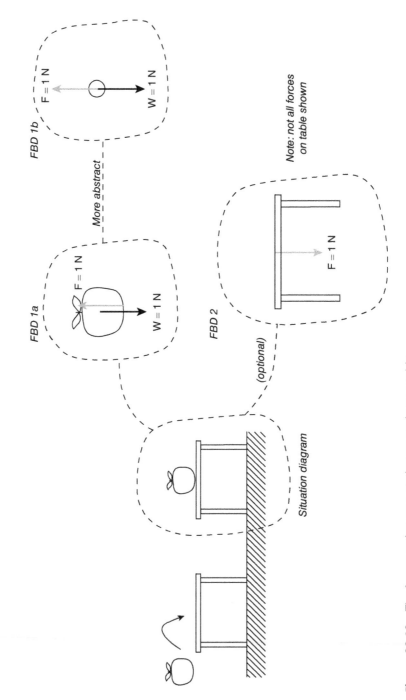

Figure 23.10 The forces acting on a stationary apple on a table

It can be difficult to provide enough examples of resultant force calculations to go through the I/we/you structure as well as for students to practise independently. Using a generic diagram and a table as in Figure 23.11 can be helpful.

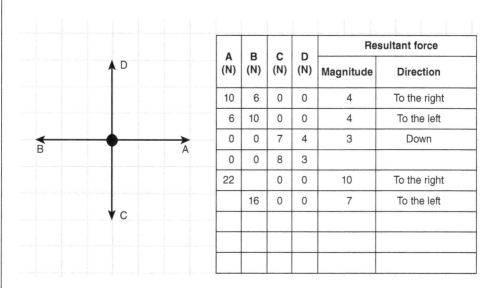

A (N)	B (N)	C (N)	D (N)	Resultant force	
				Magnitude	Direction
10	6	0	0	4	To the right
6	10	0	0	4	To the left
0	0	7	4	3	Down
0	0	8	3		
22		0	0	10	To the right
	16	0	0	7	To the left

Figure 23.11 A compact way of presenting resultant force examples

Reference

Hammer, D. (2000) Student resources for learning introductory physics. *American Journal of Physics*, 68 (S1): S52–9.

24

CURRENT AND POTENTIAL DIFFERENCE

Relevant ages

14–16 for Key Stage 4

What students should know already

- Electric current as a flow of charge.
- A qualitative understanding of electrical resistance (i.e. larger current is likely to flow along a low-resistance path).
- Correct use of an ammeter to measure current and conservation of current.

Potential misconceptions

- Might believe that electrical current is consumed by a device and that the arrangement of components affects the operation of the circuit (e.g. bulb closest to cell is always brightest).

- Might believe that the cell (battery) is a source of electrical charge or electrical current rather than a store of chemical energy.
- Will tend to treat terms such as 'current' and 'potential difference' as virtually synonymous.

What students should know by the end

- Electric current I as a flow of electric charge measured in amps or coulombs per second $I = \dfrac{Q}{t}$
- Potential difference V measured in volts or joules per coulomb $V = \dfrac{E}{Q}$
- Resistance R measured in ohms $R = \dfrac{V}{I}$
- Rate of power transfer as $P = VI$

Explanation

The suggested teaching sequence uses a 'stiff chain donation model' (following the terminology of Driver et al. 1994: 123–4) of an electric circuit called the Coulomb Train model. This allows concrete *and quantitative* explanations of abstract terms such as current, potential difference and resistance as well as a smooth transition to considering energy and power in equations such as power = potential difference x current $(P = VI)$.

Step 1: Introducing the Coulomb Train Model

This model pictures current as a flow of positively charged trucks or 'coulombs' flowing around a circuit as shown in Figure 24.1. This can be especially effective when used in combination with a demonstration circuit of real components with the Coulomb Train model diagram on the board being used to explain the behaviour of the real circuit.

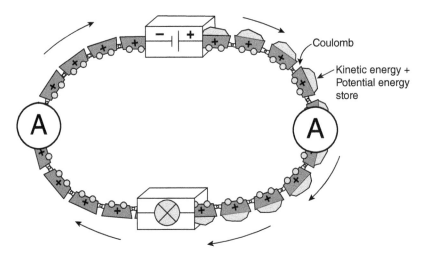

Figure 24.1 Representing current using the Coulomb Train model

The cell or battery is represented as a chemical energy store which transfers energy into the kinetic and potential energy stores of the coulombs: kinetic energy because the coulombs are moving, and potential energy because they are (essentially) being moved around the circuit by electrostatic attraction and repulsion. (Note that 'electrical energy' does not feature in the Stores and Pathways model – see Chapter 21 'Introducing energy stores and pathways'.)

A current of one amp means that one coulomb of charge passes in each second. It is also clear that if one coulomb per second passes through one ammeter then one coulomb per second will pass through the second ammeter.

If possible, add further cells to the circuit so that the current value changes and ask questions such as 'What is the current now?' ('Two amps' or similar.) 'How many coulombs will pass in one second?' ('Two coulombs'.) 'How many coulombs will pass in three seconds?' ('Six coulombs'.)

The equation charge flow = current x time ($Q = It$) can be introduced at this point.

See Chapter 22 'Electric current' for further examples for teaching electric current in parallel and series circuits that can be easily adapted to the Coulomb Train model.

Step 2: Introducing Potential Difference Using the Coulomb Train Model

Figure 24.2 shows a voltmeter being used to measure the potential difference across a resistor. Again, the picture of the Coulomb Train model is especially effective when used to explain the behaviour of a real demonstration circuit.

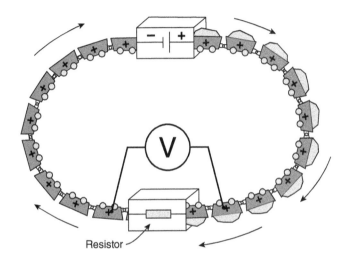

Resistor

Figure 24.2   Potential difference using the Coulomb Train model

Tips and tricks

- While bulbs are often the 'go to' component for demonstrating electric circuits, it is really useful to use other examples such as resistors, buzzers or electric motors.
- Buzzers and electric motors can also provide a visual indication of how much energy is being transferred via the coulombs, e.g. a motor will turn faster when provided with more energy.
- Terminology is important: we talk about the 'current flowing *through* a circuit' but should talk about the 'potential difference *across* a circuit'.

The potential difference is one volt when one joule of energy is transferred from each coulomb as it passes through the component. Essentially, potential difference is a measurement of the energy difference per coulomb in various parts of the circuit. Again, if we turn up the power supply or add another cell to the circuit we can ask questions such as 'How many joules is each coulomb transferring to the motor now?'

The equation $potential\ difference = \dfrac{energy\ transferred}{charge}$ or $V = \dfrac{E}{Q}$ can be introduced at this point.

Step 3: Resistance and the Coulomb Train Model

Resistance is not the 'slowing down' of electric current: for example, increasing the resistance of part of the circuit by narrowing the cross-sectional area of a conductor has the effect of increasing the speed of the charge carriers at that point!

The simplest description of resistance that is consistent with the mathematical equation is that resistance is the potential difference needed to drive one amp of current through a component. For example, a low resistance component might require (say) 0.5 V across it to allow a current flow of one amp and hence would have a resistance of 0.5 ohms. A higher resistance component might require (say) 10 V to drive a current of one amp so its resistance would be 10 ohms.

Incidentally, it is incorrect to refer to the equation *potential difference = current × resistance* ($V = IR$) as 'Ohm's Law'. Ohm's Law states that the current through a conductor is directly proportional to the potential difference across and hence only applies to 'well-behaved' *ohmic* conductors where R has a fixed, constant value over a range of physical conditions. $V = IR$ is certainly consistent with Ohm's Law but applies just as well to 'bad boy' *non-ohmic* conductors where R does not have a fixed value! It is better to refer to $V = IR$ as the 'definition of resistance' equation rather than Ohm's Law.

Step 4: Resistance and Parallel and Series Circuits

Following the 'parallel first' methodology outlined in Chapter 22 'Electric current', we can consider the resistance of placing two one-ohm resistors in parallel as shown in Figure 24.3.

We can see from the Coulomb Train model representation that the potential difference across each resistor is one volt since one joule is removed from each coulomb as they pass through the resistors. This does not violate the principle of conservation of energy: the chemical energy store of the cell will be depleted *sooner* when two resistors are connected in parallel across it since both sets of coulombs need to be filled simultaneously as they pass through the cell.

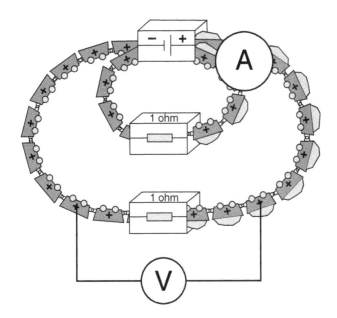

Figure 24.3 Two one-ohm resistors in parallel using the Coulomb Train model

This can be very powerful when used in combination with a demonstration circuit using the principle of continuous conversion as shown in Figure 24.4.

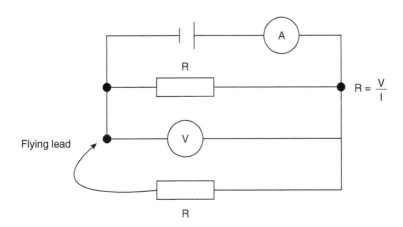

Figure 24.4 Parallel circuit by continuous conversion

A similar continuous conversion process can be applied for two resistors in series as shown in Figure 24.5.

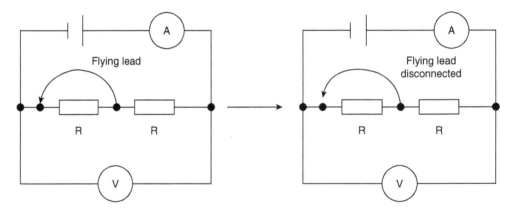

Figure 24.5   Resistors in series by continuous conversion

Step 5: Potential Divider Circuits with the Coulomb Train Model

Figure 24.6 shows a small variation on Figure 24.5 which can be used to introduce the potential divider circuit.

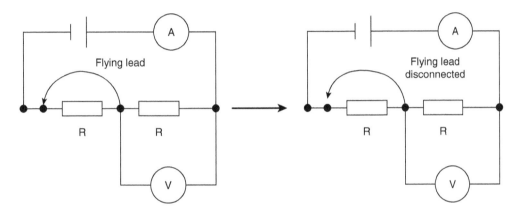

Figure 24.6 A potential divider circuit by continuous conversion

Tips and tricks

If V = 1.0 volts with the flying lead connected, then V = 0.5 volts with the flying lead disconnected (assuming both values of R are identical).

This can be explained using the Coulomb Train model as shown in Figure 24.7.

With the second resistor added, each coulomb gives up half its energy to each resistor which means the potential difference across each resistor is now (say) 0.5 V whereas previously it was 1.0 V. How do the coulombs 'know' to give up only half their energy at one resistor? They don't – it is simply a mechanical process: just as a chain being dragged through two tubes in series would experience double the resistive force when compared with being dragged through a single tube and so would lose double the amount of energy to resistive heating – plus also, the chain as a whole would be moving more slowly due to the increased resistive force. Adding a second resistor affects the whole circuit and the system must be considered holistically and not in a piecemeal fashion, which is one advantage of using a 'stiff chain model' such as the Coulomb Train.

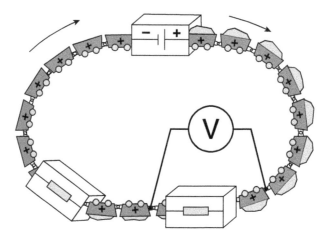

Figure 24.7 Using the Coulomb Train model to explain a potential divider circuit

Position 2

Position 1

Resistor

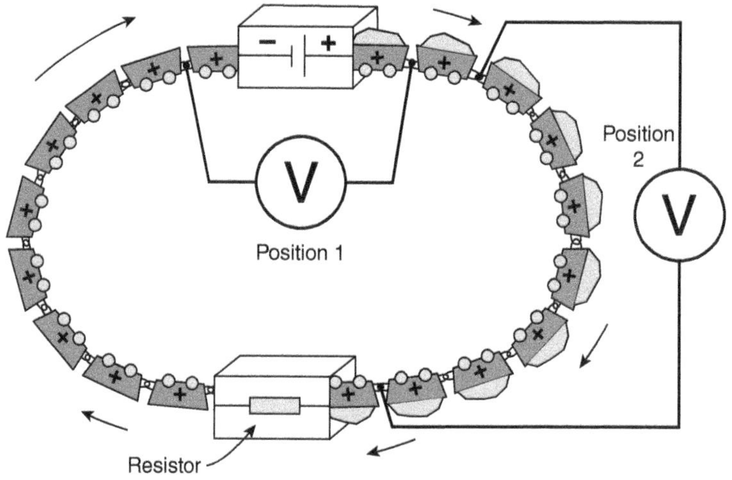

Figure 24.8 Using the Coulomb Train model to explain potential differences in a circuit

Predicting the reading of the voltmeter in position 1 and position 2 in Figure 24.8 can be useful in assessing students' understanding. In position 1 it will be equal to the potential difference across the resistor measured in Figure 24.2 because of the principle of conservation of energy: in other words, the total energy added to each coulomb will be the same as the total energy removed from each coulomb. In position 2, the voltmeter reading would be zero as no energy is transferred into or from each coulomb.

Reference

Driver, R., Rushworth, P., Squires, A. and Wood-Robinson, V. (Eds.) (2014) *Making sense of secondary science: Research into children's ideas* (2nd edn) London, New York: Routledge.

25

UNDERSTANDING WAVES

What students should know already

- Students are unlikely to have had any formal instruction on the topic of 'waves' previously.
- They may be aware from general knowledge that sound and light can be described as waves.
- Many students will have encountered 'breaking' waves on the beach, and this is the most common image that will be called up by the word 'wave'.
- Students will also be confused by usages such as 'a wave of relief' or 'she waved hello'.

Explanation

A wave is a periodic disturbance in a medium. The medium that carries the wave may be composed of particles (e.g. sound waves, water waves) or immaterial electric fields and magnetic fields (e.g. visible light and other electromagnetic waves). By 'periodic' we mean a pattern that changes and repeats over time.

We do not have scope in this book to cover the full range of wave behaviour from reflection and echoes and superposition through to refraction and polarisation. These can be covered using practical demonstrations (e.g. slinky spring or ripple tank) or on-screen simulations (https://phet.colorado.edu/ is a particularly reliable source of useful wave simulations).

Instead, in this chapter we will focus on how we can help students to understand the basic physics of wave behaviour and how it arises from simple interactions. The concept of a 'wave' will hopefully cease to be a fuzzy and ill-defined 'something to do with water' and be replaced with the idea that 'wave' describes a set of phenomena by which energy is carried through a medium by vibrations.

Step 1: Introducing Transverse Waves

We start with transverse waves as these are likely to be most familiar (at least in terms of shape) to students and we always start with the known before moving to the unknown. They can be demonstrated by ropes, rubber tubing, or slinky springs. However, one highly convincing demonstration that follows the concrete → abstract progression model makes use of dynamics trolleys linked together with springs as in Figure 25.1.

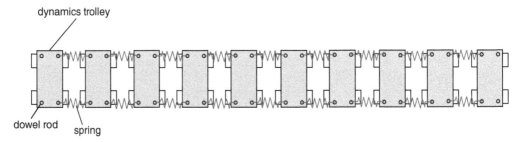

Figure 25.1 Dynamics trolleys linked with springs to demonstrate transverse waves (plan view)

Figure 25.2 shows how the displacement of a single 'particle' can produce a 'chain reaction' of moving particles, or a wave pulse that travels through the medium.

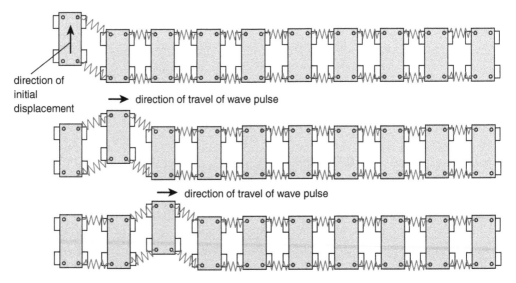

Figure 25.2 A wave pulse travelling along a line of linked dynamics trolleys (plan view from above)

Following the simple → complex progression, we next produce a *wave train* – a continuous stream of crests and troughs – by moving the first trolley up and down in the direction shown on Figure 25.3.

Figure 25.3 can also be labelled with important terms such as the amplitude A and the wavelength λ.

The wavelength can be defined as the length of a complete wave, i.e. including a crest and a trough. It is also equal to the crest-to-crest distance.

Older students can also be introduced to the wave equation $v = F \times \lambda$ at this point.

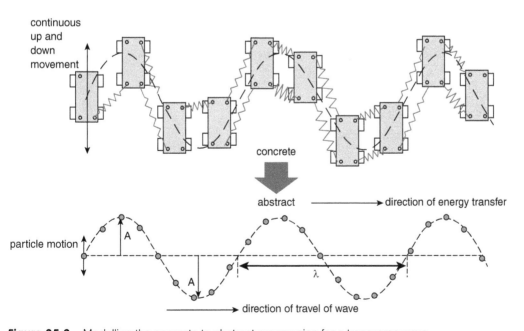

Figure 25.3   Modelling the concrete to abstract progression for a transverse wave

Step 2: Introducing Longitudinal Waves

One of the defining characteristics of a wave is that it transmits energy with no net (overall) movement of the medium. In a longitudinal wave, the particles vibrate back and forth along the same line as the wave travels. (The statement 'vibrate in the same direction as the wave travels' is confusing in my opinion as it implies there is a net movement of the medium.)

This can be modelled on a slinky spring of course, but using a variation of the dynamics trolleys and springs arrangement above can help highlight the most important features in a very effective way. Figure 25.4 shows what happens when the first trolley is moved closer to the next.

But equally importantly, energy can also be transferred via a different mechanism shown in Figure 25.5.

Once these baseline facts are established, we can use the concrete → abstract progression to draw a representation of a longitudinal wave as in Figure 25.6.

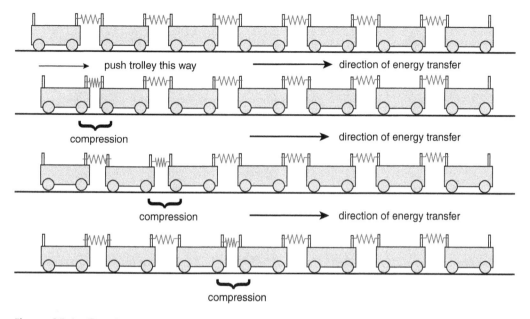

Figure 25.4   Transferring energy using a compression (side view)

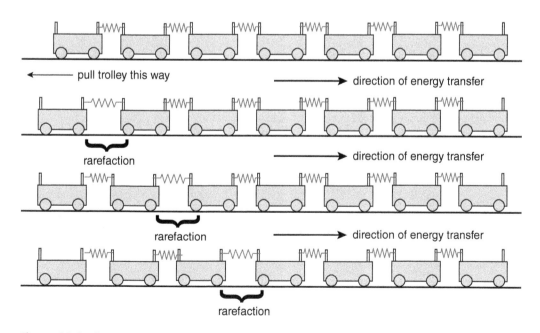

Figure 25.5   Demonstrating that a rarefaction pulse can carry energy

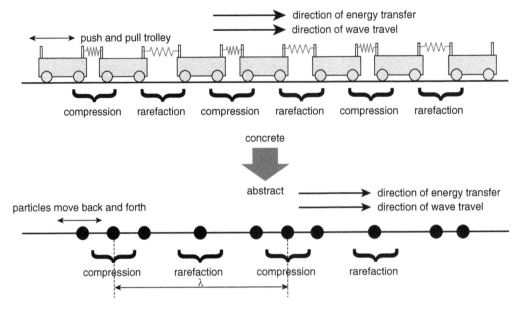

Figure 25.6 Modelling the concrete to abstract progression for a longitudinal wave

Step 3: Understanding the Ways Waves Can be Displayed

There are a number of conventions that can be used to display waves. To aid student understanding we should be as explicit as possible as to which convention we are using. The three main conventions are:

- The wave profile or side view: This is very common in introductory courses (see Figures 25.4 and 25.5). It is often replaced with the wavefront view with little explanation.

- The wavefront view: A wavefront is a line joining similar points on a wave; for example it often indicates the position of the crests of a set of waves spreading out from a single source (but it could equally show the troughs).

- Ray diagrams: This is an arrow showing the path of energy transfer. It is drawn so that it is always at right angles to the wavefront. Although we could (in theory) draw an infinite number of rays on any diagram, we usually select one or two rays with a view to predicting the direction of the reflected wave (e.g. water waves) or the location of an image (e.g. light rays).

Each row of Table 25.1 shows the same wave displayed using the three most common conventions.

Step 4: Using the Ray Convention for Reflection

We can think of moving between these conventions as moving between more concrete and abstract representations. For example, if we wanted to find the image of a candle flame reflected in a mirror as in Figure 25.7.

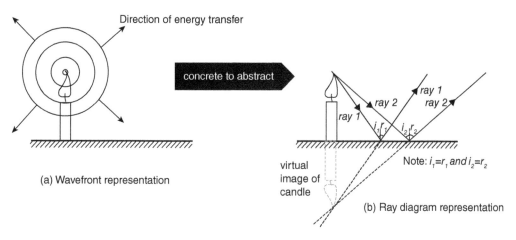

Figure 25.7 Using wavefront and ray diagrams to locate the reflected image of a candle

Table 25.1 Representing waves with increasing level of abstraction

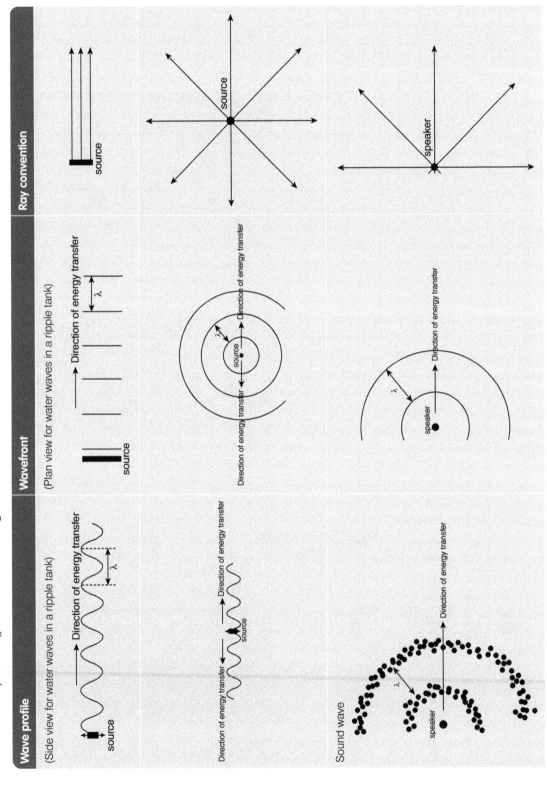

Step 5: Using a Sequence of Wave Display Conventions to Explain Refraction

Again, we start with a concrete representation of how water waves are affected by different depths of water, as in Figure 25.8. We use this representation initially because it is the most simple and direct way of showing the changes produced by a change in the speed of travel of water waves.

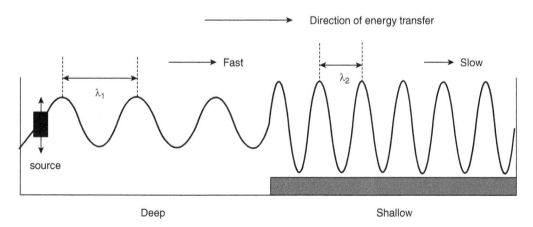

Figure 25.8 Using the wave profile convention to show the refraction of water waves in a ripple tank

After discussing Figure 25.8, we can then move on to the more abstract wavefront representation as shown in Figure 25.9. It is important to emphasise to students that both these diagrams show *exactly the same situation* and to be as explicit as possible as to which form of representation we are using and why we are using it. We are using the more abstract representation in this case because otherwise we cannot draw any conclusion about any possible change in the direction of the waves.

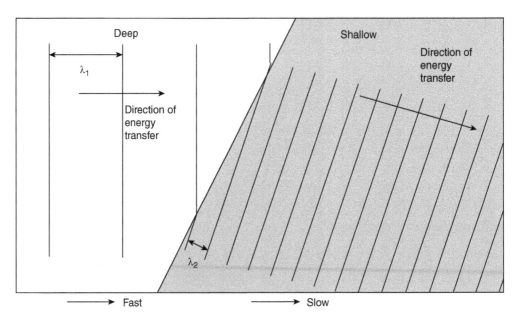

Figure 25.9 Using the wavefront convention to show the refraction of water waves in a ripple tank

Finally, we show the ray diagram representation as shown in Figure 25.10.

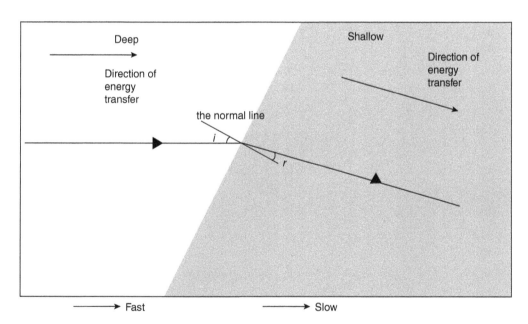

Figure 25.10 Using the ray diagram convention to show the refraction of water waves in a ripple tank

Sentence stems such as the ones below are excellent for assessing how much students have understood.

- Waves transmit ____ but ____ (energy, there is no net movement of the medium).
- The particles in a transverse wave ____ (vibrate at 90° to the direction of travel of the wave).
- A transverse wave has ____ but a longitudinal wave has ____ (crests and troughs, compressions and rarefactions).
- The particles in a longitudinal wave ____ (move back and forth along the same line as the direction of travel of the wave).

Other valuable checks for understanding are asking students to redraw a particular diagram using an alternative convention. The more abstract conventions are often physically easier to draw but sometimes are conceptually difficult to relate to the original diagram and so are a very good test of student understanding. As example is shown in Figure 25.11.

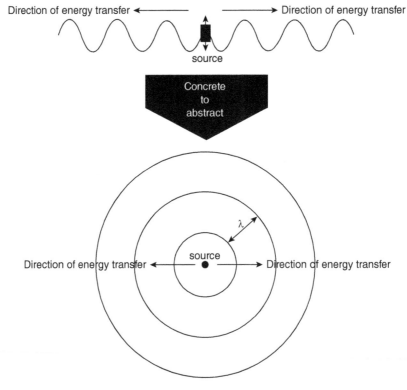

Figure 25.11 Showing the same situation using different representations

26

VECTORS AND COMPONENTS

What students should know already

All or some of the following will have been learned as part of the mathematics curriculum:

- How to use scale factors and scale diagrams.
- Measuring and drawing lines to the nearest millimetre, and measuring and drawing angles to the nearest degree.

- Examples of scalar and vector quantities.
- How to add vectors in one dimension.
- How to add vectors in two dimensions.
- How to resolve a vector into two perpendicular components.

Introduction

A vector is a quantity for which the direction in which it acts matters: for example, a force of 100 N to the right may speed up an object whereas an equal force acting to the left would slow it down. Information about their direction is essential to fully understanding these composite quantities. On the other hand, a scalar quantity such as mass has no directionality in any meaningful sense. There is a reason why *speed limits* are set and not *velocity limits*: 'But, your honour, I was travelling at 47 mph northwards. The velocity limit of 30 mph southwards applies only to vehicles travelling in the opposite direction.' A measurement of speed is a scalar quantity because we are not interested in the direction of travel.

Resultant Force as an Example of Vector Addition

One common misconception is that all vectors include compass directions, e.g. 'The velocity is 10 m/s north': the truth is that nearly any information about direction will do. For example, 'A force of +10 N' is a complete description of a vector since + (plus) and – (minus) supply enough information about its directionality in one dimension.

Tips and tricks

- The shorthand +ve for positive is a great timesaver in physics. Labelling a direction as 'positive' (usually left to right and/or upwards) is also very helpful.
- Drawing diagrams to scale on squared paper is an excellent way of making sure that the length of the arrows properly represents the magnitude of the vectors.

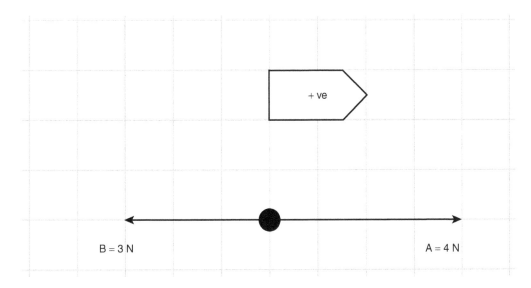

Figure 26.1 The first example of adding vector quantities

Students intuitively grasp this when (for example) they calculate a resultant force, as in Figure 26.1.

Force A = + 4 N. Force B is –3 N. Hence A + B = + 4 + (–3) = + 1 N. Therefore, the resultant vector is 1 N *to the right*.

Adding Vectors to Find a Resultant Vector in Two Dimensions

Scale drawing methods are preferable in science because they work for vectors at any angle: Pythagoras' Theorem and simple trigonometry may seem to be a useful shortcut, but it won't work for vectors at any angle other than 90°.

A good introduction to the scale drawing technique is to consider adding *displacements* (the vector version of distance).

Example question: A woman walks 8 km due east and then 10 km due south. Calculate a) the total distance walked; and b) her final displacement from the starting point.

We begin by drawing a scale drawing as in Figure 26.2.

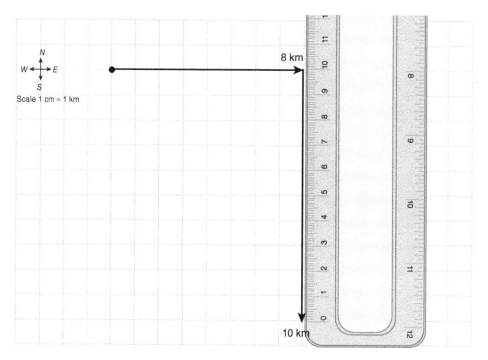

Figure 26.2 Scale diagram of vector addition

The total distance travelled is simple 8 + 10 = 18 km.

Tips and tricks

- Draw a compass rose on the diagram and note the scale selected.
- A grid is helpful but not essential as the lines can be drawn to scale using a ruler.

Figure 26.3 shows how to find the magnitude of the resultant vector R by drawing the third side of the vector triangle and measuring its length.

The length of R is 12.8 cm so this scales to a distance of 12.8 km.

Figure 26.4 shows how we find the direction of R.

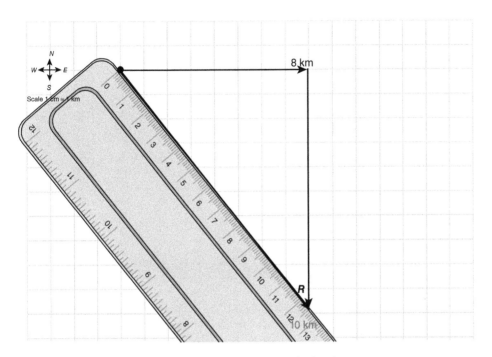

Figure 26.3 How to find the magnitude of a vector by scale drawing

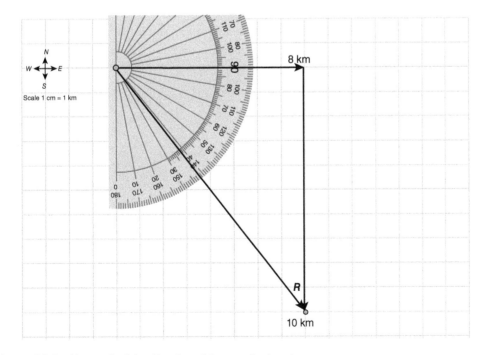

Figure 26.4 How to find the direction of the resultant vector

- Since this type of question often asks for a compass bearing, we have aligned the zero of the protractor with the N–S line.
- Since due south has a compass bearing of 180° we know that we need to use the outer scale so R is at a bearing of 143°.

So the final displacement of the woman is 12.8 km on a compass bearing of 143°.

Adding Forces in Two Dimensions

To find the correct resultant, the vectors have to be placed 'nose-to-tail'. This happens automatically when we are dealing with displacements. However, this is not the case when we consider forces. To find the resultant, we need to draw a vector diagram and place the vectors 'nose-to-tail'. Alternatively, we can draw a parallelogram of force which is a traditional 'cheat' which achieves the same object (see Figure 26.5).

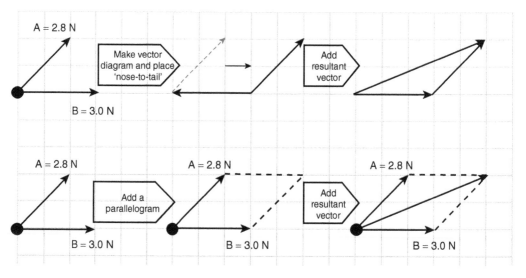

Figure 26.5 The 'nose-to-tail' method (top) and parallelogram of force (bottom) methods compared

Using Scale Drawing to Find the Components of a Force

Up to now, we have been combining two vectors to find the single resultant vector.

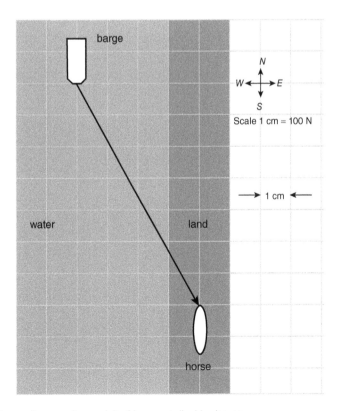

Figure 26.6   Force diagram (to scale) of barge pulled by horse

However, it is sometimes useful to divide a single vector into two separate *component* vectors (which, when added together, produce the original vector as their resultant). The two component vectors can then be analysed *independently* of each other (provided, of course, that they are 90° to each other).

To see how this is used in practice, let's look at an example question.

Example: In the 18th century, heavy loads were carried by canal barges towed by a horse as shown in Figure 26.6. The barge is moving due south at a constant velocity.

Figure 26.6 is drawn to scale so that 1 cm = 100 N. The line between the barge and the horse is 8.1 cm long and represents a force of 810 N. By a scale drawing method, find (a) the resistive force of the water on the barge which opposes its forward motion; and (b) the sideways force of the water acting on the barge. State their magnitude and directions.

We begin by drawing a parallelogram of force as in Figure 26.7.

Tips and tricks

Remember that:

- F_S and F_E are the *components* of F.
- F_S and F_E added together would produce F – so (working together) they affect the barge in exactly the same way as F.
- However, because F_S and F_E are at 90° to each other they can be *analysed independently* of each other.

The southward component of the force exerted by the rope is shown by F_S and the eastward component is shown by F_E. From the scale of the diagram we know that F_S = 700 N and F_E = 400 N.

However, the question asks for the forces exerted by the water on the barge. We know the resultant force on the barge is zero because it is moving at a constant velocity. This means that (a) is 700 N due north; and (b) is 400 N due west.

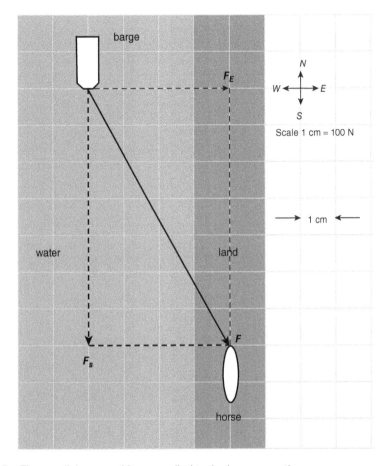

Figure 26.7 The parallelogram of force applied to the barge question

Check for understanding

It can be difficult to provide enough examples of resultant force calculations to go through the I/we/you structure as well as for students to practise independently. Using a generic diagram and a table as in Figure 26.8 can be helpful.

Figure 26.9 shows a similar arrangement that could provide plenty of challenging scale drawing practice for students.

(Continued)

Question	Vector 1 (N)	Vector 2 (N)	Angle (°)	Resultant vector Magnitude (N)	Resultant vector Angle (°)
1	6	8	90	10	53
2	6	8	45	12.9	29
3	10	5	90		
4	10	5	45		
5	10	5	60		
6	300	400	90		
7	200	200	90		
8	200	200	60		

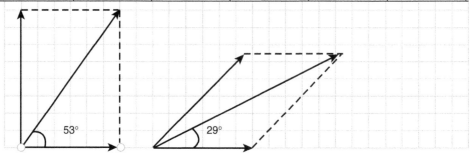

Figure 26.8 A compact way of presenting parallelogram of force examples (with answers for questions 1 and 2)

A (N)	B (N)	C (N)	D (N)	Resultant force Magnitude	Resultant force Direction
10	6	0	0	4	To the right
6	10	0	0	4	To the left
0	0	7	4	3	Down
0	0	8	3		
22		0	0	10	To the right
	16	0	0	7	To the left

Figure 26.9 A compact way of presenting resultant force examples

- Use the I/we/you structure to model answers and gradually fade support for students.
- Scale drawings for answering Q1 and Q2 are shown in Figure 26.8.

27

PRESSURE

What students should know already

- Force is measured in newtons and the size and direction can be represented as an arrow.
- How to draw free body diagrams.
- How to calculate the area of a rectangle.

What students should by the end

- Pressure measured by ratio of force over area – acting normally to any surface.
- Links between pressure and temperature of a gas at constant volume, related to the motion of its particles (qualitative).
- Pressure in liquids, increasing with depth; upthrust effects, floating and sinking.
- Atmospheric pressure, decreases with increase of height as weight of air above decreases with height.

Step 1: Introducing the Concept of Pressure

Consider holding a drawing pin between thumb and forefinger so that the blunt end is being pushed with a force of 10 N as shown in Figure 27.1. Hold it so that the skin remains unbroken at B.

The force experienced by the skin at A and B is the same. Why then does the person feel discomfort at B but not at A?

The answer is to do with the area the force is applied over. At A the force is spread out over a relatively large area. At B the force applied by the pin is concentrated into a very small area (the point of the pin). This is described as *pressure*: the pressure is low at A and high at B. It can be useful to summarise this in a table (Table 27.1).

When the applied force is constant, the pressure *increases* as the area *decreases*. Students can find inverse relationships (i.e. when quantity *x* increases then quantity *y* decreases) very difficult to understand, so it is worth labouring this point, as shown in Table 27.2.

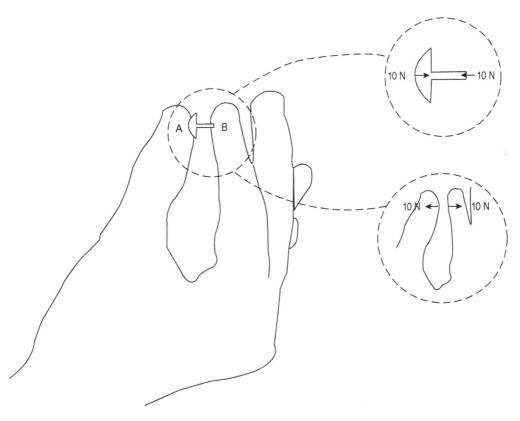

Figure 27.1 Pressure exemplified using a drawing pin

Table 27.1 Pressure and area for a drawing pin

Position	Discomfort?	Force	Area	Description	Pressure	Type of relationship
A	No	10 N	Large	Force spread out over large area	Low	Inverse relationship
B	Yes	10 N	Small	Force concentrated into small area	High	

Table 27.2 An example of an inverse relationship

Change to area	How pressure changes (assuming force is constant)
Increases	Decreases
Decreases	Increases

Step 2: Effect of Total Area and Pressure on Total Force

We will be considering a number of three-dimensional situations, so it is worth introducing a simple convention for representing them in two dimensions. This has two advantages: firstly, it makes 3D representations much easier to draw; secondly, there is less room for misinterpretation than when using perspective drawings. The one we will use is called the dot and cross convention, as shown in Figure 27.2.

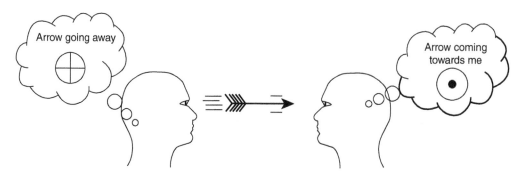

Figure 27.2 Introducing the dot and cross convention

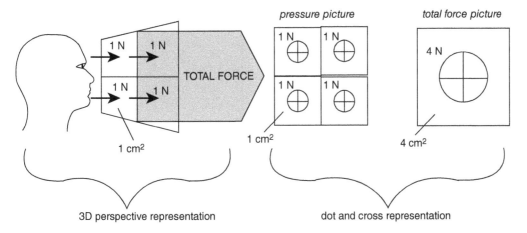

Figure 27.3 Introducing pressure quantitatively

The dot and cross convention can be used to great advantage in many areas of physics so students will gain from being exposed to it on multiple occasions.

Pressure is the force per unit area.

Figure 27.3 shows how this idea can be introduced pictorially, including making students aware of how we will be using the dot and cross convention to show the relationship between force and pressure.

Tips and tricks

- Students can see that the pressure is 1 N/cm² in the 'pressure picture'.
- They can also see that it produces a total force of 4 N over a total area of 4 cm² in the 'total force picture'.
- Once students are comfortable with the dot and cross convention, it becomes a simple matter to present a large number of examples in pictorial form (see the check for understanding section at the end of the chapter).

Figure 27.4 shows how this form of representation can be used to show the effect on the total force of (a) changing the total area; and (b) changing the pressure.

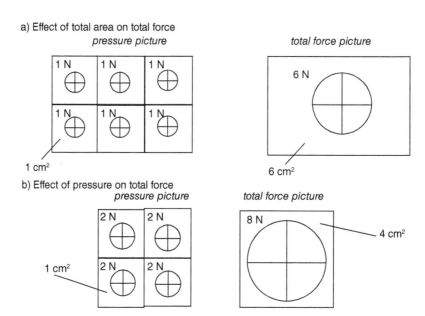

a) Effect of total area on total force

pressure picture

1 N   1 N   1 N
⊕   ⊕   ⊕

1 N   1 N   1 N
⊕   ⊕   ⊕

1 cm²

total force picture

6 N ⊕

6 cm²

b) Effect of pressure on total force

pressure picture

2 N   2 N
⊕   ⊕

2 N   2 N
⊕   ⊕

1 cm²

total force picture

8 N ⊕

4 cm²

Figure 27.4   Modelling the effect of changing total area and pressure on total force

Tips and tricks

- Change the size of the circles to represent larger and smaller values of force.
- It can help students' visualisation of this example-set to lay a transparent rectangular glass block (used in refraction experiments) over gridded paper and draw the pressure and total force picture underneath the block.
- Use as many examples as necessary to ensure students have mastered the relationships and identified them as direct or inverse relationships.
- The discussion can be summarised in a table similar to Table 27.3.

Table 27.3   Effect of changing area and pressure on the total force

Quantity	Change in quantity…	Effect on total force	Type of relationship
Area	Increase	Increase	Direct relationship
	Decrease	Decrease	
Pressure	Increase	Increase	Direct relationship
	Decrease	Decrease	

Step 3: Calculating Pressure

We have looked at how pressure and total area affects the total force. Now we look at how the total force and total area affect the pressure.

Figure 27.5 suggests a way of pictorially modelling the effect of increasing the total force on the pressure applied to a surface when we keep the area fixed.

Figure 27.6 suggests a way of pictorially modelling the effect of increasing the total area on the pressure applied to a surface when we keep the total force fixed.

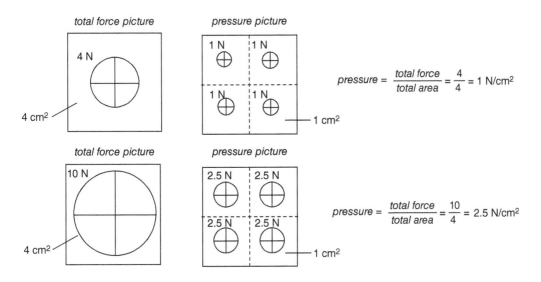

Figure 27.5 How pressure is affected by increasing total force (assuming area is constant)

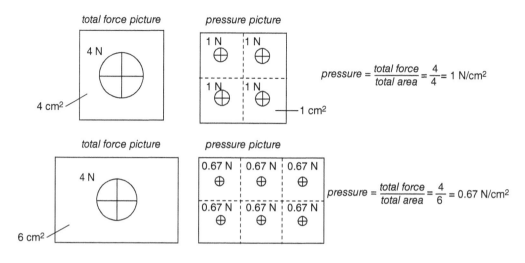

Figure 27.6 How pressure is affected by the total area (assuming total force is constant)

Table 27.4 Effect of changing total force and total area on the pressure

Quantity	Change in quantity....	Effect on pressure	Type of relationship	Description of relationship
Total force	Increase	Increase	Direct relationship	If x gets larger then y gets larger
	Decrease	Decrease		
Total area	Increase	Decrease	Inverse relationship	If x gets larger then y gets smaller
	Decrease	Increase		

Step 4: Pressure and Gases

According to kinetic theory, gas pressure is produced by the myriad collisions of billions of very small gas particles with surfaces. This is a complex picture even for older students to absorb. We can break down this model as follows.

Figure 27.7 shows an observer looking at a cubical container of gas.

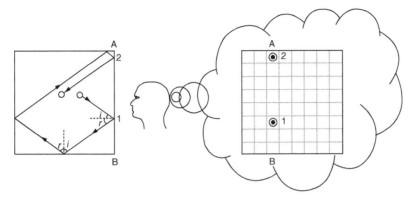

Figure 27.7   Tracking the path of one particle of gas in a cubic container

Figure 27.7 shows the effect of a single particle colliding. In reality, of course, there are hundreds of thousands of billions of billions of particles (a reasonable estimate for a container which has a volume of one litre).

This produces a situation as shown in Figure 27.8. There are so many collisions that they produce a continuous outward force, not just on side AB, but on *all* the sides of the container.

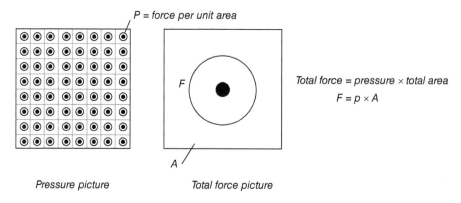

Figure 27.8 The effect of pressure on the walls of a container

If the temperature of the gas within the container is increased, then the average kinetic energy store of the particles also increases. (If we assume that there are no intermolecular forces, then there will be no potential energy stores to complicate matters – see Chapter 29 'Internal energy and heat capacity'.) This means that:

- The average speed of the particles will increase and so the number of collisions in one second will increase.

- The average momentum of the particles will increase so there will be a greater change in momentum when the particles collide with the walls of the container.

Both of these mechanisms lead to an increase in the pressure when the temperature is increased.

However, if the volume of the container is increased, then the number of collisions in one second will decrease, leading to a decrease in pressure. This is summarised in Table 27.5.

Table 27.5 A summary of how a fixed mass of gas responds to changes in temperature and volume

Quantity	Change in quantity	Effect on pressure	Type of relationship	Description of relationship
Temperature	Increase	Increase	• Direct (when temperature measured in °C) • Directly proportional (when temperature measured in kelvin, K)	• Pressure increases when temperature in °C increases • Pressure is doubled when the temperature in kelvin is doubled
	Decrease	Decrease		
Volume	Increase	Decrease	Inverse	Pressure increases when volume is decreased
	Decrease	Increase		

Step 5: Buoyancy

The fact that pressure increases with depth explains why objects which are fully or partially submerged in a *fluid* (i.e. a liquid or a gas) experience an upward force. This upward force or *upthrust* is due to differences in pressure as shown in Figure 27.9.

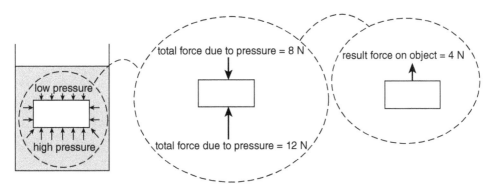

Figure 27.9   The origin of buoyancy forces from pressure differences

This upward force is experienced by all objects when placed in a fluid. It is especially noticeable when the density of the object is less than the density of the liquid; in this case the upthrust or upward force produced by the pressure difference is greater than the weight so the object floats.

Table 27.6 How pressure is affected by changes in one variable

Quantity	Change in quantity….	Effect on pressure	Type of relationship (direct or inverse)	Description of relationship
Total force	Increase			If x gets larger then y gets …………
	Decrease			
Total area	Increase			If x gets larger then y gets …………
	Decrease			

Using a rectangular block of known weight as a *manipulable* with the class can be a good way of assessing students' understanding, as shown is Figure 27.10.

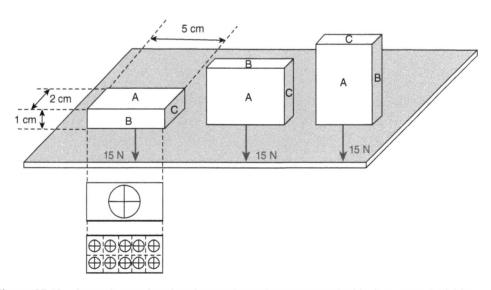

Figure 27.10 Assessing students' understanding using a rectangular block as a manipulable

Tips and tricks

- If you demonstrate a *real* physical block with the class, there is no need to even attempt to draw the top 3D section of Figure 27.10. The 'total force' and 'pressure pictures' below the main diagram will do nicely.
- Some questions to ask:
  - On which side will there be the most pressure and why? (C. Smallest area. Inverse relationship between pressure and area.)
  - In which direction will the pressure exerted by the block act? (Vertically downwards.)
  - Calculate the pressure when the block is resting on side A. ($\frac{15}{2 \times 5} = 1.5 \text{ N/cm}^2$.)

28

FORCES AND NEWTON'S LAWS OF MOTION

Relevant ages

14–16

What students should know already

- Forces as pushes or pulls, arising from the interaction between two objects.
- Using force arrows in diagrams, adding forces in one dimension.
- Moment as the turning effect of a force.
- Forces: associated with deforming objects; stretching and squashing – springs; with rubbing and friction between surfaces; with pushing things out of the way; resistance to motion of air and water.

- Newton's three laws of motion and how they can be applied, qualitatively and quantitatively, to explain the behaviour of objects and systems in the real world.

Explanation

It is fair to say that most human beings navigate the world with a fair measure of success without recourse to Newton's laws of motion. Instead, we rely on a collection of instinctual behaviours and responses learned in early childhood that can be termed as 'intuitive physics'. For example, we learn to walk carefully on a slippery surface and can predict the behaviour of a heavy log when it is pushed or pulled.

However, 'intuitive physics' applies to a very limited range of environments, namely, the surface of the planet Earth. Part of the intensive training of astronauts is to overcome this 'hard wired' parochial understanding of the universe so they can function effectively in the great beyond.

The three laws that bear Sir Isaac Newton's name were collected for the first time in his book the *Principia Mathematica* published in 1687. It is hard to overstate their importance in developing a sound understanding of the true nature of the universe, which begins with the nature of the relationship between force and motion. The three laws are summarised in Table 28.1 in a form suitable for 14–16 year old students.

Table 28.1 A summary of Newton's laws of motion

Name	Scope	Full statement	Concise summary	Examples
Newton's First Law of Motion	What happens when the total force (resultant force) on an object is zero.	An object will remain stationary or continue moving at a constant velocity (i.e. constant speed in a straight line) unless it is acted on by a resultant force.	Forces are needed to *change* (not sustain) the motion of an object.	• Two tug-of-war teams pulling with equal force in opposite directions. • A car moving at a steady speed along a straight road when engine force is equal and opposite to the air resistance force.

(Continued)

Table 28.1 (Continued)

Name	Scope	Full statement	Concise summary	Examples
Newton's Second Law of Motion	What happens when the total force (resultant force) on an object is not zero.	The acceleration of the body is: • Directly proportional to the resultant force acting on it. • Inversely proportional to the mass of the object.	$F = ma$	50 kg → 100 N, → 2.0 m/s² 25 N ← 50 kg → 100 N, → 1.3 m/s² 100 kg → 100 N, → 1.0 m/s²
Newton's Third Law of Motion	What happens when objects interact (i.e. act on each other simultaneously).	If object A exerts a force on object B, then object B exerts an equal and opposite force on object A.	Forces always occur in pairs.	• Swimming: A person pushes back against the water, so the water pushes the person forward. • Normal contact force: When an object presses down on the table, the table pushes up on the object.

Step 1: Newton's First Law

The idea that force is needed to *sustain* motion is a pernicious and perennial misconception. However, it seems consistent with our everyday experience in that moving objects on the Earth's surface do come to rest if left to themselves, and a continuous effort seemingly needs to be applied to keep an object moving at a steady speed.

Galileo Galilei was the first to argue that we can reach a deeper truth if we extrapolate beyond the range of our everyday experience and accept that a moving object free of all resistive forces would continue with unchanging speed on a horizontal plane.

This can be demonstrated to students by careful observation of the motion of a vehicle on a linear air track (the vehicles experience negligible friction as they float on a cushion of air generated by the track). However, if a linear air track is unavailable, a variation on the argument presented by Galileo in his *Dialogues Concerning Two New Sciences* published in 1638 can be very useful. This is shown in Table 28.2.

Table 28.2   A conceptual argument to illustrate Newton's First Law of Motion

Diagram	Description	Extrapolation
What we see in the real world:	The height reached by a ball rolling forward and backward on a U-shaped track gradually decreases.	This happens because friction and air resistance slows down the ball. The ball will eventually stop moving after a certain amount of time because of these resistive forces.
What we would see in a world without friction:	The ball would reach the same height each time.	This would happen because there would be no resistive forces such as friction or air resistance to slow down the ball. The ball would not stop moving because there would be no resistive forces to stop it.
What we would see in a world without friction:	One side of the U-shaped track is straightened out so that it is horizontal. The ball would keep moving in a straight line at a steady speed once it reaches the straight part.	The ball would not slow down because there would be no resistive forces to slow it down. This leads to the conclusion that forces are needed to speed up or slow down an object, but that no forces are needed to keep an object moving.

Step 2: Newton's Second Law

One of the main misconceptions to be wary of here is that 'As x increases then y increases' is an example of a *directly proportional* relationship rather than merely a vague statement of a 'positive correlation' (which is a category beloved by mathematics teachers, but is of limited utility in the physical sciences).

Newton's Second Law says that the acceleration is directly proportional to the resultant (total) force acting on an object: that is to say, if the resultant force acting on an object doubles, then the acceleration doubles; if the total force halves, then the acceleration halves.

This can be summarised as: $F = ma$ where F is the resultant force in newtons, m is the mass in kilograms and a is the acceleration in metres per second squared.

One common pitfall when carrying out an experiment to find the relationship between resultant force and acceleration, where the force is supplied by a string held in tension by a weight stack hanging vertically, is to inadvertently confound one of the main control variables. The total mass of the accelerating system must be constant and the system includes the weight stack as well as the vehicle. Weights removed from the weight stack must be placed on the vehicle to ensure that the total mass remains constant.

Another common misconception is that the opposite of a directly proportional relationship is an 'indirectly proportional relationship' rather than an inverse relationship. A table can be immensely helpful for students (see Table 28.3).

Table 28.3 A summary of the different types of relationship relevant to Newton's Second Law

Type of relationship	As applied to Newton's Second Law
Directly proportional	(Assuming mass is constant) • As F doubles, a doubles. • As F triples, a triples. • As F halves, a halves.
Inversely proportional	(Assuming resultant force is constant) • As m doubles, a halves. • As m halves, a doubles.

Step 3: Newton's Third Law

Students' misunderstandings of Newton's Third Law generally fall into two categories:

1. An active 'pushing' agent is required to generate the Newton's Third Law force. (The question 'But how can the table produce a force?' is a frequent indicator that this misconception is in play.)
2. The Newton's Third Law force acts on the same object as the first force.

Figure 23.10 in Chapter 23 'Introduction to forces' suggests a useful 'bridging analogy' that can help address the first misconception in the context of the 'normal contact force'. Also, Figures 28.1 and 28.2 show a minor variation of the classic textbook illustration of two ice skaters (or roller skaters) pushing on each other. This is achievable in the school laboratory or classroom if two students are seated in chairs on castors.

Next, arrange the students as shown in Figure 28.2.

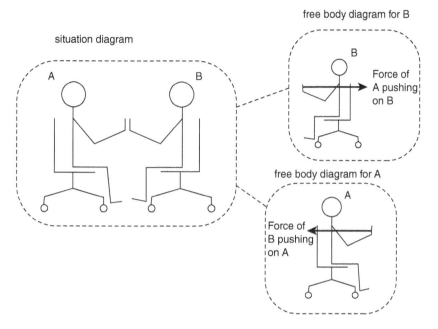

Figure 28.1   Modelling Newton's Third Law in the classroom

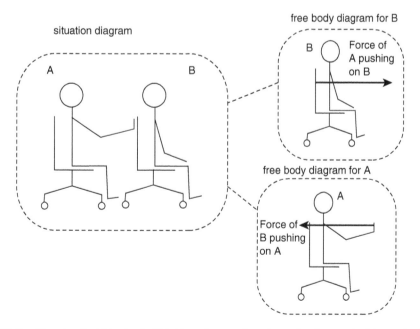

Figure 28.2   Showing that Newton's Third Law forces do not need to be created by an 'active pusher'

Check for understanding

Asking students to complete a summary of Newton's First Law in the format shown in Figure 28.3 can be very instructive.

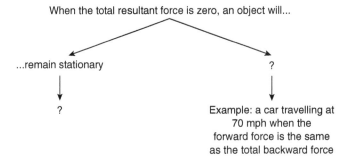

Figure 28.3   Testing understanding of Newton's First Law

Students' understanding of Newton's Second Law can be tested using a straightforward multiple choice question as shown in Figure 28.4.

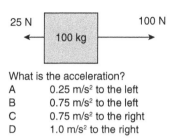

What is the acceleration?

A   0.25 m/s² to the left
B   0.75 m/s² to the left
C   0.75 m/s² to the right
D   1.0 m/s² to the right

Figure 28.4   Testing students' understanding of Newton's Second Law

Tips and tricks

- A is incorrect and indicates that although the student can carry out the $a = F/m$ operation correctly there remains a fundamental misunderstanding on the nature of a resultant force.
- B is incorrect and indicates that although the mechanical operation of calculating a resultant force and applying $a = F/m$ were carried out correctly, the student cannot reliably predict the direction of a resultant force.
- C is correct.
- D is incorrect and indicates that although the student can carry out the $a = F/m$ operation correctly there remains a fundamental misunderstanding on the nature of a resultant force.

Students' understanding of Newton's Third Law can be tested using questions such as Figure 28.5.

The picture shows a box stationary on a floor. Since the forces F and W are equal and opposite, is this a good example of Newton's Third Law in action?

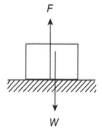

Figure 28.5   Testing students' understanding of Newton's Third Law

The answer is no. The forces F and W are acting on the same object and in Newton's Third Law the forces always act on different objects: see Figure 28.6 for a full explanation.

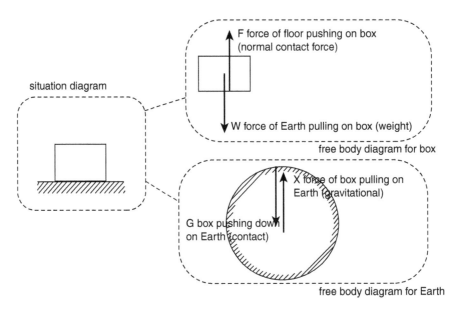

Figure 28.6   Free body diagrams for a box resting on the Earth's surface

Tips and tricks

'Newton 3 pairs' (i.e. the pair of forces generated by any interaction between two objects) must:

- Be equal and opposite.
- Act on different objects.
- Be of the same type (e.g. contact versus gravitational in this example).
- Thus, the Newton 3 pairs are forces F and G and forces W and X.

29

INTERNAL ENERGY AND HEAT CAPACITY

Relevant ages

14–16

What students should know already

- Energy is a quantity that can be quantified and calculated.
- Energy is transferred and stored in many physical processes, e.g. heating and cooling; speeding up and slowing down; stretching and squashing elastic objects; and changing position in a gravitational or magnetic field.
- Energy is measured in joules and power is measured in joules per second.
- How particles are arranged in solids, liquids and gases.

What students should know by the end

- Specific heat capacity is the change in the thermal energy store required to raise (or lower) the temperature of one kilogram of substance by one degree Celsius.
- Internal energy is the sum of the total KEs (kinetic energies) and the total potential energies of all the particles.
- The specific latent heat is the change in internal energy required to change the state of one kilogram of substance (with no change in temperature).

Explanation and Rationale

The conceptual difficulty with understanding temperature and thermal energy is that both of them are the observable, macroscopic consequences of the microscopic motion of vast numbers of particles which are nearly impossible to observe directly. Students are often asked to switch between looking through a 'macroscopic lens' at things we can observe directly and measure in the laboratory and a 'microscopic lens' where we explain those properties through the behaviour of particles which are not directly observable. It is always good to be explicit in signalling a change in perspective by saying 'Looking through a macroscopic lens, this is what we see…' or similar.

Table 29.1 summarises some of the important concepts.

Table 29.1 Looking through the macroscopic and microscopic 'lenses' at some thermal properties

Property	How we observe this property through the 'macroscopic lens'	How we think about this property when looking through the 'microscopic lens'
Temperature	The reading on a thermometer.	A measurement of the average kinetic energy store of all the individual particles in an object. The higher the temperature then the greater the average kinetic energy of the particles.
Thermal energy store	Different objects will store different amounts of thermal energy. This will depend on the mass of the object and the specific heat capacity of the substance it is made of.	The sum of all the kinetic energies of all the particles in an object. This will depend on: • The mass of the object (more particles = higher total KE). • The temperature of the object (higher KE for each particle = higher total KE).

Property	How we observe this property through the 'macroscopic lens'	How we think about this property when looking through the 'microscopic lens'
Internal energy	The behaviour of substances when they change state (e.g. ice at 0°C more effective at cooling than water at 0°C).	The sum of the kinetic and potential energy stores of all the particles in the object.
Potential energy store	Cannot be observed directly.	The energy stored as a result of intermolecular forces between the particles in an object.

Tips and tricks

- The preferred scientific temperature scale is the Kelvin scale since its zero coincides with Absolute Zero – the temperature at which particles will have zero thermal motion and zero KE.
- Temperature scales such as the Celsius scale are chosen for convenience: there is nothing scientifically 'special' about 0°C, the freezing point of water, but it's a useful reference point for humans.
- The Kelvin and Celsius scales are designed so that a temperature increase of +1 K will also be +1°C.
- An object at 0°C will *not* have zero thermal energy since 0°C = 273 kelvin.

Step 1: Heating and Cooling in Terms of Energy Stores

When energy is shifted *into* a thermal energy store, then the temperature increases. When it is shifted *out* of a thermal energy store, the temperature will decrease (see Figure 29.1).

Tips and tricks

- The direction of energy flow is always from hot to cold. In the kettle, this is from the hot element to the cold water. For the hot cup of tea, this is from the hot tea to the cooler surroundings.
- It is unhelpful to talk of 'cold' being transferred.
- The wavy lines on the energy diagrams are intended to help students picture energy as a quasi-material entity similar to a liquid which can enter or leave a store.

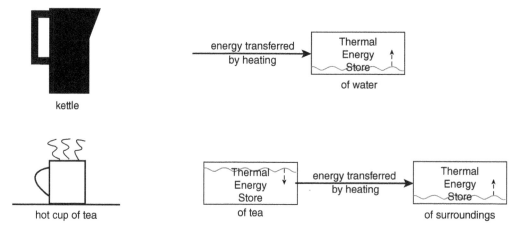

Figure 29.1 Examples of heating and cooling

If we think about what is happening to the water being heated in the kettle:

- *Looking through a macroscopic lens*, the temperature of water in a kettle increases when energy is transferred *into* its thermal energy store.

- *Looking through the microscopic lens*, its temperature increases because its particles are gaining kinetic energy so the average kinetic energy of the particles also increases.

If we think about what is happening to the tea in the cup:

- *Looking through a macroscopic lens*, the temperature of an object decreases when energy is transferred out of its thermal energy store.

- *Looking through the microscopic lens*, its temperature decreases because its particles are losing kinetic energy so the average kinetic energy of the particles also decreases.

Step 2: The Difference Between Temperature and Thermal Energy

Knowing the temperature of an object alone is not enough to be able to predict or explain its thermal behaviour. We also have to think about its thermal energy store.

For example, a spark from a firework sparkler has a much higher temperature than a hot cup of coffee, and yet the coffee will produce a much more serious injury than the spark. Let's look through our macroscopic lens to try to explain this.

The spark has a very small mass and consequently the energy in its thermal energy store is small. This means that only a small amount of energy is transferred to any cooler object that it comes into contact with. By contrast, because the mass of the hot coffee is much larger, it has a much larger of amount of energy in its thermal energy store. This energy will be transferred to any cooler object it comes into direct contact with, and would cause serious injury if dropped into a person's lap.

Step 3: Quantifying Thermal Energy Transfer by Using Specific Heat Capacity

Some substances are easier to heat up than others. For example, it takes 2000 J of energy to heat 1 kg of cooking oil by 1°C but 4200 J of energy to heat up 1 kg of water by 1°C. In other words, oil has a different *heat capacity* (or ability to hold thermal energy) than water. This is shown diagrammatically in Figure 29.2 (see also Chapter 21 'Introducing energy stores and pathways' for similar diagrams). To make the diagrams easier to interpret we have considered temperature changes of one degree Celsius exactly.

It is also important for students to realise that the heat capacity affects how substances cool down as well, which is shown in Figure 29.3.

The word 'specific' has a specific meaning in physics: it means 'per kilogram'. Thus, the *specific heat capacity* describes how one kilogram of substance responds to thermal energy.

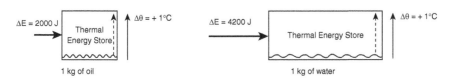

Figure 29.2 Heating 1 kg of oil and 1 kg of water to show the effect of their different heat capacities

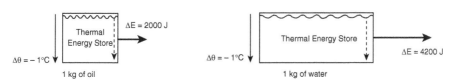

Figure 29.3 Cooling 1 kg of oil and 1 kg of water to show the effect of their different heat capacities

The formula is: change in thermal energy = mass × specific heat capacity × change in temperature or $\Delta E = mc\Delta\theta$.

Students can be introduced to specific heat capacity problems by using diagrams as shown in Figure 29.4.

This approach can also be beneficial when introducing specific heat capacity practicals which often involve electrical heating as shown in Figure 29.5 (also see Chapter 21 'Introducing energy stores and pathways').

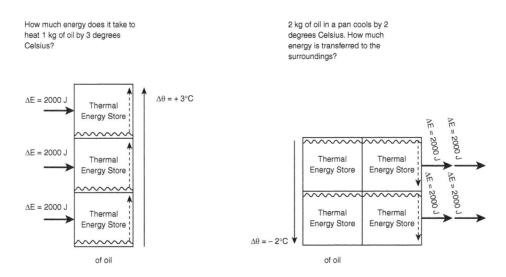

Figure 29.4 Introducing specific heat capacity problems with diagrams

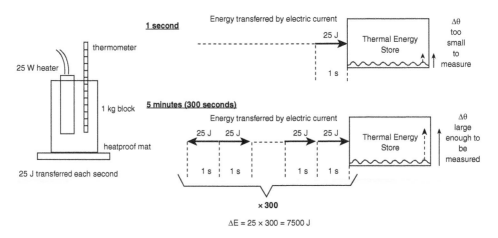

Figure 29.5 Carrying out an experiment to measure the specific heat capacity of a substance

Step 4: Recognising that Thinking Macroscopically is Not Enough to Account for All Thermal Behaviour

How does adding energy to a substance affect its temperature? Looking only through the macroscopic lens, we might naively expect a simple relationship as shown by the graph in Figure 29.6a.

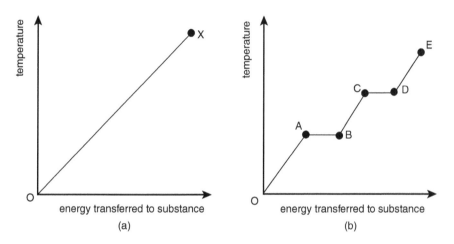

Figure 29.6 Effect of heating (a) an ideal substance and (b) a real substance

Tips and tricks

- To obtain a graph similar to 29.6b, try freezing a thermometer in a solid block of ice using a silicone 'ice lolly' mould. The thermometer should be placed where the stick is normally positioned.
- The block of ice containing the thermometer is then put in a beaker of water and heated.

However, when we heat a real substance such as ice we get a more complex relationship similar to Figure 29.6b. There are sections (AB and CD) where the temperature of a substance does not increase even though energy is being added to the substance. When the experiment is demonstrated, students can observe that AB is when the ice (or other substance) is melting and CD is when the water is boiling. In other words, the temperature 'pauses' when the substance is changing state.

Figure 29.6a shows a situation where there are no changes of state. To understand why this might happen, we have to look through the microscopic lens and think about the particles. Substance (a) cannot condense into a liquid or freeze into a solid because there are no forces of attraction between its particles: substance (a) is a gas and can only ever be a gas. No substance like this exists in nature so this 'theoretical' substance is called an 'ideal gas' (and can be very useful when we want to model the behaviour of gases at high temperatures and low pressures).

If we look at Figure 29.6a through the macroscopic lens we can see that none of the energy is 'hidden': any energy transferred to the substance is 'visible' as a change in temperature. Looking through the microscopic lens, this is because any energy transferred makes its particles move faster. Faster particles have a larger kinetic store and so the average kinetic energy of the particles is larger. Since temperature is a measurement of the average kinetic energy of the particles in a substance, this is why the temperature increases.

Looking through the macroscopic lens, the same is obviously not true of Figure 29.6b: some of the energy transferred is 'hidden'; in other words, it is absorbed by the substance but is not always 'visible' as an increase in temperature. Looking through our microscopic lens, we can surmise that this will have something to do with the intermolecular forces between the particles affecting the energy stores of the particles.

Step 5: Modelling a Change in State

We can use the 'spotting tray in a box' model (see Figure 29.7) to represent what happens to the energy stores of particles as a substance is heated.

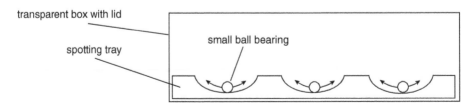

Figure 29.7 The spotting tray in a box model: a concrete representation of the energy stores of particles during melting

Tips and tricks

- Use Blu Tack or glue to secure the spotting tray to the bottom of the box.
- If the area of the box is larger than the area of the tray, fill in the edges with plasticine.
- If ball bearings are unavailable, use the small silver sugar balls used for cake decoration.

When the box is shaken very gently, the ball bearings oscillate in the bottom of each 'well' – the curved shape of each well provides an 'intermolecular force' that keeps each ball in the same relative position. The potential energy of the molecules is represented by their gravitational potential energy as they are raised out of the well. The procedure is summarised in Table 29.2.

We can then annotate the graph as shown in Figure 29.8.

Table 29.2 Representing a change of state using the spotting tray model

| Motion of tray | Microscopic lens (thinking about particles) | | | Macroscopic lens (what we can see or measure) | |
	Motion of particles	Total kinetic energy of particles	Total potential energy of particles	Temperature	Phase
Completely still	Not moving	Zero	Zero	Absolute zero	Solid
Shaken very very gently	Vibrating around a fixed position	Small	Zero	Slightly warmer	Solid
Shaken very gently so that balls reach upper edge of well	Vibrating around a fixed position with larger amplitude	Increased	Very small	Approaching melting point	Solid
Shaken gently so that balls climb out of well but often get trapped in each well	They no longer stay in the same positions	Same as before, since some kinetic energy → potential energy	Increased	At melting point	Solid → liquid
Shaken so that balls can move easily across surface of spotting tray	Move easily over the wells	Larger	Same as before	Above melting point	Liquid

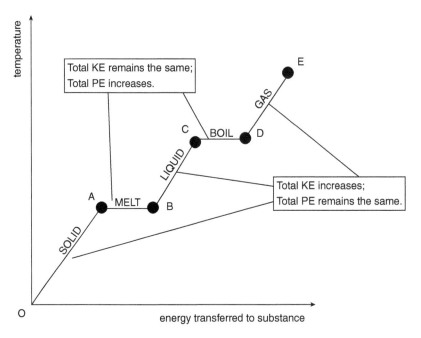

Figure 29.8 Effect of heating on temperature

Step 6: Thermal Energy, Latent Heat and Internal Energy

Internal energy only makes sense when viewed through the microscopic lens. The internal energy is the sum of the kinetic energy and potential energy stores of all the particles in a substance.

It is not identical to the thermal energy since this depends on only the kinetic energy stores of the particles and does not take account of potential energy. A change in thermal energy occurs when the kinetic energies of the particles change, i.e. when they speed up or slow down. In other words, a change in thermal energy is always associated with a change in temperature.

The potential energy stores come into play when a substance changes state. Until the potential energy store of each particle has been filled, the average kinetic energy of the particles will not increase and so the temperature of the substance remains constant until this happens. The energy that the substance absorbs without increasing the temperature during a change of state is called the *latent heat*.

Check for understanding

To establish that students have understood the distinctions between these concepts, ask questions such as:

- Which has the most thermal energy: a hot cup of tea or an iceberg? (An iceberg, since although the average KE of its particles is smaller, there are many more of them.)
- Which object has the particles with the highest average KE: the 'spark' from a firework sparkler or a hot cup of coffee? (The 'spark' at about 1500°C. The cup of coffee has a lower temperature of about 80°C.)

For checking student understanding of internal energy, asking students to complete a partially incomplete version of Table 29.3 is really useful.

Table 29.3 Checking student understanding of internal energy

Part of graph (see Figure 29.8)	Microscopic lens – what the particles are doing			Macroscopic lens – what we could observe
	Kinetic energy of particles	Potential energy	Internal energy	
OA	Increases	Constant	Increases	Solid. Temp increases.
AB	Constant	Increases	Increases	Melting. Temp constant.
BC	Increases	Constant	Increases	Liquid. Temp increases.
CD	Constant	Increases	Increases	Boiling. Temp constant.
DE	Increases	Constant	Increases	Gas. Temp increases.

30

MAGNETISM AND ELECTROMAGNETISM

What students should know already

- Magnetic poles, attraction and repulsion.
- Earth's magnetism, compasses and navigation.
- The magnetic effect of a current, electromagnets, DC motors (principles only).

What students should know by the end

- Exploring the magnetic fields of permanent and induced magnets, and the Earth's magnetic field, using a compass.
- Magnetic fields by plotting with a compass, representation by field lines.
- Magnetic effects of currents, how solenoids enhance the effect.
- How transformers are used in the national grid and the reasons for their use.

Many centuries ago, certain types of rock found in the region of Magnesia were observed to attract iron – this mysterious phenomenon was called 'magnetism'. Another observation that was inexplicable at the time was that when suspended, some of these 'magnetic' rocks pointed north – they had a 'north-seeking pole' or 'north pole'.

We now know that every magnetic phenomenon ever observed has the same underlying cause: they are produced by moving electric charges.

Step 1: Permanent and Temporary Magnets

In most atoms, the separate magnetic fields produced by the movement of groups of electrons within each atom cancel each other out. However, in certain atoms belonging to *ferromagnetic* materials (notably iron, cobalt and nickel) this is not the case: each atom produces its own magnetic field.

In a typical sample of iron, the atoms within a small region about 0.1 mm across called a *domain* will line up in the same direction and produce a measurable magnetic field. However, the atoms in neighbouring domains will be lined up in a different and random orientation as shown in Figure 30.1. This means the total magnetic field of the sample is zero since the magnetic fields due to each magnetic domain within the sample will cancel each other out. This sample is *unmagnetised*.

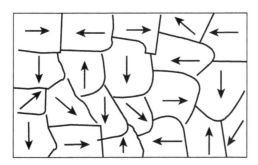

Figure 30.1   Randomly oriented domains in a ferromagnetic material

The arrows show the end that would point north if the domain was able to turn freely.

By chance or by design, the domains in a sample can be oriented the same way. Such an arrangement produces a total overall magnetic field and the sample is said to be magnetised as in Figure 30.2.

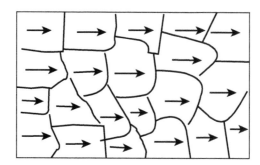

Figure 30.2 Domains in a ferromagnetic sample oriented so as to produce an overall magnetic field; if the orientation of domains is stable over time, then the material is said to be a permanent magnet

The orientation of the domains can be altered by a strong external magnetic field (e.g. by placing it near to a strong permanent magnet). If the change in domain orientation is temporary, then the material is a temporary magnet since they will return to their random orientations when the external field is removed. This type of material is described as *magnetically soft*. If the domains keep their 'new' orientations when the external magnetic field is removed then the material is referred to as *magnetically hard*. Permanent magnets are made out of magnetically hard materials.

This is summarised in Table 30.1

Table 30.1 Types of magnetic material

Type of material	Effect of external magnetic field	Type of magnetism
Magnetically hard (e.g. steel).	Orientation of domains is not affected (unless the external field is very strong).	Permanent magnet.
Magnetically soft (e.g. pure iron).	The orientation of domains is affected – but will return to random orientations when the external field is removed.	Temporary magnet – only magnetised when placed in an external magnetic field.

Note that the only true test of whether a sample is a permanent magnet is repulsion: samples may become attracted when they become temporarily magnetised but only a permanent magnet will repel another permanent magnet.

Step 2: Magnetic Fields

Magnetic forces are, of course, non-contact or action-at-a-distance forces. Figure 30.3 shows a memorable demonstration of this where a steel paper clip is made to levitate because of the magnetic field of a bar magnet.

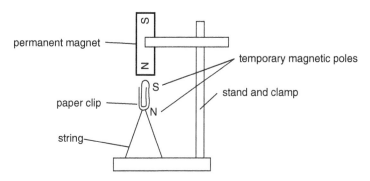

Figure 30.3   Levitating a steel paper clip to show the effect of a magnetic field

Tips and tricks

- Use a wooden stand and clamp if one is available.
- Pass a sheet of paper between the paper clip and the magnet to emphasise that it is a non-contact force. The magnetic field lines should penetrate most metallic and non-metallic materials with the exception of a thin sheet of a ferromagnetic material, e.g. a thin sheet of steel.
- Since steel is a magnetically hard material, then the paper clip may become a weak permanent magnet if it remains in the external field of the permanent magnet for a long time or if it has come into direct contact with the permanent bar magnet (where the magnetic field is strongest).
- Test the paper clip to see if it attracts an unmagnetised paper clip. However the only reliable test of permanent magnetisation is whether it repels another permanently magnetised paper clip.

In physics, we describe the behaviour of non-contact forces using the concept of a *field of force*. A field is a region of space around an object where a similar object will experience a non-contact force.

A magnetic field is a region of space around a permanent magnet or electromagnet where another 'magnetic object' will experience a force of attraction or repulsion.

Examples of 'magnetic objects' are permanent magnets, temporary magnets and wires carrying electric currents.

An indication of the 'shape' of a magnetic field can be obtained by sprinkling iron filings around a permanent magnet. The small pieces of iron become temporary magnets which line up with the magnetic field. However, a more precise picture can be obtained by using a small magnetic plotting compass as shown in Figure 30.4.

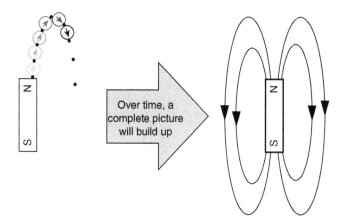

Figure 30.4   Using a plotting compass to map the magnetic field lines of a permanent magnet

Tips and tricks

- Place the plotting compass at a random point near to the permanent magnet. Draw a dot to show the position of the 'north seeking pole' (or 'south seeking pole') of the compass needle.
- Move the compass so the base of the needle is at this dot, and repeat the first step.
- Repeat the steps, until multiple magnetic field line 'loops' have been mapped.
- The magnetic field is strongest where the field lines are close together: in this case, at the poles of the magnet where the field lines emerge and disappear.

The magnetic field of the Earth is similar to that of a bar-shaped permanent magnet (but it is actually thought to result from electric currents flowing in the liquid outer core).

Note that the imaginary bar magnet would have to be oriented as shown in Figure 30.5 in order for compass needles (where the sharp end is typically a 'north-seeking pole') to point in the accustomed direction towards the geographic north pole of the Earth.

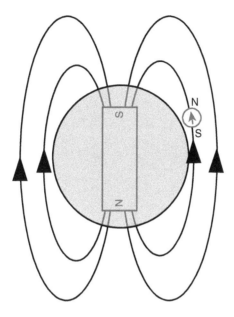

Figure 30.5 A model of the magnetic field of the Earth

Step 3: Electric Currents and Magnetic Fields

All magnetic fields are produced by moving electric charges. Even a humble copper wire is surrounded by a weak magnetic field when a current flows through it: the larger the current, the stronger the magnetic field.

The magnetic field has a three dimensional cylindrical structure which is centred on the wire as shown in Figure 30.6.

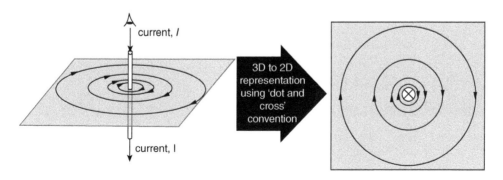

Figure 30.6 The magnetic field associated with a long, straight, current-carrying conductor

Step 4: Increasing the Magnetic Field Strength by Building a Solenoid

A solenoid is a coil or 'spiral' of wire. The magnetic field of a long, straight conductor is amplified by 'folding' the wire so that the magnetic field produced by one part of the wire overlaps with the magnetic field produced by an adjacent part of the wire as shown in Figure 30.7.

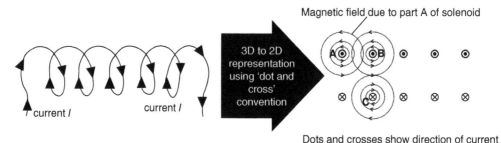

Figure 30.7 How a solenoid produces a strong magnetic field

- The magnetic fields produced by parts A and B 'support' each other both inside and outside of the solenoid.
- Also, the magnetic field of C 'supports' the magnetic field of B inside the solenoid, producing a much stronger magnetic field at the centre.

The magnetic fields of all the small current elements of the solenoid sum to produce the magnetic field shown in Figure 30.8.

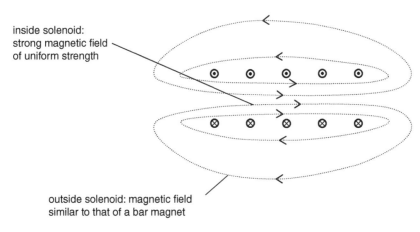

inside solenoid:
strong magnetic field
of uniform strength

outside solenoid: magnetic field
similar to that of a bar magnet

Figure 30.8   The magnetic field produced by a solenoid

Tips and tricks

- Placing an iron core in the centre of the solenoid can increase the strength of the magnetic field by a factor of 1000.
- There should be no current flow through the iron core so the solenoid should be made of insulated wire.
- Since the field lines emerge from the right hand end of the solenoid shown, this is the north pole of the solenoid.

Step 5: Strengthening Understanding of Fleming's Left Hand Rule

A current-carrying conductor in a magnetic field will experience a force, the direction of which can be predicted using Fleming's left hand rule. We do not have space for a full treatment of the rule and its application here, but analysing the situation using the tools outlined above can help students understand how the Fleming's left hand rule force originates due to the interaction of magnetic fields, and also provide a check on their application of it. This is shown in Figure 30.9.

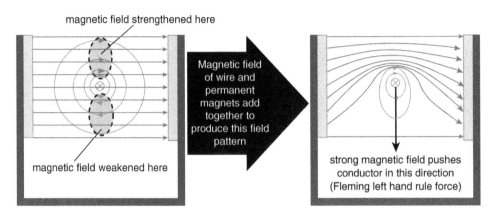

Figure 30.9 Modelling the interaction between a current-carrying conductor and magnetic field

Step 6: Explaining the Operation of a Transformer

Moving electric charges produce magnetic fields. Conversely, a changing magnetic field can make stationary electric charges move: in other words, a changing magnetic field can generate or *induce* an electric current.

Electromagnetic induction is used in transformers which enable the efficient transfer of energy through large networks of electrical supply cables such as the National Grid. Because of the efficiency gains due to *step up* and *step down transformers*, alternating current is used in the National Grid. Alternating current produces the changing magnetic field necessary for electromagnetic induction (see Figure 30.10).

Tips and tricks

- 'Step up' and 'step down' always refers to the effect on the potential difference; for example, for a step up transformer, the output potential difference from the secondary coil will be larger than the input potential difference into the primary coil.
- Due to the principle of conservation of energy, the total output power cannot be greater than the input power. In the best case scenario for a transformer that is 100% efficient, the output power will be equal to the input power.
- Since $P = VI$, if the potential difference is, for example, doubled then the output current will be halved.

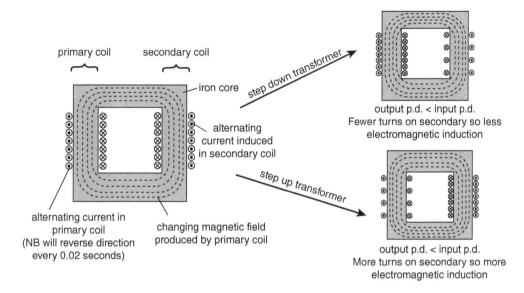

primary coil   secondary coil

iron core

step down transformer

output p.d. < input p.d.
Fewer turns on secondary so less
electromagnetic induction

alternating
current induced
in secondary coil

step up transformer

alternating current in
primary coil
(NB will reverse direction
every 0.02 seconds)

changing magnetic field
produced by primary coil

output p.d. < input p.d.
More turns on secondary so more
electromagnetic induction

Figure 30.10   Explaining how step down and step up transformers work

Check for understanding

Have students paid due attention to the salient features of many of the diagrams they are presented with when studying magnetic fields? For example, students could be asked to decide if the following statements about Figure 30.4 are true or false:

- The needle of a plotting compass is a permanent magnet. (True.)
- We can tell it is a permanent magnet because it's attracted to the S pole of the bar magnet. (False: repulsion is the key observation to check if an object is a permanent magnet.)
- The magnetic field lines begin at the S pole of the bar magnet and end at the N pole. (False.)
- The magnetic field lines around a bar magnet are equally spaced. (False: they are closer together at the poles where the field is strongest.)

One of the enduring difficulties with students' understanding of magnetic fields is their ability to analyse complex spatial arrangements in three dimensions. Asking them to convert a 3D perspective drawing into a simplified 'flat' 2D representation (as shown in Figures 30.6 and 30.7) can be an invaluable diagnostic check.

INDEX